SOVEREIGNTY INTACT

This book examines the relationship between the UK Parliament and the European Court of Human Rights, and the relationship Parliament had previously with the Court of Justice of the European Union. It examines these relationships in the context of the highly politicised area of immigration.

The book illustrates, despite frequent claims to the contrary, that the adjudication of rights by 'foreign' courts in cases involving immigration has not in fact impeded Parliament's work or its sovereignty. By applying the democratic dialogue model to the relationship between the Parliament and these courts, the book illustrates the dynamic and interactive nature of the relationships. The institutions, working together, produce moderated and normatively advantageous human rights protections.

Tackling the contentious issue of UK sovereignty, this important book, through rigorous analysis, expertly dismantles one of the most charged political claims of recent times.

Sovereignty Intact

The UK Parliament, Foreign Courts and Immigration

Matilda Gillis

•HART•

OXFORD • LONDON • NEW YORK • NEW DELHI • SYDNEY

HART PUBLISHING

Bloomsbury Publishing Plc

Kemp House, Chawley Park, Cumnor Hill, Oxford, OX2 9PH, UK

1385 Broadway, New York, NY 10018, USA

Bloomsbury Publishing Ireland Limited, 29 Earlsfort Terrace, Dublin 2, D02 AY28, Ireland

HART PUBLISHING, the Hart/Stag logo, BLOOMSBURY and the Diana logo are trademarks of Bloomsbury Publishing Plc

First published in Great Britain 2026

A catalogue record for this book is available from the British Library.

A catalogue record for this book is available from the Library of Congress.

ISBN: HB: 978-1-50998-449-7
ePDF: 978-1-50998-451-0
ePub: 978-1-50998-450-3

Typeset by Compuscript Ltd, Shannon

For product safety related questions contact productsafety@bloomsbury.com

To find out more about our authors and books visit www.hartpublishing.co.uk. Here you will find extracts, author information, details of forthcoming events and the option to sign up for our newsletters.

ACKNOWLEDGEMENTS

Peterhouse funded the research upon which this book is based, through a Graduate Research Studentship. I am very grateful to Peterhouse and also to Trinity College, which funded my initial postgraduate studies and brought me to Cambridge.

I completed this book as the Hong Kong Link Research Fellow and Lecturer in Law at Corpus Christi College, Cambridge. I am sincerely thankful to Corpus and to the benefactors of this fellowship for funding me to continue this research. At Corpus, Jonathan Morgan, Oleh Stupak and Andrew Sanger have been particularly supportive (and fun!) colleagues, and I am very grateful to them. My thanks too to my colleagues at the Lauterpacht Centre for International Law, for providing such a wonderful community and place to work over the past years.

Alison Young and Andrew Sanger supervised the PhD thesis, which forms the basis of this book, and I could not have asked for two more brilliant, dedicated and thorough supervisors.

Hart Publishing has been great to work with, and my thanks especially to Sinead Moloney for initially contracting this book, and to Verity Stuart, Tom Adams and Sasha Jawed for all their work on the manuscript. My thanks also to Libby Evans for her excellent research and editorial assistance in the final stages.

On a personal level, I feel so immensely lucky to have the most wonderful friends both in Cambridge and afar – especially in Australia, and I am so grateful for this friendship. Of course, my deepest thanks and love go to my husband, Tim.

This book is dedicated to my parents, Jonathan and Patricia, to whom I owe everything.

CONTENTS

TABLE OF CASES AND LEGISLATIVE INSTRUMENTS

Domestic

ECtHR

CJEU

ICJ

Other

Related Documents

Legislative Instruments

Hansard

Treaties

Introduction

As I begin to write the introduction to this book, Prime Minister Keir Starmer is announcing sweeping new immigration reforms in the United Kingdom (UK). It is May 2025. The reforms include tightening the rules on who can obtain a skilled work visa, ending overseas recruitment for social care visas, lengthening the time it takes to obtain indefinite leave to remain in the UK, and making it easier to remove visa-holders from the UK who have committed crimes.[1] Weeks earlier, Starmer had told MPs that: 'it should be parliament that makes the rules on immigration. It should be the government who makes the policy'.[2]

This sentiment is not new. The UK government has long expressed concerns about courts – particularly about 'foreign' courts like the European Court of Human Rights (ECtHR) and the Court of Justice of the European Union (CJEU) – interfering with the UK Parliament's democratic sovereignty and preventing it from implementing its legislative agenda. These concerns have been acted upon and expressed explicitly in recent years.

In December 2021, the UK's Conservative government began its campaign to replace the Human Rights Act 1998, which incorporates the European Convention on Human Rights (ECHR) into UK domestic law, with what it called a 'modern' Bill of Rights.[3] The repeal of the Human Rights Act was needed, according to some ministers at the time, 'to stop Strasbourg dictating to us',[4] and to 'shore up the sovereignty of elected law-makers in Parliament'.[5] While the bill of the Bill of Rights was ultimately withdrawn from Parliament in June 2023, Parliament then passed the Illegal Migration Act 2023 in July 2023. The Illegal Migration Act, the purpose of which is to regulate unlawful immigration into the UK, significantly: (i) disapplies section 3 of the Human Rights Act, which provides that legislation, so far as is possible, be read and given effect in a way which is compatible with ECHR rights;[6] and (ii) gives the government power to ignore interim measures of

[1] Peter Walker, 'Skilled Visa Rules, Deportations and Higher Fees: What's in the Immigration White Paper' *Guardian* (12 May 2025): www.theguardian.com/uk-news/2025/may/12/whats-in-uk-immigration-white-paper-visa-rules-deportations-fees.

[2] Becky Morton, 'Keir Starmer Pledges to Close Loophole That Let Gazan Family Settle in UK' *BBC News* (12 February 2025): www.bbc.com/news/articles/cpdx0yn6v7lo.

[3] Ministry of Justice, Human Rights Act Reform: A Modern Bill of Rights. A Consultation to Reform the Human Rights Act 1998 (2021) 5.

[4] Edward Malnick, 'Dominic Raab: I'll Overhaul the Human Rights Act to Stop Strasbourg Dictating to Us' *Telegraph* (16 October 2021): www.telegraph.co.uk/politics/2021/10/16/dominic-raab-sets-plans-overhaul-human-rights-act-reform-judicial/. See also Lord Leonard Hoffmann, 'The Universality of Human Rights' (2009) 125 *LQR* 416.

[5] Ministry of Justice, *Human Rights Act Reform* (n 3) 4.

[6] Illegal Migration Act 2023, s 5(1).

the ECtHR and, therefore, in one minister's words, 'to unilaterally decide whether the UK should uphold its international obligations'.[7]

The Illegal Migration Act seemed to respond, at least in part, to the ECtHR's 2022 decision to grant an injunction to prevent planes taking off pursuant to the government's plan to send those seeking asylum in the UK to Rwanda.[8] The decision did not determine the lawfulness of the Rwanda plan, and the interim measure was granted only to allow time for the delivery of the domestic decision in the applicant's judicial review proceedings. Nevertheless, it led several Conversative MPs to argue openly that the UK should leave the ECHR and, accordingly, the ECtHR's jurisdiction, on the basis of a perceived need to 'defend our borders and [] bring order to our asylum system',[9] and to 'end the ECHR's trespass on our parliamentary democracy'.[10] In April 2024, UK Prime Minister Rishi Sunak commented to the *Sun* newspaper, in discussing the government's Rwanda plan, that 'border security and controlling illegal migration is more important than our membership of any foreign court'.[11] The UK had, of course, already withdrawn from the European Union (EU) and, therefore, from the direct application of EU law and from the CJEU's jurisdiction.

This book is about the relationship between the UK Parliament and the ECtHR, and the relationship that the UK Parliament in the past had with the CJEU. It provides an empirical and analytical account of those relationships, specifically in the highly charged, controversial and politicised context of immigration.

I. Argument

The central argument made here is that those relationships have been highly interactive and dynamic. These 'foreign' courts, to use Sunak's terminology, have not in fact significantly impeded the UK Parliament's work, as the UK government has, for some time, argued that they have. Rather, Parliament and these 'foreign' courts have worked together, and indeed have quite consciously worked together, to produce moderated protections of rights, even where decisions of these courts have in effect provided non-nationals with a form of legal protection to enter or remain

[7] HC deb 26 Apil 2023, vol 731, col 802. See Illegal Migration Act 2023, s 55.

[8] *NSK v UK* App no 2877/22 (ECtHR, 14 June 2022).

[9] See Jessica Elgot, 'Tory MPs to Push for UK Exit from European Convention on Human Rights' *Guardian* (5 February 2023): www.theguardian.com/politics/2023/feb/05/tory-mps-to-push-for-uk-exit-from-european-convention-of-human-rights; Rowena Mason, 'UK Would Be Outlier with Russia If It Left ECHR, Law Society Says' *Guardian* (9 August 2023): www.theguardian.com/world/2023/aug/09/uk-could-leave-european-convention-on-human-rights-to-stop-channel-migrant-boats; Matthew Weaver, 'Suella Braverman Says "We Will Do Whatever It Takes" If Strasbourg Thwarts Rwanda Plan' *Guardian* (28 August 2023): www.theguardian.com/politics/2023/aug/28/suella-braverman-strasbourg-rwanda-european-convention-human-rights.

[10] HC deb 14 December 2022, vol 724, col 1136.

[11] Martina Bet and Jack Elsom, 'Rwanda WILL Keep Taking Illegal Migrants Even If Britain Quits ECHR' *Sun* (4 April 2024): www.thesun.co.uk/news/27126580/rishi-sunak-echr-rwanda-boats-flights/.

in the country. This argument is made by demonstrating that the UK Parliament's relationship with the ECtHR, and the relationship it had with the CJEU, can be explained by the domestic constitutional model of democratic dialogue.

The metaphor of 'dialogue' has often been used to explain different kinds of institutional interactions at the domestic level,[12] as well as to describe interactions in the international and transnational space.[13] When I use the word 'dialogue' in this book, however, I am referring specifically to 'democratic dialogue': a constitutional model of rights protection with distinct descriptive and normative claims.

The democratic dialogue model will become familiar over the course of the book. For now, it suffices to know that the model is characterised by constitutional and judicially developed mechanisms which allow a legislature to respond to a court decision which has struck down legislation, in a way that is respectful of the court's decision, while nonetheless achieving the original policy goal behind the impugned law. The legislative response may take the form of amending or repealing the relevant legislation or explicitly ignoring the court's decision. Hogg and Bushell were the first scholars to articulate the dialogue model, which has since entered the mainstream of constitutional theory. They did so by examining instances in which the Supreme Court of Canada struck down legislation on the basis of its incompatibility with the Canadian Charter of Rights and Freedoms,[14] and in which the Canadian legislature subsequently took further action in light of the Court's decision. They initially described their analytical model as follows:

> [Whenever] a judicial decision is open to legislative reversal, modification, or avoidance, then it is meaningful to regard the relationship between the Court and the competent legislative body as a dialogue … The legislative body is in a position to devise a response that is properly respectful of the *Charter* values that have been identified by the Court, but which accomplishes the social or economic objectives that the judicial decision has impeded.[15]

In 2007, Hogg and Bushell, writing with Wright, further expanded and clarified their analysis:

> The legislature and the executive may act on their interpretation of the *Charter* … However, where the interpretive task takes place against the backdrop of a prior relevant

[12] See, eg, Christine Bateup, 'The Dialogic Promise – Assessing the Normative Potential of Theories of Constitutional Dialogue' (2005) 71 *Brooklyn Law Review* 1109.

[13] See, eg, Devika Hovell, 'A Dialogue Model: The Role of the Domestic Judge in Security Council Decision-Making' (2013) 26 *Leiden Journal of International Law* 579; Kent Roach, 'Constitutional, Remedial, and International Dialogues about Rights: The Canadian Experience Symposium: Globalization and the Judiciary' (2004) 40 *Texas International Law Journal* 537; Anne-Marie Slaughter, 'A Typology of Transjudicial Communication Symposium: Human Rights International Law' (1994) 29 *University of Richmond Law Review* 99; Anne-Marie Slaughter, 'A Global Community of Courts Focus: Emerging Fora for International Litigation (Part 2)' (2003) 44 *Harvard International Law Journal* 191.

[14] See pt 1 of the Constitution Act 1982, sch B to the Canada Act 1982 (UK) 1982, c 11.

[15] Peter W Hogg and Allison A Bushell, 'The Charter Dialogue between Courts and Legislatures (Or Perhaps the Charter of Rights Isn't Such a Bad Thing after All)' (1997) 35 *Osgoode Hall Law Journal* 75, 79.

> judicial decision, the legislature and the executive may not act on an interpretation of the *Charter* which conflicts with an interpretation provided by the Courts.[16]

Mechanisms that facilitate legislative responses to court decisions have since been identified in Australia,[17] New Zealand[18] and the United Kingdom.[19] In her comprehensive study of democratic dialogue in the UK context, Young found that there are no necessary or sufficient criteria that need to be met to facilitate dialogue.[20] Rather, she found that there are various and diverse mechanisms and constitutional structures which can enable legislative responses to court decisions.[21]

Young concluded that constitutional mechanisms that facilitated democratic dialogue broadly fall into two groups. The first group are those mechanisms that give rise to '*constitutional collaboration*', in that they enable the legislature and the courts 'to work together by drawing on their relative strengths and weaknesses when reasoning about rights', thereby allowing each institution 'to take account not just of reasons for and against a particular resolution of rights issues, but also other reasons which would require each institution to give weight to the resolution of the other'.[22]

The second group are mechanisms which give rise to '*constitutional counter-balancing*' because they ensure that both the legislature and court contribute to determining rights issues, while making sure that one institution's analysis does not always dominate or override the contribution of the other.[23] The argument is that, while constitutional collaboration should be the primary focus of the institutions, constitutional-counterbalancing mechanisms should be available for 'when one institution believes the other has transgressed the proper scope of its constitutional powers'.[24] Constitutional counter-balancing, according to Young, indirectly

[16] Peter M Hogg, Allison A Bushell Thornton and Wade K Wright, 'Charter Dialogue Revisited – or Much Ado about Metaphors Charter Dialogue: Ten Years Later' (2007) 45 *Osgoode Hall Law Journal* 1, 33.

[17] These mechanisms have been identified only in some Australian jurisdictions, such as Victoria and the Australian Capital Territory. See, eg, Scott Stephenson, 'Constitutional Reengineering: Dialogue's Migration from Canada to Australia' (2013) 11 *International Journal of Constitutional Law* 870; Leighton McDonald, 'Rights, "Dialogue" and Democratic Objections to Judicial Review' (2004) 32 *Federal Law Review* 1.

[18] See, eg, Andrew Geddis, 'Inter-Institutional "Rights Dialogue" under the New Zealand Bill of Rights Act' in Tom Campbell, Keith Ewing and Adam Tomkins (eds), *The Legal Protection of Human Rights: Sceptical Essays* (Oxford University Press 2011); Léonid Sirota, 'Constitutional Dialogue: The New Zealand Bill of Rights Act and the Noble Dream' (2017) 27 *New Zealand Universities Law Review* 897.

[19] TRS Allan, 'Constitutional Dialogue and the Justification of Judicial Review' (2003) 23 *Oxford Journal of Legal Studies* 563; Alison L Young, 'Deference, Dialogue and the Search for Legitimacy' (2010) 30 *Oxford Journal of Legal Studies* 815.

[20] Alison L Young, *Democratic Dialogue and the Constitution* (Oxford University Press 2017) 22.

[21] ibid 31, 174–75.

[22] ibid 33, 161. See also Bateup (n 12) 1175; Sara Jackson, 'Designing Human Rights Legislation: Dialogue, the Commonwealth Model and the Roles of Parliaments and Courts' (2007) 13 *Auckland University Law Review* 89, 92.

[23] Young, *Democratic Dialogue and the Constitution* (n 20) 32–33, 117.

[24] ibid 161.

facilitates constitutional collaboration because it maintains the model's stability by ensuring that there is a way to resolve constitutional conflicts.[25] These mechanisms must, however, be used rarely, if they are to facilitate dialogue.[26]

Hogg and Bushell's aim was to show that the Canadian Charter is more democratic (and judicial review is weaker) than might be otherwise supposed,[27] and they emphasised that they did not, from their study, want to draw conclusions as to whether judicial review is good or bad.[28] Despite their reticence, however, the democratic dialogue model has subsequently been described as normatively advantageous and it is the normative justifications for the dialogue model that make it unique. It is a model that is not only reflective of practice and one grounded in 'real facts and assumptions', but it is also a model that provides an 'aspirational ideal'.[29]

The key normative claim of the model is that when courts and legislatures engage in dialogue, the rights protection produced by the interaction is 'better' than it would be if the institutions were acting alone. What is meant by this use of the word 'better' is not that a stronger protection of the individual's legal rights is necessarily produced. Nor does the use of the word 'better' mean that a stronger political protection of rights is produced that allows governments, through legislatures, to achieve exactly their agenda. Rather, a 'better' protection of rights here means one that draws on both a political and legal protection of rights; specifically, a protection of rights which 'maximises the advantages and minimises the dangers of purely legal or purely political protections of human rights' by providing a balance between or a 'hybrid' of the two systems.[30]

Gardbaum and Young unpack and refine this claim. Their argument is that a 'better' protection of rights is produced not because that protection provides a balance between a purely legal or political protection of rights, but because the protection produced draws on the strengths of how both courts and political branches reason about rights. That is, because the protection draws on accounts of both legal and political constitutionalism.[31] Briefly, those who argue for a strong *legal* protection of human rights, usually rely on similar arguments to those which underpin legal constitutionalism.[32] Their argument is that courts are best placed

[25] ibid 161, 171.
[26] ibid 268.
[27] Hogg and Bushell (n 15) 80; Hogg, Bushell Thornton and Wright (n 16) 29.
[28] Hogg and Bushell (n 15) 105.
[29] Young, *Democratic Dialogue and the Constitution* (n 20) 174.
[30] ibid 4, 148–52. See also Stephen Gardbaum, *The New Commonwealth Model of Constitutionalism: Theory and Practice* (Cambridge University Press 2013) 51–61; Tom Hickman, *Public Law after the Human Rights Act* (Hart Publishing 2010) 71–80; Emmett Macfarlane, 'Dialogue or Compliance? Measuring Legislatures' Policy Responses to Court Rulings on Rights' (2013) 34 *International Political Science Review* 39, 39; Jeffrey Goldsworthy, 'Homogenizing Constitutions' (2003) 23 *OJLS* 483.
[31] Young, *Democratic Dialogue and the Constitution* (n 20) 6, 32, 148–49; Gardbaum (n 30). Neil Walker describes constitutionalism as being 'the set of beliefs associated with the idea of constitutional government': cited in Alec Stone Sweet, 'Constitutionalism, Legal Pluralism, and International Regimes' (2009) 16 *Indiana Journal of Global Legal Studies* 621.
[32] Young, *Democratic Dialogue and the Constitution* (n 20) 7.

to decide on rights because they are unelected institutions and thus function as 'forum[s] of principle',[33] which can focus on individual and minority interests. Those who argue for a *political* protection of rights tend to rely on arguments similar to political constitutionalism. They contend that the legislature is best placed to decide on rights issues because it is a democratically elected institution and thus directly accountable to electors.[34]

Constitutional collaboration mechanisms enable both legislatures and courts to play a role in protecting rights, 'applying their relative strengths and weaknesses in a complementary manner', and it is for this reason that those mechanisms are more likely to afford this 'better' protection of rights.[35] Constitutional counter-balancing mechanisms, by indirectly supporting constitutional collaboration by ensuring a means to smooth over constitutional conflict, also therefore indirectly facilitate the achievement of this normative claim.[36]

The second normative claim of the model is that it produces greater and more diverse deliberations on rights because, when rights are being openly discussed by the different institutions, more individuals and groups, with differing and diverse points of view, are able to contribute to the discussion.[37] Again, constitutional collaboration mechanisms are likely to facilitate this normative benefit. As Young describes it,

> [d]eliberation is facilitated when legislatures and courts provide clear reasons for their decisions. Not only does this help to ensure that there is value-oriented as well as interest-formed collaboration, but … it also helps to frame debate between institutions and that taking place in society at large.[38]

The third normative claim is that dialogue produces a system of checks and balances between courts and legislatures. This is because the court can assess the decisions being made by the legislature and ensure that it does not overstep its competence, and, in turn, the legislature can ensure that the judiciary is not acting politically.[39] This normative claim is more likely to be achieved through constitutional counter-balancing,[40] given that those mechanisms should only be used when one institution is considered to have overstepped its competence.

[33] Grégoire CN Webber, 'The Unfulfilled Potential of the Court and Legislature Dialogue' (2009) 42 *Canadian Journal of Political Science/Revue canadienne de science politique* 443, 444; Kent Roach, *The Supreme Court on Trial: Judicial Activism or Democratic Dialogue* (Irwin 2016) 285.

[34] Luc B Tremblay, 'The Legitimacy of Judicial Review: The Limits of Dialogue between Courts and Legislatures' (2005) 3 *International Journal of Constitutional Law* 617, 619; Young, *Democratic Dialogue and the Constitution* (n 20) 148.

[35] Young, *Democratic Dialogue and the Constitution* (n 20) 159.

[36] ibid 160.

[37] ibid 31, 154; Rosalind Dixon, 'Creating Dialogue about Socioeconomic Rights: Strong-Form versus Weak-Form Judicial Review Revisited' (2007) 5 *International Journal of Constitutional Law* 391, 407.

[38] Young, *Democratic Dialogue and the Constitution* (n 20) 159.

[39] ibid 31; Jackson (n 22) 114. See also *Vriend v Alberta* [1998] 1 SCR 493 [120].

[40] Young, *Democratic Dialogue and the Constitution* (n 20) 159.

The democratic dialogue model is not without its critics. Manfredi and Kelly consider that only 'negative responses' or those responses that show some disagreement with the court decision on the part of the legislature can properly be 'dialogue'. On this view, if legislatures simply agree with the judicial decision, a relationship of equality between the institutions (which is necessary, in their view, for real and meaningful dialogue) does not exist.[41] Tremblay, for his part, argues that the 'dialogue' label should only really be used if both parties to the interaction are trying to reach a common goal,[42] while Rosas suggests that 'genuine' dialogue needs some kind of mutual exchange of opinion and experience between the two institutional parties to the interaction.[43] For King, true dialogue requires domestic courts and legislatures to be in a relationship of at least 'approximate equality'.[44] Kavanagh provides an excellent and comprehensive overview of the critiques and critics of dialogue, and argues that we should move beyond the dialogue model because it oversimplifies the roles of legislatures and courts.[45]

The purpose of this book is not to engage directly with these critiques. The aim is simply to demonstrate that the democratic dialogue model, despite its flaws, can usefully and accurately explain the relationship between the UK Parliament and, respectively, the ECtHR and CJEU, even in the area of immigration, and that there are normative benefits to those dialogic relationships.

II. Contribution

The argument that the UK Parliament and the ECtHR engage in democratic dialogue, and Parliament previously did so with the CJEU, represents a new approach to rights adjudication by international courts, and an approach that addresses the problems with the more conventional theoretical approaches to that adjudication. Those traditional approaches are polarised and polarising insofar as they view rights adjudication by international courts as either highly negative (the view taken by political constitutionalists) or highly positive (the view taken by legal constitutionalists).

Legal constitutionalists consider international courts best suited to the role of adjudicating rights because they are the institutions most experienced and skilled in legal reasoning and, also, because courts are (at least in theory) impartial and

[41] Christopher P Manfredi and James B Kelly, 'Six Degrees of Dialogue: A Response to Hogg and Bushell Forum' (1999) 37 *Osgoode Hall Law Journal* 513, 520–21.

[42] See generally Tremblay (n 34) 617.

[43] Allan Rosas, 'The European Court of Justice in Context: Forms and Patterns of Judicial Dialogue' (2007) 1 *European Journal of Legal Studies* 1, 15.

[44] Jeff King, 'Dialogue, Finality and Legality' in Geoffrey Sigalet, Grégoire Webber and Rosalind Dixon (eds), *Constitutional Dialogue: Rights, Democracy, Institutions* (Cambridge University Press 2019) 189.

[45] Aileen Kavanagh, 'The Lure and the Limits of Dialogue Public Law for the Twenty-First Century' (2016) 66 *University of Toronto Law Journal* 83, 90.

apolitical institutions. Courts are, on this basis, institutionally highly and uniquely capable of protecting the interests of individuals and minorities and are in fact designed to focus on those interests. This is in contradistinction to legislative bodies which, according to legal constitutionalists, are inevitably subject to shifting political influence and are, at their worst, even susceptible to a potentially oppressive and individual rights-denying 'tyranny of the majority'.[46] As Kavanagh argues more fully, because a court: 'has no interests of its own to further, and is relatively unaccountable to the various political interests in society, it can provide an impartial forum in which the issues can be decided in light of constitutional principles'.[47]

These constitutionalists argue that courts are independent not only because they are unelected institutions but also because a key role of courts (at least in many Commonwealth jurisdictions) is to actively protect the constitution against the potential abuse of power by the political branch. This argument is articulated by, among others, Bellamy:

> Legal constitutionalists regard the political system as being established through and constrained by a judicially protected legal constitution that operates as a 'higher' law, above the ordinary legislation issuing from the democratic process. In such systems, ordinary legislation can be disapplied by 'strong', rights-based, judicial review on the part of a constitutional court.[48]

The legal constitutionalist argument becomes even more forceful in the context of international (as opposed to domestic) courts because, while international courts are set up by treaties concluded between states, they function externally to states. International courts, as O'Cinneide argues, therefore have another level of independence and separation 'from the political pressures and prevailing ideological prejudices that may apply at national level', and they function as an 'external point of scrutiny' before which states must dispute allegations that they have infringed international human rights law or before which states must justify infringements of such law.[49]

Political constitutionalists, on the other hand, argue in favour of decision-making on rights being left to legislative bodies which, unlike courts, are elected bodies and are (again, at least in theory) both representative of a population and

[46] See generally Ronald Dworkin, 'The Forum of Principle' (1981) 56 *New York University Law Review* (1950) 469, 461; Webber (n 33) 444; Roach, *The Supreme Court on Trial* (n 33) 285.

[47] Aileen Kavanagh, 'Participation and Judicial Review: A Reply to Jeremy Waldron' (2003) 22 *Law and Philosophy* 451, 472.

[48] R Bellamy, 'The Democratic Legitimacy of International Human Rights Conventions: Political Constitutionalism and the European Convention on Human Rights' (2014) 25 *European Journal of International Law* 1019, 1021 (citations omitted).

[49] Colm O'Cinneide, 'Saying "No" to Strasbourg: When Are National Parliaments Justified in Refusing to Give Effect to Judgments of International Human Rights Courts?' in Matthew Saul, Andreas Follesdal and Geir Ulfstein (eds), *The International Human Rights Judiciary and National Parliaments: Europe and Beyond* (Cambridge University Press 2017) 318. See generally Andreas Follesdal, 'The Legitimacy of International Human Rights Review: The Case of the European Court of Human Rights' (2009) 40 *Journal of Social Philosophy* 595.

accountable to that population. Legislatures, unlike courts, are capable of balancing the views of competing groups and interests and of dealing with a broad range of issues.[50] As Waldron argues, domestic legislatures can 'hold general inquisitorial hearings', 'tak[e] evidence from anyone who might have a stake' and 'open themselves to hearings and, less formally, to lobbying and consultation of all kinds'.[51] This means, Young argues, that legislatures are well placed to focus on 'general, forward-looking measures to resolve broad problems or issues facing society as a whole'.[52]

The political constitutionalist opposition to courts adjudicating rights is further strengthened in the context of international courts (as opposed to domestic courts) making such decisions. This is because: (i) international courts, unlike domestic courts, are not set up by domestic constitutions or domestic law, and so, as Bellamy describes it, 'the transfer of powers from the state to such bodies tends to lack appropriate democratic authorization in the first place';[53] and (ii) international court decisions are made by reference to laws that are not enacted by an elected body or laws made so as to respond to voters' demands or needs.[54] While some domestic systems provide for legislatures to have some say over which international treaties are ratified and how treaties should be incorporated into domestic law, international law may not have had any democratic scrutiny by domestic institutions at all. Treaty law, which international courts apply, and by reference to which international courts assess the legality of domestic law and policy, is, rather, usually negotiated by the executive, and not by the legislative branches of states.[55]

[50] Tremblay (n 34) 619; Young, *Democratic Dialogue and the Constitution* (n 20) 148; Gardbaum (n 30). This describes Habermas' 'Parliamentary Principle': Jürgen Habermas, *Between Facts and Norms: Contributions to a Discourse Theory of Law and Democracy* (William Rehg tr, MIT Press 1996) 170.

[51] Jeremy Waldron, 'Refining the Question about Judges' Moral Capacity' (2008) 7 *International Journal of Constitutional Law* 69, 81–82.

[52] Young, *Democratic Dialogue and the Constitution* (n 20) 148–49; Gardbaum (n 30) 51–61.

[53] See, eg, Bellamy (n 48) 1020–21. See generally Ronald Dworkin, 'A New Philosophy for International Law' (2013) 41 *Philosophy & Public Affairs* 2; O'Cinneide (n 49) 312; Eyal Benvenisti and George W Downs, *Between Fragmentation and Democracy: The Role of National and International Courts* (Cambridge University Press 2017) 179, citing Thomas Nagel 'The Problem of Global Justice' (2005) 33 *Philosophy and Public Affairs* 113, 138. Miguel Schor, 'Constitutional Dialogue and Judicial Supremacy' in Gary Jacobsohn and Miguel Schor (eds), *Comparative Constitutional Theory* (Edward Elgar 2018); Ran Hirschl, *Towards Juristocracy: The Origins and Consequences of the New Constitutionalism* (Harvard University Press 2004).

[54] Jamie Mayerfeld, *The Promise of Human Rights: Constitutional Government, Democratic Legitimacy, and International Law* (University of Pennsylvania Press 2016) 186.

[55] See generally Jed Rubenfeld, 'Unilateralism and Constitutionalism' (2004) 79 *New York University Law Review* 1971, 1976; Kenneth Anderson, 'The Ottawa Convention Banning Landmines, the Role of International Non-Governmental Organizations and the Idea of International Civil Society' (2000) 11 *European Journal of International Law* 91, 103. John R Bolton, 'Is There Really Law in International Affairs?' (2000) 10 *Transnational Law & Contemporary Problems* 1, 3–4; Allen Buchanan and Russell Powell, 'Constitutional Democracy and the Rule of International Law: Are They Compatible?' (2008) 16 *Journal of Political Philosophy* 326, 329–30. The argument that international law is undemocratic in this way is exacerbated by the fact that the states controlling the treaty negotiation processes are usually those politically and economically powerful states, which Bellamy describes as the 'unaccountable elites': see, eg, Bellamy (n 48) 1020.

The ECtHR's interpretation of the ECHR as a 'living instrument' provides a particularly good example of how the political constitutionalist argument against courts undertaking judicial review becomes even more persuasive when that review is undertaken by international courts. The 'living instrument doctrine' is a doctrine which provides that the ECHR's scope evolves with time to reflect changing social views and, accordingly, that the Convention should be interpreted in light of present-day conditions.[56] By virtue of this doctrine, the law (as set out in the ECHR) applied by the ECtHR is not only that negotiated by the executive branches of states, but is also the law which has been developed significantly by the ECtHR itself. This gives rise, as Horne and Tyrrell describe in the UK context, to an 'inevitable tension with the sovereignty of Parliament in the sense that the Convention rights may evolve in directions that were not anticipated or intended by the domestic legislatures ratifying the instrument'.[57]

The likely political constitutionalist opposition to this doctrine is encapsulated well by Lord Murray of Blidworth: [t]his doctrine enabled the Strasburg judges to reform social arrangements, even very fundamental ones, either without debate and approval from democratic legislatures or with a retrospective approval.[58]

***

I have so far deliberately presented the conflicting approaches of legal constitutionalists and political constitutionalists to rights adjudication by international courts in a simplified way in order to illustrate and outline an immensely complicated debate. It is, however, precisely this kind of simplification which is frequently employed in a particularly unhelpful way by the ardent proponents on either side of the debate. That is, they situate the opposing side in precarious straw-man positions and often demonstrate little appreciation (or, at least, little overt appreciation) for the particular strengths of the institution against which they are arguing.

Political constitutionalists who denounce the 'undemocratic' nature of the rights adjudication process by international courts on the basis that the process does not involve directly elected institutions, often, for instance, fail to consider the fact that states parties have consented to be bound by international court judgments,[59] and that states have a say in the composition of the court.[60] Some political constitutionalists also argue that the process is 'undemocratic' on the basis

[56] *Tyrer v UK* (1978) 2 EHRR 1 [31].

[57] Alexander Horne and Hélène Tyrrell, 'Sovereignty, Privilege and the European Convention on Human Rights' in Alexander Horne and Andrew Le Sueur (eds), *Parliament: Legislation and Accountability* (Hart Publishing 2016) 281.

[58] HL deb 20 March 2025, vol 844, col 1373.

[59] O'Cinneide (n 49) 316; George Letsas, 'The ECHR as a Living Instrument: Its Meaning and Legitimacy' in Andreas Føllesdal, Birgit Peters and Geir Ulfstein (eds), *Constituting Europe: The European Court of Human Rights in a National, European and Global Context* (Cambridge University Press 2013) 139–41; James W Nickel, *Making Sense of Human Rights*, 2nd edn (Blackwell 2007) 47.

[60] O'Cinneide (n 49) 315.

that courts only ever hear 'all sides of a two-sided argument' (which is a problem when, as Waldron argues, arguments about rights issues are, in fact, multifaceted and complex).[61] These constitutionalists thereby fail to acknowledge that (domestic and international) courts might be capable, through the trial process, of giving a platform to numerous and diverse voices. These voices might include those who might not otherwise be heard, such as victims of, and witnesses to, rights abuses, as well as, for example, policy experts in their capacity as intervenors.[62]

Legal constitutionalists can, for their part, fail to acknowledge that legislatures are not inherently 'bad' or ineffective at protecting individual rights or minorities. As Young points out, political branches can also effectively uphold individuals' and minorities' rights precisely because these branches are themselves 'made up of groups representing divergent minority interests who need to group together to form a majority'.[63]

There is also frequently little recognition by theorists on either side of the debate as to the internal deficiencies of their own arguments, and, even where there is such recognition, attempts are often made to rectify such internal weaknesses by, for instance, changing or reconceptualising even the basic terms on which the debate is conducted, particularly with respect to the meaning of 'democracy'.[64] Eisgruber, for instance, in order to defend judicial review of national legislation by international courts, adopts for his argument what has come to be known as the 'thick' definition of democracy. The 'thick' definition of democracy focuses on the outcome of the deliberative process rather than on the democratic nature of the process itself. He argues that there is only a 'loss for democracy whenever democratic procedures produce non-democratic outcomes'.[65] Accordingly, on this conceptualisation of democracy, Eisgruber says that '[a]ny democratic deficits that judicial review may retain can be compensated for by its overall legitimacy, rooted in its contribution to the protection of individual rights'.[66]

To take another example: Geary, Morrison and Jago defend judicial review as being democratically legitimate (or, at least, not necessarily undemocratic) not by focusing on the outcome of the deliberative process, but by recharacterising judges as democratic players. This is despite the fact that judges are (usually) not elected

[61] Waldron (n 51) 81.

[62] See, eg, Steven Wheatley, 'A Democratic Rule of International Law' (2011) 22 *European Journal of International Law* 525; Eyal Benvenisti and George W Downs, 'National Courts, Domestic Democracy, and the Evolution of International Law' (2009) 20 *European Journal of International Law* 59, 69.

[63] Young, *Democratic Dialogue and the Constitution* (n 20) 7, 148. See also Bateup (n 12) 1152.

[64] See generally A von Bogdandy and I Venzke, 'In Whose Name? An Investigation of International Courts' Public Authority and Its Democratic Justification' (2012) 23 *European Journal of International Law* 7; Wheatley (n 62).

[65] Christopher L Eisgruber, *Constitutional Self-Government* (Harvard University Press 2001) 4.

[66] Andreas von Staden, 'The Democratic Legitimacy of Judicial Review beyond the State: Normative Subsidiarity and Judicial Standards of Review' (2012) 10 *International Journal of Constitutional Law* 1023, 1030. Mayerfeld takes a similar position, arguing that democracy is strengthened by international human rights law because the policies and laws that international human rights law prevents governments from adopting are those in respect of which governments should not be, in his view, legislating on anyway: see Mayerfeld (n 54) 187, 216.

to their positions by a popular vote of citizens. The argument is that, in upholding the rule of law, judges are asserting the values of a democratic culture whereby government should only act in accordance with human rights.[67] On this view, if judges appear to act against the legislated intentions of an elected government in human rights cases, they are, at a deeper level, acting in accordance with the 'true' meaning of democracy. Grossman similarly focuses on the deliberative process as opposed to the outcome of the process in her examination of rights adjudication by international courts. She argues that international courts are not necessarily undemocratic because they derive their 'justified authority' not just from their 'fair and unbiased nature', but, in part, from the courts' 'transparency and relationship with other democratic values'.[68]

Other theorists have attempted to deal with the internal deficiencies of their side of the argument by presenting a whole new model according to which rights adjudication by international courts should take place. De Búrca suggests that the entire global legal order should be reconceptualised, and she proposes an approach to transnational governance which she labels the 'democratic-striving approach'. The 'democratic-striving approach', as she describes it, involves taking key elements and values of domestic constitutional orders (such as participation of the citizenry in decision-making and representation of the citizenry) and translating these 'upwards' to the international level.[69] By including democratic values in the rights adjudication process, on de Búrca's view, the political constitutionalist's counter-majoritarian objection could be answered.

Pinto-Duschinsky, for his part, argues that there should be a formalised 'democratic override' mechanism built into the rights adjudication process at the domestic level, whereby national parliaments could in effect override decisions made by international courts (and, specifically, in his example, the ECtHR).[70] He makes this argument on the basis that democracy (again, specifically, in his example, democracy in the UK), is 'too important and too intimate to be sacrificed for the supposed but unproven advantage of other peoples'.[71] This unjustified sacrifice, in his view, occurs when authority is given to the ECtHR to decide on rights issues. O'Cinneide makes a similar argument to Pinto-Duschinsky. O'Cinneide

[67] Adam Gearey, Wayne Morrison and Robert Jago, *The Politics of the Common Law: Perspectives, Rights, Processes, Institutions*, 2nd edn (Routledge-Cavendish 2013) 207.

[68] Nienke Grossman, 'Legitimacy and International Adjudicative Bodies' (2009) 41 *George Washington International Law Review* 107, 110. *cf* von Staden (n 66) 1030. Von Staden is critical of Grossman. He says that Grossman talks about this infusion with democratic norms as 'enhancing judicial legitimacy', without actually saying, aside from transparency, what these norms are.

[69] See, eg, Gráinne de Búrca, 'Developing Democracy beyond the State' (2008) 46 *Columbia Journal of Transnational Law* 221. *cf* Anne Peters, 'Dual Democracy' in Jan Klabbers, Anne Peters and Geir Ulfstein (eds), *The Constitutionalization of International Law* (Oxford University Press 2009).

[70] Michael Pinto-Duschinsky, *Bringing Rights Back Home: Making Human Rights Compatible with Parliamentary Democracy in the UK* (Policy Exchange 2011). See generally O'Cinneide (n 49).

[71] Pinto-Duschinsky (n 70) 65.

puts forward a proposal according to which national legislatures and other state organs should:

> [B]e entitled to 'disobey' a judgment of an [international human rights court], or even to repudiate an entire ['strong' international human rights law] regime, if such an act of disobedience can legitimately be shown to be necessary to vindicate popular sovereignty.[72]

He makes this proposal on the basis that, in his view, the justified authority of international human rights courts is limited by democratic first principles.

There can of course be considerable value in reconceptualising debates and in rethinking the terms on which the debates are fought. But these reconceptualisations by legal and political constitutionalists with respect to rights adjudication by international courts have usually been promulgated without acknowledgement that they are redefining key terms and that their proposals are often purely aspirational. This has resulted in an outcome where the debate is not being fought on a level playing field, and where both sides end up 'talking' past each other.

This book addresses and supplants the traditional conceptualisation and, ultimately, the oversimplification of the rights adjudication process by legal and political constitutionalists. It rejects the polarised nature of those existing approaches, and instead takes the empirically based view that domestic parliaments and international courts, such as the UK Parliament and the ECtHR and CJEU, can in fact significantly interact, specifically by engaging in democratic dialogue with one another, and that this interaction in and of itself produces a more legitimate protection of rights.

III. Structure

A small point before I explain the book's structure: for ease of understanding, I sometimes in the book refer to democratic dialogue between a domestic legislature (such as the UK Parliament) and international courts (such as the ECtHR and the CJEU) as 'transnational democratic dialogue'. This is to reflect the fact that dialogue between these particular institutions does not take place solely in the domestic sphere nor solely in the international sphere.[73]

At the domestic level, the best kinds of rights issues with which to test the claims of the democratic dialogue model are said to be rights issues about which there is disagreement: (i) as to their resolution ('contestable rights issues'); or (ii) as to which institution (of courts and legislatures) should resolve them (rights issues which give rise to 'institutional contestability'). Chapter one argues that these kinds of rights issues should also be the best kinds of issues with which to test whether

[72] O'Cinneide (n 49) 321.

[73] See generally Philip C Jessup, *Transnational Law* (Yale University Press 1956) 2; Harold Koh, 'Why Transnational Law Matters' (2006) 24 *Penn State International Law Review* 745.

the UK Parliament and the ECtHR and the CJEU have engaged in (transnational) democratic dialogue. It is against this background that the immigration-based case study of this book is introduced. The provision to non-nationals of a right, or some protection, to enter and remain in a country can be characterised as a contestable rights issue. Significantly, it is also a rights issue about which we would expect there to be reasonable disagreement as to which institution (of a domestic legislature or an international court) should have the authority to decide upon and resolve it.

Chapter two demonstrates that there in a framework in place by which the UK Parliament and the ECtHR can engage in democratic dialogue, and by which the UK Parliament could previously do so with the CJEU. It does so by identifying mechanisms which can facilitate interaction between the UK Parliament and the two courts in the sense of 'constitutional collaboration'; that is, that can facilitate the institutions working together by drawing on their strengths when reasoning about rights. It also identifies mechanisms that can facilitate interaction between the UK Parliament and the ECtHR and CJEU in the sense of 'constitutional counter-balancing'; that is, mechanisms that ensure no one institution can always override the contribution of the other.

Having set up the framework by which democratic dialogue can happen between these institutions, chapter three begins the examination of whether the framework has indeed been used in practice, and it specifically examines interactions that have taken place between the UK Parliament and the ECtHR. The chapter looks at decisions of the ECtHR concerning: (i) protection from deportation to non-nationals who have been illegally residing in the country; (ii) protection from deportation to non-nationals who have committed criminal offences while residing in the country; (iii) protection to non-nationals to enter a country for the purpose of family and, specifically, spousal, reunification; and (iv) protection from deportation to non-nationals whose proposed deportation has resulted in, or would result in, a violation of other Convention rights owed to them. For the most part, the chapter shows that: (i) the UK Parliament and the ECtHR engage in democratic dialogue with respect to non-nationals who wish to enter and remain in a foreign country; and (ii) the normative claims of the democratic dialogue model are achieved when those interactions take place.

Chapter four examines decisions of the CJEU which had the effect of providing protection from deportation to: (i) a non-European Economic Area (EEA) national who seeks to remain in a Member State, on the basis of having first arrived in the Member State with an EEA-national spouse; and (ii) a non-EEA national, who has entered the EEA unlawfully, and who seeks to remain in the EEA with an EEA-national spouse. The chapter argues that the UK Parliament and the CJEU previously engaged in democratic dialogue with respect to this rights issue, and that the normative claims of the democratic dialogue model were, at least to some extent, achieved when the institutions engaged in dialogue.

In the process of writing this book, the UK government's attacks on the ECtHR, from both sides of politics, have continued. The concluding chapter will reflect on these attacks in light of the findings made in chapters three and four of the book. It demonstrates that these attacks are unwarranted and misplaced. There is a dynamic relationship between the ECtHR and the UK Parliament, with attendant normative advantages, and the institutions have for the most part worked together to produce moderated protections of rights. Significantly, being part of the ECHR and subject to the ECtHR's jurisdiction has not diminished Parliament's sovereignty, even when the Court has engaged Parliament on the subject of immigration and as to which kinds of non-nationals can enter and remain in the country. The same can be said for the relationship the UK Parliament had with the CJEU. The book, accordingly, leaves us with a framework with which to critically examine the government's attacks on these 'foreign' courts.

IV. A Note to the Reader

The focus of this book is on the UK Parliament and its relationship with the ECtHR and the CJEU. The ECtHR and CJEU each represent a different and contrasting model of human rights protection at the international level, despite both being based in Europe. The implication of this is that the democratic dialogue model should also be able to explain the relationship between domestic legislatures and these two courts, and indeed, the relationships between domestic legislatures and international courts and tribunals, beyond the specific case studies chosen here.

By showing that domestic legislatures and international courts work consciously together to produce protections of rights, criticisms that the process of rights adjudication at the international level, by international courts, is undemocratic, can be addressed. The following extract from the UK's Human Rights Joint Committee in its 2009 Report entitled 'Enhancing Parliament's Role in Relation to Human Rights Judgments' seems to support this view:

> [P]arliamentary involvement in the implementation of Court judgments on human rights has many advantages. It not only raises awareness of human rights issues in Parliament, but it increases the political transparency of the Government's response to Court judgments. *In so doing it helps both to ensure a genuine democratic input into legal changes following Court judgments and to address the perception that changes in law or policy as a result of Court judgments lack democratic legitimacy. It facilitates the co-ordination of the various actors, raises the political visibility of the issues at stake and provides an opportunity for public scrutiny of the justifications offered by the Government for its proposed response to the judgment or for its delay in bringing such a response forward.* Parliamentary involvement is also an essential aspect of *strengthening national mechanisms for ensuring compliance with the Convention* and the Court's interpretation of the Convention and therefore for reducing the flood of applications to the Court.[74]

[74] Joint Committee on Human Rights, 'Enhancing Parliament's Role in Relation to Human Rights Judgments' (House of Commons 2010) Fifteenth Report of Session 2009–2010, para 17 (emphasis added).

Responding to the counter-majoritarian concern in this way, by involving political branches in the rights adjudication process, also functions to enhance the credibility and authority of the international human rights legal system. As Torbisco-Casals says:

> Legitimacy, in a sociological sense, is even more important at the international level than domestically, as [international courts] can only resort to coercion in a very limited way in order to compel state actors to comply with their decisions. Normatively, insofar as the international judiciary generates binding rules, it becomes even more important from a democratic angle that those who are legally bound by such normative system feel that they are so 'in their own name'.[75]

Buchanan and Keohane discuss the normative legitimacy of global governance institutions and they similarly note that, because the perception of legitimacy is itself of considerable significance, then international organisations 'will only thrive if they are viewed as legitimate by democratic publics'.[76] This is particularly the case in the current political climate, where international human rights law and, in particular, the adjudication of rights by international courts, are continually, and increasingly, faced with scepticism and attack. As Torbisco-Casals describes it:

> These concerns about legitimacy have become even more pressing in the current context of rising conservative populist regimes that appeal to democratic deficits to debunk and dismantle international governance. The backlash against human rights and global governance typical of this movement also entails a backlash against international courts and quasi-judicial mechanisms.[77]

Enhancing the actual and perceived legitimacy of the international human rights legal system in this way, by recognising a role for domestic political branches in the protection of rights, is of particular importance because it helps to ensure that states continue: (i) to participate in developing international law through treaty making; and, relatedly, (ii) to consent to the exercise of jurisdiction by international courts. International courts interpret, apply and develop international human rights law, but it is those states which are parties to international human rights treaties which draft and negotiate those treaties, and which thus confer jurisdiction on international courts to function in that way. States can, also, always withdraw from such treaties or amend how treaties are incorporated into and given effect in domestic law.[78] That states can, and might, withdraw from international treaties when the

[75] Neus Torbisco-Casals, 'The Legitimacy of International Courts: The Challenge of Diversity' (2021) 52 *Journal of Social Philosophy* 491, 494 (citations omitted).

[76] Allen Buchanan and Robert O Keohane, 'The Legitimacy of Global Governance Institutions' (2006) 20 *Ethics & International Affairs* 405, 407.

[77] Torbisco-Casals (n 75) 492.

[78] See generally Peters (n 69) 263 for this argument. See also Başak Çalı, 'ESIL Reflection: The Disciplinary Account of the Authority of International Law: Does It Stand Firm against Its External Critics?' (European Society of International Law, 9 May 2016): esil-sedi.eu/esil-reflection-the-disciplinary-account-of-the-authority-of-international-law-does-it-stand-firm-against-its-external-critics-2/. As Torbisco-Casals points out, however, withdrawing from a treaty

political branch is excluded from the process of rights adjudication (or, perhaps, when there is even a mere perception that the political branch is excluded), is demonstrated by the UK's withdrawal from the EU and, in turn, from the CJEU's exercise of jurisdiction. As Ekins states, 'the United Kingdom's decision to leave the EU follows in large part from alienation from EU decision-making and recognition of its incompatibility with parliamentary democracy'.[79]

That alienation (or at least that perceived alienation), according to Ekins, resulted directly from the fact that domestic political branches are not involved in EU decision-making. He argues that the EU's structure:

> [P]rivileges an elite conversation amongst heads of government, which is unavoidably *detached from ordinary citizens and wider parliamentary processes*. And the resulting institutional form is not clearly responsible to anyone, pursuing a centralizing agenda that is arguably not supported by any (or very few) member states. The position of the CJEU is particularly important and its willingness to depart from legal commitments *compounds the undemocratic nature of supranational government made by way of international agreements*.[80]

That states can also (and do) amend their domestic implementation of international human rights treaties is demonstrated by the UK government's proposal to replace the Human Rights Act with a Bill of Rights, without withdrawing from the ECHR.

Of course, not everyone will agree that recognising that the state has a voice and a role to play in human rights protection beyond the domestic sphere enhances the legitimacy of the system. Doing so fragments and therefore undermines a universal application of international human rights law, weakening the enforcement of international human rights law,[81] and calling into question the authority and function of international courts in the context of interpreting, applying and developing international human rights law.[82] A key role of international courts, in the context of human rights, is to protect, or at least to consider, the rights and interests of minorities or other individuals who do not necessarily fall within the political majority.[83] Legislatures, as elected institutions can have, 'an incentive to minimize and even trivialize the rights of the truly unpopular',[84] which results in the disenfranchisement of 'discreet and insular minorities', such as 'ethnic, cultural,

regime does come with consequences. He describes how 'although states can formally withdraw from treaties, there are serious limitations, uncertainties and costs in the "right to exit", which might make it problematic in practice … as the whole "Brexit" process has evidenced'. See Torbisco-Casals (n 75) n 5.

[79] Richard Ekins, 'Constitutional Conversations in Britain (in Europe)' in Geoffrey Sigalet, Grégoire Webber and Rosalind Dixon (eds), *Constitutional Dialogue*, 1st edn (Cambridge University Press 2019) 464.

[80] ibid (emphasis added).

[81] Eyal Benvenisti, 'Margin of Appreciation, Consensus, and Universal Standards' (1998) 31 *NYU Journal of International Law and Politics* 843, 843.

[82] Roach, 'Constitutional, Remedial, and International Dialogues about Rights' (n 13) 565.

[83] O'Cinneide (n 49) 325.

[84] Kent W Roach, 'Sharpening the Dialogue Debate: The Next Decade of Scholarship' (2007) 45 *Osgoode Hall Law Journal* (1960) 169, 172.

religious, racial and national' minorities, by the political branch.[85] Accordingly, recognising that international courts are in partnership with domestic legislatures may, to some, function to delegitimise the international human rights system. Taking this viewpoint and overlooking this partnership, however, the book argues, ignores both what is actually happening in practice and the significant benefits of that practice.

[85] Eyal Benvenisti, 'The Margin of Appreciation, Subsidiarity and Global Challenges to Democracy' (2018) 9 *Journal of International Dispute Settlement* 240, 241. Benvenisti also acknowledges that minorities can effectively engage in national politics and be 'highly influential' in 'outweighing diffuse majorities'.

1

Testing Transnational Democratic Dialogue

Decisions by the ECtHR and CJEU about immigration and, in particular, decisions which have effected a protection or right for a non-national to enter and remain in the country, have particularly antagonised the UK government over the past several decades. This is not entirely surprising given that a non-national's enjoyment of protection to enter and remain in a country is a rights issue which can be characterised as: (i) '*contestable*' because there are multiple available ways to resolve the rights issue, and (ii) '*institutionally contestable*' because there is reasonable disagreement as to which institution should resolve it.

Contestable and institutionally contestable rights issues are considered to be the best kinds of rights issues with which to test the claims of the democratic dialogue model, as that model exists at the domestic level. This chapter demonstrates that this is also the case for transnational democratic dialogue. That is, when the dialogue is between a domestic legislature and an international court. It is on this basis that I justify this book's central focus on interactions between the UK Parliament and the ECtHR and CJEU about immigration and, specifically, on interactions between these institutions concerning the enjoyment of a right to enter and/or remain in the country for a non-national.

I. The Right to Enter and Remain in a Country

Every person has the right to enter the territory of the state of which they are a national or citizen and, in turn, to reside in that territory, without fear or threat of deportation.[1] The right to enter is also sometimes conceived of as, or at least formulated textually to

[1] See Office of the UN High Commissioner for Human Rights, 'Discussion Paper: Expulsions of Aliens in International Human Rights Law' (2006) 1. I use the terms 'national' and 'citizen' interchangeably. Edwards explains that, the two concepts have such a close relationship 'such that making such a clear distinction is not always necessary or helpful': see Alice Edwards, 'The Meaning of Nationality in International Law in an Era of Human Rights' in Alice Edwards and Laura van Waas (eds), *Nationality and Statelessness under International Law* (Cambridge University Press 2014) 14. *cf* Weis who wrote that the terms are 'two different aspects of the same notion: State membership. "Nationality" stresses the international, "citizenship" the national, municipal, aspect': see Paul Weis, *Nationality and Statelessness in International Law*, 2nd edn (Sijthoff & Noordhoff 1979) 4–5. On this understanding, nationality is about the state being able to exercise jurisdiction over the individual vis-a-vis other states, while citizenship is about the conferral of particular rights and duties at domestic law: see Alfred Michael Boll, 'Nationality and Obligations of Loyalty in International and Municipal Law' (2005) 24 *Australian Year Book of International Law* 37, 37, fn 3.

be, a 'right to return' to one's country of nationality or as a 'right of re-entry' to one's country of nationality.[2]

The right to enter (or return) and the right to remain in a country are distinct rights, but because the two are inevitably inextricably connected to and inform one another, I refer to them as a singular right in this book: 'the right to enter and remain'. As Dame Rosalyn Higgins explained:

> [T]he rights of entry, sojourn and exit are indivisible: the denial of any one makes the assertion of the others a chimera rather than a reality. Moreover, they flow inexorably from the right of freedom of movement and residence within the borders of a state. Further, these rights of mobility are inextricably intertwined with certain other human rights.[3]

Two duties arise on the part of the state with respect to the right to enter and remain.[4] The first is a *positive duty* on the state to (re)admit its nationals to the territory of the state. The second is a *negative duty* on the state to not expel nationals of the state from the state's territory. These duties were, at least from the perspective of international law, historically owed only to other states, or, on a broader view, to the international community at large.[5] This position makes sense from a public ordering perspective because a state's expulsion of one of its nationals would, practically speaking, mean that another state, in order not to leave the individual stateless (which is itself contrary to international law), would need to admit a non-national.[6] As I discuss later in this chapter, a state's refusal to admit its own national would therefore be considered a violation of the expelling state's territorial supremacy and sovereignty.[7] This position has developed, however, and, more recently, it has been accepted that a state, in addition to owing the duty of

[2] Alison Kesby, *The Right to Have Rights: Citizenship, Humanity, and International Law* (Oxford University Press 2012) 17; Vincent Chetail, 'Freedom of Movement and Transnational Migrations: A Human Rights Perspective' in T Alexander Aleinikoff and Vincent Chetail (eds), *Migration and International Legal Norms* (TMC Asser Press 2003) 57.

[3] Rosalyn Higgins, 'The Right in International Law of an Individual to Enter, Stay in and Leave a Country' (1973) 49 *International Affairs* 341, 342.

[4] See generally Weis (n 1).

[5] Edwards (n 1) 30. See generally Guy S Goodwin-Gill, 'The Limits of the Power of Expulsion in Public International Law' (1976) 47 *British Yearbook of International Law* 55. This position does not hold true from a domestic, constitutional law perspective. The English Crown's 'duty of protection' owed to its subjects in exchange for their allegiance can be traced back to at least the 17th century, evidenced by Lord Coke LCJ's statement in 1608 that: 'between the Sovereign and the subject there is without comparison a higher and greater connexion: for as the subject oweth to the King his true and faithful ligeance and obedience, so the Sovereign is to govern and protect his subjects': see *Calvin's Case* (1608) 7 Co Rep 1a, 4b, 77 ER 377, cited in Campbell McLachlan, *Foreign Relations Law* (Cambridge University Press 2014) 353–54.

[6] See Weis (n 1) 45.

[7] Kesby (n 2) 16; Weis (n 1) 47; Francesca de Vittor, 'Nationality and Freedom of Movement' in Serena Forlati and Alessandra Annoni (eds), *The Changing Role of Nationality in International Law* (Taylor & Francis 2013) 96–97; Higgins (n 3) 350.

(re)admission and non-expulsion of its nationals to other states and to the international community, also owes these duties to its own nationals, as individuals.

Although the right to enter and remain is sometimes framed more broadly as being a right to enter and remain in one's 'own country' (as opposed to one's country of nationality),[8] nationality remains the key characteristic which triggers the above-mentioned duties on the part of the state. 'Nationality' itself is a contested concept and there are different ways of defining it as a matter of international law. In *Nottebohm*,[9] the International Court of Justice (ICJ) defined nationality in a substantive and holistic way because it suggested that something more (ie, a genuine link to the state) is required in order to be considered a national of a state:[10] 'nationality is a legal bond [between the state and an individual] having as its basis a social fact of attachment, a genuine connection of existence, interest and sentiments, together with the existence of reciprocal rights and duties'.[11]

This understanding of nationality stands in contradistinction to the 'formal' or 'thin' understanding of nationality, which views the concept as 'an international legal status denoting membership of a state'; a status which 'serves an ordering function between states as the status by which individuals are ascribed to states and distinguished from "aliens"'.[12]

[8] See, eg, art 12(4) of the ICCPR provides that 'no one shall be arbitrarily deprived of the right to enter his own country'. The UN HRC has stated that the reference to 'own country' encompasses 'an individual who, because of his or her special ties or claims in relation to a given country cannot be considered to be a mere non-national'. However, the UN HRC has acknowledged that there are only very limited circumstances in which someone might be considered not to be a 'mere non-national'. The Committee gives the example of a stateless person 'arbitrarily deprived of the right to acquire the nationality of the country' in which the stateless person is a resident, as being someone who would fall within this category: see, eg, UN HRC, 'General Comment No 27, Freedom of Movement' (UN Doc CCPR/C/21/Rev1/Add9 1999) para 20. See also Kesby (n 2) 17; Marc J Bossuyt, *Guide to the 'Travaux Préparatoires' of the International Covenant on Civil and Political Rights* (M Nijhoff 1987) 261; Stig Jägerskiöld, 'The Freedom of Movement' in Louis Henkin (ed), *The International Bill of Rights: The Covenant on Civil and Political Rights* (Columbia University Press 1981) 180. See, eg, *Stewart v Canada* [1996] UN Doc CCPR/C/58/D/538/1993 [12.8]; *Canepa v Canada* [1997] UN Doc CCPR/C/59/D/558/1993 [11.3]; *Francesco Madafferi v Australia* [2004] UN Doc CCPR/C/81/D/1011/2001 [9.6].

[9] *Nottebohm Case (Liechtenstein v Guatemala) (Second Phase)* [1955] ICJ Reports 4. Nottebohm was both a Guatemalan citizen and a citizen of Liechtenstein. He had obtained the latter citizenship through the process of naturalisation. The issue which arose for determination by the ICJ was whether Liechtenstein could exercise diplomatic protection on behalf of Nottebohm. The majority in *Nottebohm* held that Liechtenstein could not exercise diplomatic protection in these circumstances because there was no 'genuine connection' between it and Nottebohm: at 26.

[10] See generally Kim Rubenstein and Niamh Lenagh-Maguire, 'More or Less Secure? Nationality Questions, Deportation and Dual Nationality' in Alice Edwards and Laura Van Waas (eds), *Nationality and Statelessness under International Law* (Cambridge University Press 2014) 269–70; Anne Peters, 'Extraterritorial Naturalizations: Between the Human Right to Nationality, State Sovereignty and Fair Principles of Jurisdiction' (2010) 53 German Yearbook of International Law 624, 685.

[11] *Nottebohm Case (Liechtenstein v Guatemala) (Second Phase)* (n 9) 23.

[12] Kesby (n 2) 40, 42.

While the Organization for Security and Co-Operation in Europe (the OSCE)'s High Commissioner on National Minorities stated in 2008 that states should not confer citizenship on a person in the absence of a genuine link to the state,[13] by-and-large it is the formal conception of nationality which seems to have been preferred in subsequent practice to *Nottebohm*, with the 'genuine link' requirement being confined to the particular facts of that case.

In *Flegenheimer*, for example, the Italian–US Conciliation Commission, only a few years after *Nottebohm* was decided, limited the 'genuine-link' requirement for nationality (or, as it referred to it, the 'effective nationality principle') to situations involving dual nationals.[14] Additionally, in *Barcelona Traction*, the ICJ held, in the context of determining corporate nationality, that there was no need to show a 'genuine link' between an injured corporation and a state for the latter to exercise diplomatic protection on the former's behalf.[15] The ICJ also did not adversely comment when Guinea sought to exercise diplomatic protection over an individual in *Diallo* despite the relationship between Guinea and Diallo having been similar to that of Liechtenstein and Nottebohm.[16]

The 'formal' conception of nationality is also the conception which was adopted by the International Law Commission (the ILC) in its Articles on Diplomatic Protection.[17] Article 4 of the Articles on Diplomatic Protection provides that nationality is a status which an individual 'has acquired in accordance with the law of that State, by birth, descent, naturalization, succession of States, or in any other manner, not inconsistent with international law'.

The ILC also explicitly, in its commentaries to the Articles on Diplomatic Protection, limited the 'genuine link' requirement to the specific facts of *Nottebohm*:

> [C]ertain factors ... served to limit *Nottebohm* to the facts of the case in question, particularly the fact that the ties between Mr. Nottebohm and Liechtenstein (the Applicant State) were 'extremely tenuous' ... the Court did not intend to expound a general rule applicable to all States but only a relative rule according to which a State in Liechtenstein's position was required to show a genuine link between itself and

[13] High Commissioner on National Minorities, 'The Bolzano/Bozen Recommendations on National Minorities in Inter-State Relations' (Organization for Security and Co-operation in Europe 2008) para 11.

[14] *Flegenheimer* [1958] 25 ILR 91, 150.

[15] *Case Concerning the Barcelona Traction, Light and Power Company, Limited (Belgium v Spain) (Second Phase) (Merits)* [1970] ICJ Reports 3, 42.

[16] *Ahmadou Sadio Diallo (Republic of Guinea v Democratic Republic of the Congo) (Preliminary Objections)* [2007] ICJ Reports 582 [41]. Mr Diallo was a Guinean national, but he had not lived in Guinea for 32 years. This is comparable to Nottebohm who had lived in Guatemala for 34 years before the case had been brought before the ICJ. See generally Phoebe N Okowa, 'Case Concerning Ahmadou Sadio Diallo (Republic of Guinea v Democratic Republic of the Congo) Preliminary Objections' (2008) 57 *ICLQ* 219.

[17] International Law Commission, 'Draft Articles on Diplomatic Protection with Commentaries', *Report of the International Law Commission on the Work of its 58th Session* (UN Doc A/61/10 2006) ('Draft Articles on Diplomatic Protection').

> Mr. Nottebohm in order to permit it to claim on his behalf against Guatemala with whom he had extremely close ties.[18]

On either definition of nationality, however, the duty on the part of the state both to admit its nationals and not to expel its nationals has been described as the very 'essence of nationality'.[19] As Kesby articulates more fully, nationality is viewed as 'the primary status of admission and residence',[20] and it is the legal status which 'enables a person to be physically and legally emplaced (in the sense of acquiring a place of lawful residence) in the international system of states with all the consequent legal ramifications for the enjoyment of rights'.[21]

II. Applying a Right to Enter and Remain in a Country to Non-Nationals

When a right to enter and remain in a country is applied to non-nationals, it can be characterised as a 'rights issue'. Young, in her examination of how the democratic dialogue model functions under the UK Human Rights Act 1998, explains what a rights issue is by distinguishing it from rights generally: 'Rights are broader, more general and more abstract than rights-issues, which focus upon the way in which a particular human right is to be defined or applied in a particular situation'.[22]

Young expands further on the two ways in which a rights issue is less abstract than a right. First, a rights issue might involve looking at the question of whether or not a specific kind of activity is within the right's scope.[23] Young draws on the application to prisoners of the right to vote as an example to demonstrate this, and finds that 'determining whether the right to vote includes the right for prisoners to vote in general elections for legislatures' is a rights issue.[24] Second, a rights issue might involve determining how the right applies to a particular individual and under which certain circumstances it so applies. Again, with respect to the application to prisoners of the right to vote, Young notes that, whether or not the right to vote should be enjoyed by particular prisoners, such as those who have committed particularly violent crimes or who have been sentenced to a particularly long sentence, is a rights issue.[25] In basic terms, we can say that a rights issue is 'a question about how human rights should apply in a particular situation'.[26]

[18] ibid 30 (citations omitted).
[19] Kesby (n 2) 16. See also Edwards (n 1) 41.
[20] Kesby (n 2) 13.
[21] ibid 16; Kristin Henrard, 'The Shifting Parameters of Nationality' (2018) 65 *Netherlands International Law Review* 269, 285.
[22] Alison L Young, 'Is Dialogue Working under the Human Rights Act 1998?' [2011] *Public Law* 773, 776.
[23] Alison L Young, *Democratic Dialogue and the Constitution* (Oxford University Press 2017) 111.
[24] ibid.
[25] ibid.
[26] ibid 11.

The application to non-nationals of the right to enter and remain in a country involves questions both as to whether a specific activity is within the scope of the right and as to whether a right to enter and remain in a country can be applied to individuals of a particular status. More precisely, it involves: (i) determining whether the right's scope includes the right for non-nationals to enter into a state and to remain in a state; and also (ii) determining how and under what circumstances the right applies to non-nationals.

As set out above, the right to enter and remain in a country turns on the concept of nationality. The right exists with respect to one's country of nationality and the correlating duties arise on the part of the state only with respect to the state's own nationals. Although there is no precise or agreed upon definition of 'non-national' at international law, a non-national is generally understood to be the opposite of a national or citizen and is often defined in the negative as such.[27] In part as a consequence of this, a non-national is, more generally, often considered to be, in effect, 'an outsider, a non-member of the state',[28] and the ordinary definition of a non-national is 'a person who does not belong to a particular family, community, country, etc; a foreigner, a stranger, an outsider'.[29]

Non-nationals are, therefore, generally understood to have no right to enter a country of which they are not a national and, when in a foreign state's territory, non-nationals remain vulnerable to deportation to the country of their nationality.[30] It is immigration law that attaches to non-nationals and non-citizens, and it is that body of law which determines, as Plender describes it, 'the circumstances and conditions in and on which those who are not citizens of a state are permitted to enter and remain within it'.[31] The application to non-nationals of a right to enter and remain thus challenges directly, or at least gives rise to, questions concerning the scope of that right. It also gives rise to questions about how and under what circumstances the right applies and should apply to non-nationals.

III. Contestable Rights Issues

Young, in her examination of how the public law democratic dialogue model functions under the UK Human Rights Act, uses the terminology of 'contestable

[27] ILC, 'Draft Articles on the Expulsion of Aliens, with Commentaries', *Report of the International Law Commission on the Work of its 64th Session* (UN Doc A/67/10 2012) art 2(b); John P Grant and J Craig Barker, *Parry and Grant Encyclopaedic Dictionary of International Law*, 3rd edn (Oxford University Press 2009) 23.

[28] Myres S McDougal, Harold D Lasswell and Lung-chu Chen, 'The Protection of Aliens From Discrimination and World Public Order: Responsibility of States Conjoined with Human Rights' (1976) 70 *American Journal of International Law* 432, 467.

[29] *Oxford English Dictionary*, 'Alien'.

[30] Higgins (n 3) 444, 450; United Nations Human Rights Committee, 'General Comment No 15: The Position of Aliens under the Covenant' (UN Doc HRI/GEN/1/Rev9 1986) para 5.

[31] Richard Plender, 'Nationality Law and Immigration Law' in Richard Plender (ed), *Issues in International Migration Law* (Brill 2015) 1; Hiroshi Motomura, 'Immigration Law After a Century of Plenary Power: Phantom Constitutional Norms and Statutory Interpretation' (1990) 100 *Yale Law Journal* 545, 547.

rights issues'. By 'contestable rights issues', she means those rights issues about which there is 'reasonable disagreement' as to their resolution, and, in turn, those issues the resolution of which 'we would expect legislatures and the judiciary, and national, international, and supranational courts to disagree'.[32]

Reasonable disagreement can come about for a range of reasons. There might be social or political reasons for reasonable disagreement. Disagreement might also arise because of differences in legal reasoning; for example, there might be disagreement as to which legal doctrine applies or as to the existence of, or interaction between, the application of different legal principles or norms. Social, political and legal reasons are, of course, often intrinsically intertwined. As Allan argues, '[l]egal reasoning embodies our ideal of moral reasoning as that ideal applies when we try to reason in the name of the whole society'.[33] But, for Young, the focus is specifically on the differences in the legal reasoning processes available to be undertaken in the resolution of rights issues and it is those differences that give rise to the labelling of a rights issue as 'contestable'.[34] In the context of the UK Human Rights Act, Young says: 'Contestable rights-issues arise when it is reasonable to disagree [either] as to whether legislation contravenes Convention rights, or as to the best means through which to render legislation Convention-compatible'.[35]

This focus on the difference in the legal reasoning process being what, according to Young, gives rise to contestability with respect to a rights issue, seems to make it narrower than Waldron's concept of 'watershed' rights,[36] as does the fact that reasonable disagreement might not exist with respect to watershed issues.[37] This being the case, I consider it useful here to set out briefly Waldron's concept of watershed rights in order to understand the foundations of contestable rights issues and, also, to understand the relationship between contestable and non-contestable rights issues, and how differences in legal reasoning processes are what give rise to the label and characterisation of contestability.

Waldron describes as watershed rights those rights that are particularly, or at least usually, controversial when judicially reviewed. Watershed rights issues are those issues that first appear simply to concern narrow issues of legal interpretation, but that, in fact, 'raise unresolved questions of considerable practical moment for the political community',[38] and that often have 'significant ramifications for the lives of many people'.[39] Watershed rights are

[32] Young, *Democratic Dialogue* (n 23) 111.

[33] TRS Allan, 'The Moral Unity of Public Law' (2017) 67 *University of Toronto Law Journal* 1, 16.

[34] Young, 'Is Dialogue Working under the Human Rights Act 1998?' (n 22) 776.

[35] ibid 775. See also Alison L Young, *Parliamentary Sovereignty and the Human Rights Act* (Hart Publishing 2009) ch 5.

[36] Jeremy Waldron, 'The Core of the Case against Judicial Review' (2006) 115 *Yale Law Journal* 1346, 1367.

[37] There is of course an argument that contestable rights issues can be wider than watershed issues because contestable rights issues are not necessarily new or controversial, but this analysis focuses on the difference in legal reasoning specifically.

[38] Waldron, 'The Core of the Case against Judicial Review' (n 36) 1367.

[39] ibid.

those rights issues that, accordingly, Waldron says, 'define the major choices that any modern society must face, choices that are the focal points of moral and political disagreements in many societies', and about which we would not expect there to be consensus.[40] Watershed rights are thus not those rights that are tied to any specific society, as they are not grounded in some particular constitutional text or legal doctrine.[41] Examples of watershed rights issues are: 'abortion, affirmative action, the legitimacy of government redistribution or interference in the marketplace, the rights of criminal suspects, the precise meaning of religious toleration, minority cultural rights, the regulation of speech and spending in electoral campaigns, and so on'.[42]

Contestable rights issues are, of course, watershed issues, but some non-contestable rights issues will also fit that description. Some rights are 'non-contestable' because of the presence of some circumstance or circumstances which provide an answer to the rights issue, or which render no room for reasonable disagreement on the issue. One such circumstance might be, according to Young, the presence of a clear line of case law or the presence of constitutional provisions which address the issue.[43] Other such circumstances include the presence of 'background social conditions, moral rights or other principles', which establish clearly the scope of the right, and establish which individuals may enjoy the right and under which circumstances they may do so.[44] From this, we can see how the concept of contestable rights is narrower than Waldron's concept of 'watershed' rights, precisely because of the differences in legal reasoning available to be drawn on to resolve the rights issue.

A. Contestable Rights Issues and Democratic Dialogue

We know from the introductory chapter that legal constitutionalists consider courts to be the best institutions to decide on rights issues, while political constitutionalists argue that legislatures best fulfil that role. When it comes to contestable rights issues in particular, these arguments are, or at least should be, at their strongest because there is, by definition, disagreement on these issues and, specifically, on the legal reasoning process which should be engaged to decide their resolution. Accordingly, we would expect legal and political

[40] Jeremy Waldron, 'Judges as Moral Reasoners' (2009) 7 *International Journal of Constitutional Law* 2, 22; Waldron, 'The Core of the Case against Judicial Review' (n 36) 1368.

[41] Waldron, 'Judges as Moral Reasoners' (n 40) 22.

[42] Waldron, 'The Core of the Case against Judicial Review' (n 36) 1367.

[43] Young, 'Is Dialogue Working under the Human Rights Act 1998?' (n 22) 775, 781–82.

[44] ibid. Young uses the consensus approach of the ECtHR as evidence of this. That is, where the ECtHR finds there is consensus on a rights issue, it would be incorrect to say that the right is contestable, even though it might be described as a 'watershed' right in Waldron's terms. See generally Kanstantsin Dzehtsiarou, 'Does Consensus Matter? Legitimacy of European Consensus in the Case Law of the European Court of Human Rights' [2011] *Public Law* 534.

constitutionalists to approach contestable rights issues differently, although the argument as to which institution should determine contestable rights issues frequently depends on the particular way in which contestable rights are defined and on the particular way their nature is understood.[45]

Allan provides a good example of how a legal constitutionalist might approach contestable rights issues. Allan argues that these kinds of rights issues should be decided by courts because courts are able to reason by principle and do so either in the abstract or in the particular social, cultural, or legal context in which they are situated. Courts also focus on the particular nature of the right. The latter is particularly important because, Allan argues, contestability with respect to rights issues arises from the right in question itself. He also considers that courts are the best institution to resolve these kinds of issues because they are the institution able: (i) to recognise the importance of legislatures and executives having some part in resolving contestable rights issues and to give decision-making discretion to these other institutions; but also, importantly, (ii) to nonetheless constrain these other institutions in their decision-making.[46]

Griffith, on the other hand, provides a good example of how a political constitutionalist might approach contestable rights issues. According to Griffith, legislatures should predominantly resolve contestable rights issues because: (i) legislatures are institutionally able to consider the differing and competing views of multiple groups; and (ii) particularly where there is disagreement and tension as to the resolution of a rights issue (which he views as inevitable given his characterisation of rights as being, in effect, interest claims), it is more legitimate for an institution which is democratically elected to decide on contestable rights issues.[47]

It is on this basis that contestable rights issues are said to be the best kinds of issues to test the normative claims of the democratic dialogue model, and, in turn, the claims of the model should be at their most persuasive when it comes to these kinds of rights.[48] As Young explains:

> Contestable rights-issues are difficult to resolve. They therefore provide a good example from which to determine whether democratic dialogue can make good on its promise to provide a better protection of human rights, maximising the advantages and minimising the disadvantages of a purely legal or purely political protection of rights.[49]

[45] See generally Young, *Democratic Dialogue* (n 23) 111.

[46] ibid 112. See generally TRS Allan, *Law, Liberty, and Justice: The Legal Foundations of British Constitutionalism* (Oxford University Press 1994); TRS Allan, *The Sovereignty of Law: Freedom, Constitution and Common Law* (Oxford University Press 2013).

[47] Young, *Democratic Dialogue* (n 23) 111–12. See generally JAG Griffith, 'The Political Constitution' (1979) 42 *MLR* 1, 18.

[48] See generally Stephen Gardbaum, *The New Commonwealth Model of Constitutionalism: Theory and Practice* (Cambridge University Press 2013) 93; Young, *Democratic Dialogue* (n 23) ch 3.

[49] Young, *Democratic Dialogue* (n 23) 11.

B. Contestable Rights Issues and Transnational Democratic Dialogue

Does this same claim about contestable rights issues and democratic dialogue work when the interaction is between a domestic legislature, like the UK Parliament, and an international (as opposed to a domestic) court, like the ECtHR and the CJEU? It should. Again, as we know from the introductory chapter, we can expect legal constitutionalists to argue that international courts, when compared with domestic legislatures, are best placed to decide on rights issues. Conversely, we can expect political constitutionalists to argue that domestic legislatures, when compared with international courts, are best placed to decide on rights issues.

Given this, we can expect those same arguments made at the domestic level for applying the democratic dialogue model to contestable rights issues, to also exist when the model is applied to the relationship between a domestic legislature and an international court. That is, we can expect contestable rights issues to similarly provide the best test of whether the UK Parliament and, respectively, the ECtHR and the CJEU have engaged in (transnational) democratic dialogue because these are the kinds of issues with respect to which the arguments for legal constitutionalism and political constitutionalism are at their strongest.

There are, however, some differences as to how we might consider and frame the nature of contestable rights issues in the international or transnational sphere as opposed to at the domestic level. One such point of difference is the characterisation of what, precisely, gives rise to the contestable nature of a rights issue. As I have already noted, Young's focus is on differences in legal reasoning processes, as opposed to moral or social reasons, as the thing that gives rise to the contestable nature of rights issues. Gardbaum's characterisation of contestability as arising from a combination of political, social, moral and legal reasons might, however, be more persuasive in the international or transnational sphere.

Gardbaum, with respect to the application of the dialogue model to contestable rights at the domestic level, argues that Young's separation of the legal, the moral and the political in her characterisation of contestable rights issues is unnecessary, and overly artificial, particularly in light of the abstract way rights are framed and the role of proportionality in rights analysis.[50] Gardbaum's characterisation might be more persuasive here because politics and political reasoning arguably have a more significant influence on legal reasoning with respect to rights when rights adjudication is being undertaken by international courts. This is because international and regional human rights law rely for their continued existence and, in turn, their credibility and legitimacy, on states accepting them. Although states cannot of course withdraw from customary international law, if states do not accept convention law at this level, then states may withdraw from human rights conventions and the jurisdiction of courts which enforce those treaties.

[50] Gardbaum (n 48) 93.

Accordingly, legal reasoning by international courts is particularly interlinked with political reasoning.

There is another point of difference that should also be borne in mind when testing transnational democratic dialogue by applying it to contestable rights issues. That difference lies in a potential criticism that international human rights lawyers and legal constitutionalists, in particular, might make – namely, that international human rights should not be accepted as being of a 'contestable' or 'watershed' nature in the first place. Acknowledging that there might be a reasonable argument to be made on the part of the state or that there are even 'two sides' to rights issues, at least from a legal constitutionalist viewpoint and particularly with respect to absolute rights, arguably goes against the very purpose of international and regional human rights law, which is primarily to protect individuals (and, in particular, marginalised and oppressed individuals) against the state. Further, accepting that some rights have 'two sides' or are 'contested' can function to disrupt what is, at least usually, the desired universal application of the international human rights project, and this can itself, in turn, result in abuse on the part of states at the resolution (of the rights issue) stage.

These criticisms can, however, be addressed by: (i) the argument that accepting some rights as contestable or as open to different interpretations is precisely why states are willing to be part of and 'on board' with the international human rights project at all and that, therefore, the project is maintained precisely because some rights are accepted as contestable; (ii) accepting that there are some rights issues, such as those arising with respect to absolute rights, which, for their resolution, it would be appropriate for there to be 'barriers to dialogue' and for international courts to have the 'final word' (I will say more on this in the next chapter); and, even, at a more abstract level, (iii) re-framing how we think about and perceive contestable rights in the first place.

With respect to this third point of response, Waldron, at the domestic level, with respect to his 'watershed' rights concept describes a way to reframe the way we look at these kinds of rights to counter concerns that might arise on the part of international human rights lawyers or legal constitutionalists at the international level. Waldron proposes beginning from the position that there is 'a general commitment to rights' and that disagreement about rights does not mean that rights are not being taken seriously.[51] He argues that, while 'it is tempting to infer that that general commitment covers the core of each right and that the right only becomes controversial at the outer reaches of its application', thinking in that way would be a mistake.[52] In Waldron's view, disagreements about rights are not limited to the marginal applications of the right, but often go to the core of the right and that, '[a] commitment to rights can be wholehearted

[51] Waldron, 'The Core of the Case against Judicial Review' (n 36) 1367.
[52] ibid.

and sincere even while watershed cases remain controversial'.[53] He provides the following example:

> [T]wo people who disagree about whether restrictions on racist hate speech are acceptable may both accept that the right to free speech is key to thinking through the issue and they may both accept also that the case they disagree about is a central rather than marginal issue relative to that right.[54]

Although Waldron does accept that there are inevitably some positions that are held disingenuously or ignorantly by 'scoundrels (who care nothing for rights) or that are held by moral illiterates (who misunderstand their force and importance)',[55] he does say that it would be wrong to assume, at least in most cases, that the disagreement with respect to rights is not being pursued both in a reasonable manner and in good faith.[56] Waldron also draws on Rawls' argument that we cannot claim, whenever we disagree on rights, that such disagreement comes from a place of ignorance or from some perversity or rivalry or desire for social or economic gain.[57] With respect to the example about racist hate speech above, on this view, the two people may hold different conceptions of the right, but it would be wrong or at least misjudged to question their commitment to or sincerity about rights.[58]

C. Contestable Rights Issues and a Non-National's Right to Enter and Remain

Insofar as a contestable rights issue is a 'rights issue' the resolution of which we would expect a domestic legislature (such as the UK Parliament) and international courts (such as the ECtHR and CJEU) to disagree, a right to enter and remain in a country, as it applies to non-nationals, is capable of being so characterised.

We know from the introductory chapter that legislatures, being popularly elected institutions (desirably, in the political constitutionalist's view), reason in such a way as to balance competing interests and groups and, also, reason in such a way as to consider broad issues facing the whole of society (as opposed to focusing on an individual's circumstances). This seems to be borne out in the context of the application to non-nationals of a right to enter and remain in a country, and legislatures appear to take into account those factors which affect the entire body politic, such as national security and economic stability. In practice, this has resulted in legislatures restricting the scope of the application to non-nationals of this right, as the allowing of more non-nationals to

[53] ibid.
[54] ibid.
[55] ibid 1368.
[56] ibid.
[57] See John Rawls, *Political Liberalism*, expanded edn (Columbia University Press 2005) 58.
[58] Waldron, 'The Core of the Case against Judicial Review' (n 36 1367; Ronald Dworkin, *Taking Rights Seriously* (Harvard University Press 1977) 134–36.

enter into and remain in a country seems usually to be positioned as being a threat to these kinds of factors, or as, at least, not facilitating the achievement of those factors.[59]

Goodwin Gill describes how the right on the part of states to deny entry to and expel non-nationals is often justified by reference to the 'public interests' of the state,[60] and how the 'essential function' of the state's right to expel non-nationals, in particular, serves to 'protect' and to 'preserve' public order, morality and health.[61] Walters, for his part, frames the practice of refusing to admit non-nationals and the practice of expelling non-nationals in relation to 'police', and he argues that the exercise of these powers is a form of policing both territory and people.[62] Nowak, on the other hand, discusses how states seek to 'safeguard' against the presence of 'undesirable non-nationals' being on their territories.[63] As Torbisco-Casals describes it, in the current context: 'of growing populist authoritarian politics, democratic backsliding and renewed hostility against minority rights … Populist leaders typically deploy a politics of fear to unite and mobilize people against minority groups that are represented as threats to stability and community'.[64]

The UK Parliament provides a persuasive example of a domestic legislature essentially focusing on problems facing the domestic constituency as a whole and, in turn, of a domestic legislature positioning the entry and subsequent remaining of non-nationals in a country as a threat to, or at least as being contrary to, the public interest. Griffiths and Yeo describe how the political rhetoric and policy-making on immigration in the UK has 'become especially harsh in recent years'.[65] In 2012, the UK government announced what it labelled its 'hostile environment policy' for immigrants, although:

> Unlike most major policy reforms, no White Paper presaged [the hostile environment policy's] introduction. There is no central policy document, no official definition nor clear aims and objectives. The policies are spread across various Immigration Acts, rules

[59] Feldman argues, in the UK context, that human rights generally (and not just immigration rights) are positioned as a threat to these kinds of factors. He notes: '[i]n the UK, which enacted a Human Rights Act in 1998, the government and opposition currently profess to see human rights as threats to democratic politics and constraints on their ability to advance the public interest through policies and legislation, especially in relation to combating terrorism and crime, and controlling immigration'. See David Feldman, 'Democracy, Law and Human Rights: Politics as Challenge and Opportunity' in Murray Hunt, Hayley Hooper and Paul Yowell (eds), *Parliaments and Human Rights: Redressing the Democratic Deficit* (Bloomsbury Publishing 2015) 96.

[60] Guy S Goodwin-Gill, *International Law and the Movement of Persons between States* (Clarendon Press 1978) 203.

[61] Goodwin-Gill, 'The Limits of the Power of Expulsion in Public International Law' (n 5) 77.

[62] William Walters, 'Deportation, Expulsion, and the International Police of Aliens' (2002) 6 *Citizenship Studies* 265, 281.

[63] Manfred Nowak, *U.N. Covenant on Civil and Political Rights: CCPR Commentary*, 2nd rev edn (NP Engel 2005) 290–92.

[64] Neus Torbisco-Casals, 'The Legitimacy of International Courts: The Challenge of Diversity' (2021) 52 *Journal of Social Philosophy* 491, 495.

[65] Melanie Griffiths and Colin Yeo, 'The UK's Hostile Environment: Deputising Immigration Control' (2021) 41 *Critical Social Policy* 521, 524. See generally Colin Yeo, *Welcome to Britain: Fixing Our Broken Immigration System* (Biteback Publishing 2020); Maya Goodfellow, *Hostile Environment: How Immigrants Became Scapegoats* (Verso Books 2020).

> and regulations and affect numerous sectors and policy arenas. The term's meaning is also shifting, expanding in academic and media discourses to refer to a general stance of nastiness towards migrants.[66]

Griffiths and Yeo set out to understand what the 'hostile environment policy' means, and they ultimately characterise it as being 'a new approach intended to dissuade illegal residence in the UK by preventing people from accessing basic services'.[67] The policy can be, according to Griffiths and Yeo, 'characterised by restrictive policies, absurdly complex and ever-changing Immigration Rules, harsh and arbitrary decision-making, criminalisation of mobility and indefinite immigration detention'.[68]

One example of a measure which falls under this broader policy of creating a 'hostile environment' for immigrants can be seen in the UK government's announcement in April 2022 of its plan to send those seeking asylum in the UK to Rwanda, which I briefly mentioned in the introductory chapter.[69] While the plan was ultimately abandoned on the election of the Labour government in 2024, under the Memorandum of Understanding for the plan, concluded between the UK and Rwanda, people seeking asylum in the UK would have had their asylum claims processed in Rwanda and the UK would not have had any legal responsibilities with respect to those people.[70] The positioning of immigrants (specifically here, asylum seekers) entering and remaining in the UK as a threat to the general public interest (which Parliament seeks to ensure), is well articulated in a speech given by former UK Prime Minister Boris Johnson on the introduction of the policy when he said the following:

> We can't ask the British taxpayer to write a blank cheque to cover the costs of anyone who might want to come and live here. Uncontrolled immigration creates *unmanageable demands on our NHS and our welfare state, it overstretches our local schools, our housing and public transport, and creates unsustainable pressure to build on precious green spaces*.[71]

As well as by Baroness Lawlor, who stated the following in May 2023 during the Lords debate on the Illegal Migration Bill:

> Today, the system is significantly different. It is more expensive and far more reliant on tax funding, with higher expectations for social security, healthcare and education. As families struggle to pay the bills, it is right to take the rising costs of illegal migration,

[66] Griffiths and Yeo (n 65) 522.

[67] ibid.

[68] ibid 524. See generally Goodfellow (n 65).

[69] The Home Office, 'World First Partnership to Tackle Global Migration Crisis' (2022): www.gov.uk/government/news/world-first-partnership-to-tackle-global-migration-crisis.

[70] ibid 3.

[71] Rt Hon Boris Johnson MP, 'PM speech on action to tackle illegal migration' (UK Government, 14 April 2022): www.gov.uk/government/speeches/pm-speech-on-action-to-tackle-illegal-migration-14-april-2022 (emphasis added).

for which we are all paying through an increased tax base for that and other things … *[v]oters now want their borders controlled.*[72]

International courts, on the other hand, as a reminder, essentially reason by principle and in such a way as to focus on individual and minority interests, as opposed to focusing on the majority and the citizenry. This again seems to be borne out in the immigration context and international courts appear to reason by looking at the individual non-national's circumstances and, therefore, to find, in effect, some kind of right on the part of non-nationals to enter and remain in a foreign country.

Joppke and Menzal argue that courts have been given a key role in expanding immigration rights because, structurally, they are neutral institutions which are uninfluenced by popular influence and pressure.[73] That international courts act in this way is evidenced by how the ECtHR has in effect been able to provide some protection to non-nationals wishing to enter into, and to not be deported from, a foreign country. This is despite there being no such right contained within the text of the ECHR. The ECtHR has found that a non-national cannot be deported in circumstances where that deportation would violate Article 3 of the Convention (the right to be free from torture), Article 5 of the Convention (the right to liberty and security), or Article 8 of the Convention (the right to respect for private and family life). The Court has also found that a denial of entry to a non-national, or the deportation of a non-national, pursuant to discriminatory immigration law, would violate Article 14 of the Convention (the right to be free from discrimination).[74]

The locating in different articles of protection or even a kind of right to enter and remain in a country as a non-national in this way, albeit perhaps implicitly, also demonstrates a focus on the part of international courts on non-nationals' individual circumstances. It does so because it shows an understanding of the broader effects that the denial of admission to, and the exclusion from, a country can have for individuals and their communities. As de Aguiar, Special Rapporteur to the Committee on Migration, Refugees and Demography of the Council of Europe's Parliamentary Assembly, stated in her report to that committee, there can be 'lifelong consequences for the expelled person, often resulting in separation from his family life and uprooting from his environment'.[75] Wojnowska-Radzinska similarly writes about how deportation can remove a non-national not just from territory, but from their enjoyment of an established social and family life,[76] and

[72] HL deb 10 May 2023, vol 829, col 1904.

[73] Christian Joppke and Elia Marzal, 'Courts, the New Constitutionalism and Immigrant Rights: The Case of the French Conseil Constitutionnel' (2004) 43 *European Journal of Political Research* 823, 824.

[74] Goodwin-Gill, 'The Limits of the Power of Expulsion in Public International Law' (n 5). The UN HRC in a General Comment has made a similar comment with respect to the ICCPR, noting that, 'in certain circumstances [aliens] may enjoy the protection of the Covenant even in relation to entry or residence … when considerations of non-discrimination, prohibition of inhuman treatment and respect for family life arise'. See, eg, UN HRC (n 8) para 5.

[75] Aguiar cited in Julia Wojnowska-Radzinska, *The Right of an Alien to Be Protected against Arbitrary Expulsion in International Law* (Brill 2015) 46.

[76] ibid 3–4.

Kanstroom describes how, while deportations may be in theory characterised as civil, they function as a punishment.[77] The denial of entry to a state of course means that a non-national is denied the potential of ever enjoying those other rights and protections.

Fragmented law also functions to further the contestable nature of rights. Young makes this argument at the domestic level with respect to the contestability of the issue of prisoner voting rights. She points out how prisoner voting is a prima facie contestable rights issue because, if we look at how the issue of prisoner voting is regulated by the law in common law countries, we can see how the issue has been resolved in different ways. Importantly, Young points out how these differing resolutions have been reached usually following interventions on the part of both legislatures and courts.[78]

The location of a kind of right to enter and remain in a country for foreign nationals in various rights has resulted in highly fragmented law in this context. This fragmentation is perhaps best illustrated by how the ECtHR has not only located protections for non-nationals to enter and remain in a country in different articles, but has done so inconsistently *within* those articles – such as, most significantly, with respect to Article 8 of the European Convention.[79] Klaassen describes how the ECtHR has located, well beyond the actual text of Article 8, a particular new kind of obligation on the part of the state with respect to certain types of non-nationals:

> The Court is not consistent in the test it uses to determine whether there is a violation of Article 8 in cases in which the applicant is already residing in the host State, developing family life there, but not in possession of a valid right of residence. [These types] of cases, labelled as 'hybrid obligation cases' because they cannot be considered purely positive obligation cases as the applicant has already entered and lived in the host state … This residence in the host State can either concern residence without a valid residence permit, or lawful residence in the past which was voluntarily disrupted by leaving the country.[80]

There are, however, arguably, certain types of non-nationals with respect to whom the application of a right to enter and remain is not contestable in light of the existence of clear law providing for how the issue is resolved, or, more broadly, clear social or political conditions which decide the issue.[81]

The application of a right to enter and remain to refugees and asylum seekers is, arguably, one such example. Refugees and asylum seekers are, of course, 'non-nationals', in the sense of being non-citizens, with respect to the country into which

[77] Daniel Kanstroom, 'Deportation as a Global Phenomenon: Reflections on the ILC Draft Articles on the Expulsion of Aliens' (2017) 30 *Harvard Human Rights Journal* 49, 51.

[78] Young, *Democratic Dialogue* (n 23) 16.

[79] Kesby (n 2) 26.

[80] Mark Klaassen, 'Between Facts and Norms: Testing Compliance with Article 8 ECHR in Immigration Cases' (2019) 37 *Netherlands Quarterly of Human Rights* 157, 164.

[81] See generally Office of the United Nations High Commissioner for Human Rights (n 1) 1. See also Wojnowska-Radzinska (n 75) ch 1.

they seek to enter and remain, or, more precisely, with respect to the country in which they seek asylum or refuge. Article 14 of the Universal Declaration of Human Rights sets out that 'everyone has the right to seek and to enjoy in other countries asylum from persecution', and the 1951 Convention relating to the Status of Refugees provides that refugees have the right to seek asylum in a country and that they cannot be returned to their country of nationality.[82] This principle of 'non-refoulement' exists also at customary international law.[83]

There are, and inevitably will be, layers of contestability in the application of the non-refoulement principle, as is demonstrated by differences in precisely how states determine whether someone is in fact a refugee or not. Further, as the UK–Rwanda Memorandum of Understanding set out above demonstrates, just because the application of a law is uncontested, does not mean it is not, and cannot, be broken. The fact that non-nationals who are refugees can seek asylum and not be expelled to their country of nationality, is not, however, a matter giving rise to contestability in light of the *sui generis* application and operation of international refugee law,[84] and as Gammeltoft-Hansen concludes in his study, international refugee law does place 'a constraint on the otherwise well-established right of any state to decide who may enter and remain on its territory'.[85]

Non-nationals who might face torture on their return to their country of nationality if expelled from a country is another such example of a circumstance where the application to non-nationals of a right to enter and remain is not contestable. Article 3(1) of the Convention against Torture provides that: 'No State Party shall expel, return ("refouler") or extradite a person to another State where there are substantial grounds for believing that he would be in danger of being subjected to torture',[86] and a similar positive obligation has been held to be owed on the part of states at regional human rights law.[87] There are again, of course, further layers of contestability in the application of a right to enter and remain to non-nationals

[82] Convention relating to the Status of Refugees, opened for signature 28 July 1951; 189 UNTS 150 arts 32–33. See also Ruth Rubio-Marín, 'Introduction' in Ruth Rubio-Marín (ed), *Human Rights and Immigration* (Oxford University Press 2014) 5.

[83] See United Nations High Commissioner for Refugees, 'Advisory Opinion on the Extraterritorial Application of Non-Refoulement Obligations under the 1951 Convention Relating to the Status of Refugees and Its 1967 Protocol' (2007) 7, fn 30; Guy S Goodwin-Gill and Jane McAdam, *The Refugee in International Law*, 3rd edn (Oxford University Press 2007) ch 5.

[84] In the UK, s 2 of the Asylum and Immigration Appeals Act 1993 provides that: '[n]othing in the immigration rules (within the meaning of the [Immigration] 1971) Act shall lay down any practice which would be contrary to the Convention [on the Status of Refugees' and Lord Steyn in *R (European Roma Rights Centre) v Immigration Officer at Prague Airport* [2005] 2 AC 1 at [42] held that it was clear, given s 2 of the Asylum and Immigration Appeals Act, 'that the Refugee Convention has been incorporated into our domestic law'.

[85] Thomas Gammeltoft-Hansen, *Access to Asylum: International Refugee Law and the Globalisation of Migration Control* (Cambridge University Press 2011) 12–13.

[86] United Nations Convention Against Torture and Other Cruel, Inhuman or Degrading Treatment or Punishment, Opened for Signature 10 December 1984; 1465 UNTS 85.

[87] With respect to the European human rights regime and the interpretation of art 3 of the European Convention: see, eg, *A v United Kingdom* [1998] 27 EHRR 611 [22]; *Al-Adsani v United Kingdom* [2001] ECHR 752 [38]; *Assenov and Others v Bulgaria* [1998] 28 EHRR 652 [102].

who might face torture if returned to their country of nationality. For example, assurances may be provided by the non-national's country of nationality and the definition of torture is itself contested. The legal context, however, is such that at the general application level of a right to enter and return, there is no significant issue of contestability with respect to non-nationals who might face torture if returned to their country of nationality.

The above two examples illustrate situations in which there is no real element of contestability because it is clear how the law applies. In addition, there are also types of non-nationals for whom the application of a right to enter and remain raises no real contestability issues because of particular political and social conditions and status. It is generally accepted that non-nationals for whom a special status attaches, such as being an accredited diplomat, or a member of the armed forces, are generally exempt from the imposition of immigration law.[88]

There would also likely be little, if any, contestability arising with respect to the application to non-nationals of a right to enter and remain where such non-nationals could be described as transient non-nationals. These kinds of non-nationals would, at least usually, not be seeking out the protection of a right to enter and remain.[89] These non-nationals are better characterised as 'non-immigrants' and include 'foreign workers who have temporary permission to remain, foreign students, business visitors, tourists, and unsuccessful asylum seekers'.[90]

I am, therefore, only concerned with some types of non-nationals in this book (specifically, those to whom the application of a right to enter and remain would be contestable). I am principally concerned with the expulsion of those non-nationals for whom the expelling state is considered their permanent home, and with the denial of admission and residency to those persons who seek to migrate permanently (more or less). These are the kinds of non-nationals whom the Rapporteur to the Committee on Migration, Refugees and Demography of the Parliamentary Assembly of the Council of Europe described as 'virtual nationals',[91] and whom Wojnowska-Radzinska would describe as being those immigrants who may,

> share the culture, language, education, traditions and everyday life with its nationals and frequently have very tenuous or even non-existent links with their country of origin … [and who] have integrated into the host society through long-standing residence and the emotional and professional links they have forged.[92]

[88] See discussion in Alessia di Pascale, 'Exceptional Duties to Admit Aliens' in Richard Plender (ed), *Issues in International Migration Law* (Brill 2015) 203; James AR Nafziger, 'The General Admission of Aliens under International Law' (1983) 77 *American Journal of International Law* 804, 806.

[89] A similar approach was taken by Nafziger: see Nafziger (n 88) 806.

[90] David Weissbrodt, *The Human Rights of Non-Citizens* (Oxford University Press 2008) 2.

[91] Manuela Aguiar, 'Report of the Committee on Migration, Refugees and Demography of the Council of Europe on the Non-Expulsion of Long-Term Immigrants' (2001).

[92] Wojnowska-Radzinska (n 75) 47.

IV. Institutional Contestability

The term 'institutional contestability' is used here to describe the situation where there is not just disagreement between the institutions as to how a rights issue should be resolved, but where a question exists as to which institution (here, between an international court or domestic legislature) should resolve the rights issue.

A. Institutional Contestability and Democratic Dialogue

It is sometimes argued that the democratic dialogue model may not solely function to solve contestable rights issues, but it may also be able to resolve questions as to which institution should resolve the rights issue. The model does this, the argument goes, by functioning to allocate, at least provisional, normative authority to either a court or legislature. Gardbaum is the most prominent theorist of this argument, claiming that, at the domestic level, the democratic dialogue model can function: (i) to allocate authority, or, more precisely, in his words, to disperse responsibility to either the legislature or courts to decide upon rights issues; and (ii) to provide normative constraints on when such authority or responsibility should be used.[93] Gardbaum makes this claim specifically with respect to what he calls 'the new Commonwealth model of constitutionalism', which he identifies as being the particular dialogue model present in the constitutional and legal systems of New Zealand, Canada, the United Kingdom and some jurisdictions within Australia.

Gardbaum argues that the democratic dialogue model, or specifically the Commonwealth model of constitutionalism, is able to function in this way because of four key institutional characteristics, or 'jointly necessary and sufficient conditions', namely:[94] (i) a codified bill of rights or a judicially created charter of rights with legal enforceability, such as EU human rights law as it existed prior to the EU Charter of Fundamental Rights; (ii) pre-enactment political review by the political branches of legislation with respect to human rights; (iii) weak-form judicial review of the legislation by the judiciary, which is framed as a 'power' of the courts which *can* be exercised, as opposed to a 'duty' which *must* be;[95] and (iv) a formal power, again not a duty, held by the legislature to articulate what the law is.

[93] Gardbaum (n 48) 88, 94.

[94] ibid 30–31.

[95] Gardbaum argues that it is particularly this provision of a legal power to courts in these models without the additional mandating of its exercise that is what makes this feature different from traditional models of both legal and political constitutionalism: see ibid 27.

The way in which these features come together to allocate and constrain normative authority can be demonstrated by the following flow chart:

Figure 1 Flow chart showing how the dialogue model allocates normative authority

legislation proposed

↓

pre-enactment review of proposed legislation

↓

legislature passes the legislation

↓

court *may* review legislation with respect to rights issue

↓

legislature *may* respond to the review with respect to the rights issue

The rights issue is first allocated to the political branches for a pre-enactment review of the legislation for its compatibility with human rights and for the subsequent debate on and passing of the legislation. The authority to examine the legislation for its compatibility with rights may then be allocated to the judiciary, though the legislature retains the power to respond to any exercise of that power by the judiciary that may take place. It is worth exploring in more detail what this process looks like in practice. The UK Human Rights Act and how it functions to allocate provisional normative authority to decide on rights is used as the key example here.

Sections 3 and 4 of the UK Human Rights Act are the key mechanisms which currently facilitate dialogue between Parliament and the judiciary in the UK. As a reminder, section 3 provides that courts should read and give effect to legislation in a manner compatible with ECHR rights, so far as it is possible to do so, and thus, courts can, through section 3, 'provide a remedy for the individual through reading the law so as to protect their human rights'.[96] Section 4 of the Human Rights

[96] Young, *Democratic Dialogue* (n 23) 5.

Act, on the other hand, empowers the judiciary to issue a declaration that legislation is incompatible with ECHR rights where the primary legislation concerned prevents removal of the incompatibility. Section 4(6) of the Act provides that a declaration of incompatibility has no legal effect.

These sections operate in such a way as to allocate normative authority to either the court or the UK Parliament to decide, provisionally at least, upon rights issues. Section 3, according to Young, functions to tip the authority and power to decide on the rights issue towards the court. Section 3 gives domestic courts the power to issue a specific remedy to the individual. This means that it is more likely to be used with respect to, and courts are more likely to have the power to decide upon, those rights issues which are characterised as non-contestable. Non-contestable rights issues are of course, because of their nature, inevitably more likely to be resolved with a specific remedy. It is perhaps for this reason that Gardbaum finds that legal systems with codified rights are more likely to be those with judicial supremacy, while systems with no codified rights are more likely to be those with parliamentary supremacy, which take the view that 'rights are not limits on legislation but its product and are changeable by it'.[97]

Section 4 of the Human Rights Act, on the other hand, tips the balance in favour of the political branch, as the Parliament has the power to respond to a court decision. This is because rights remain unprotected until (and unless) the UK Parliament responds to the court's declaration of incompatibility by amending or repealing the legislation in question or by enacting a different piece of legislation.[98]

Because a declaration of incompatibility issued by a court under section 4 of the Human Rights Act does not result in a specific remedy to an individual, the declaration is more likely to be used for contestable rights issues, and the UK Parliament is thus more likely to have the authority to decide upon the issues. As Young explains, even in the context of non-contestable rights where a court cannot provide a remedy to the individual or is otherwise unable to provide a legal protection of the right, then the UK Parliament has an even greater duty to intervene and to provide a political protection of the right. By the same token, when a court exercises its power under section 3 of the Human Rights Act, Parliament should not interfere in the process unless there are compelling reasons to do so. The political process should function to ensure Parliament only intervenes in this way when it is legitimate to do so.[99]

Of course, the allocation of normative authority with respect to the UK Human Rights Act is only provisional and Parliament does, as Gardbaum outlines in his general model, retain the power to exercise its authority under either avenue or mechanism. If the court exercises its powers under section 3 of the Act, the UK Parliament can respond with new or amended legislation. But this is not achieved by giving more power to Parliament, in a sense, to protect democracy from an

[97] Gardbaum (n 48) 1.
[98] Young, *Parliamentary Sovereignty and the Human Rights Act* (n 35) 129.
[99] ibid 142–43.

intrusive and legally strong protection of rights.[100] Rather, the judiciary is given restrained powers and duties to provide a legal protection of rights by way of providing remedies for breaches of rights in the face of 'unwarranted intrusion' by the political branches.[101] As Young summarises it, 'sections 3 and 4 only give relative greater authority, as opposed to a definitive authority, to resolve a human rights issue to either the legislature or the courts'.[102]

Gardbaum draws on, but ultimately distinguishes, his theory from Young's analysis of how authority is provisionally allocated to institutions to determine rights issues. Gardbaum characterises Young's model as in fact beginning with the question of whether a right is contestable or not. He argues that, unlike his model which is, in a sense, self-triggering of the presumptive allocation process by reason of constitutional structure and design, Young's theory in effect allocates provisional normative authority 'by type or nature of the issue' in question 'based on the contestability criterion'.[103] Gardbaum confines Young's analysis to its context, saying it must be understood in the context of the UK and the Human Rights Act. Young is, according to Gardbaum, in effect simply providing an account of how courts should use their powers under sections 3 and 4 of the Human Rights Act; namely, that courts should use their interpretive power contained in section 3 of the Act for non-contestable issues and their ability to issue a declaration of incompatibility in section 4 of the Act for contestable issues.[104]

Young does seem to argue that contestable issues are best decided by legislatures, and that non-contestable issues are best resolved by courts,[105] and she appears to suggest there is an additional advantage to the democratic dialogue model in this respect because, she argues, allocating normative authority in this way makes the model work in at least a semi-plausible and stable way. But this is an additional normative element to her argument about the operation of the model itself. As set out above, the way that the democratic dialogue model is structured by way of sections 3 and 4 of the Human Rights Act, means that courts are simply more likely to decide on non-contestable rights issues and the UK Parliament on contestable rights issues because of the nature of the remedies or lack thereof provided for by those sections. Section 3 enables the courts to give specific remedies to individuals and this is more likely to be the relevant remedy in non-contestable rights cases.

[100] ibid 132, 139.

[101] See, eg, *Reference by the Attorney General and the Advocate General for Scotland – United Nations Convention on the Rights of the Child (Incorporation) (Scotland) Bill; Reference by the Attorney General and the Advocate General for Scotland – European Charter of Local Self-Government (Incorporation) (Scotland) Bill* [2021] UKSC 42.

[102] Young, *Parliamentary Sovereignty and the Human Rights Act* (n 35) 131.

[103] Gardbaum (n 48) 93.

[104] ibid.

[105] Young, 'Is Dialogue Working under the Human Rights Act 1998?' (n 22) 774–78.

In any case, as I discuss in chapter two, this distinction as to whether the model begins with the nature of the rights issue or with the mechanism itself is largely irrelevant when the democratic dialogue model is being applied to the relationship between a domestic legislature, such as the UK Parliament, and an international court, such as the ECtHR and the CJEU.

B. Institutional Contestability and Transnational Democratic Dialogue

The function of the democratic dialogue model at the domestic level to allocate at least provisional normative authority to an institution to resolve rights issues should also apply when an international court is undertaking the rights adjudication. I make this argument by: (i) drawing on another model and system of normative allocation that already exist in the transnational sphere which claims to allocate normative authority, namely, the model of EU constitutional pluralism; and, in turn (ii) demonstrating how the democratic dialogue model might work in a similar (albeit distinguishable) manner to that model, when it is applied to the relationship between a domestic legislature (such as the UK Parliament) and an international court (such as the ECtHR or the CJEU).

i. EU Constitutional Pluralism

MacCormick was one of the first people to discuss the concept and model of 'EU constitutional pluralism'. He examined the interactions between EU national constitutional courts and the CJEU, and described the relationship as being one of constitutional pluralism on the basis that it is a system

> [w]here there is a plurality of institutional normative orders, each with a functioning constitution (at least in the sense of a body of higher-order norms establishing and conditioning relevant governmental powers) [and where] it is possible that each acknowledge the legitimacy of every other within its own sphere, while none asserts or acknowledges constitutional superiority over another.[106]

MacCormick stated, specifically with respect to the interactions between the EU national courts and the CJEU, that:

> It is for the European Court of Justice to interpret in the last resort and in a finally authoritative way the norms of Community law. But equally, it must be for the highest constitutional tribunal of each Member State to interpret its constitutional and other

[106] Neil MacCormick, *Questioning Sovereignty: Law, State, and Nation in the European Commonwealth* (Oxford University Press 1999) 104.

> norms, and hence to interpret the interaction of the validity of [European Community] law with higher level norms of validity in the given state system.[107]

The 'in principle' normative basis for the pluralist constitutional system is not, MacCormick emphasised, because of 'an absence of legal answers to given problems', but, rather, because there is 'a superfluity of legal answers'.[108]

Maduro takes this understanding of EU constitutional pluralism and, significantly, draws out a normative dimension to the model. He argues that there are three claims to be made with respect to the EU model of constitutional pluralism: (i) the descriptive or empirical; (ii) the normative; and (iii) the thickly normative.[109] The 'core' of the descriptive claim of EU constitutional pluralism, according to Maduro, is that there are 'competing constitutional claims of final authority among different legal orders (belonging to the same legal system)' and also 'judicial attempts at accommodating them'.[110]

The normative claim of the model, according to Maduro, is that it is actively desirable to have a constitutional system, such as that in the EU, where competing claims as to which institution should have the 'final authority' to decide on a particular legal issue are not simply decided by a system of hierarchy. He specifically makes this normative claim on the basis that a 'heterarchical' system, specifically in the EU context: (i) 'promotes inclusiveness in national democracies by requiring national political processes to take into account out-of-state interests that may be affected by the deliberations of those political processes'; (ii) allows 'national democracies to collectively regain control over transnational processes that evade their individual control'; and (iii) 'constitute[s] a form of self-imposed external constitutional discipline on national democracies', which can function to correct 'domestic political malfunctions'.[111] Maduro's thickly normative claim is that constitutional pluralism also, desirably, 'provides a closer approximation to the ideals of constitutionalism than either national constitutionalism or a form of EU constitutionalism modelled after state constitutionalism'.[112]

Maduro also begins to touch on the question of 'who' within the EU constitutional pluralist framework should have at least provisional authority to decide upon contentious legal issues. More precisely, he suggests that there are circumstances where a particular issue may, at least presumptively, be better decided by one institution over the other. He states, with respect to national constitutional courts, that such courts need to realise that 'the protection of the fundamental

[107] Neil MacCormick, 'The Maastricht-Urteil: Sovereignty Now' (1995) 1 *European Law Journal* 259, 264; see also Neil MacCormick, 'Beyond the Sovereign State' (1993) 56 *MLR* 1.

[108] MacCormick, 'The Maastricht-Urteil' (n 107) 265.

[109] Miguel Poiares Maduro, 'Three Claims of Constitutional Pluralism' in Matej Avbelj and Jan Komárek, *Constitutional Pluralism in the European Union and Beyond* (Hart Publishing 2012).

[110] ibid 70.

[111] ibid 76–77.

[112] ibid 77–78.

values of their legal order may be better achieved by another institution or that the respect owed to the identity of another legal order should lead them to defer to that jurisdiction' and that, accordingly, national courts should 'both develop instruments for institutional comparison and [work] to set the limits for jurisdictional deference at the level of systemic identity'.[113]

Kumm examines more directly the question of 'who' should, at least provisionally, decide upon particular legal issues within the EU constitutionalist framework. He considers how and under what circumstances such normative authority might be allocated where there is a constitutional conflict between the EU legal order and the national legal order. Kumm accepts the basic premise of EU constitutional pluralism that there should be no institution which has final authority on questions of constitutionality in Europe, and, against that basic premise, he develops guidelines and principles as to when and under what circumstances normative authority should, at least provisionally, be allocated to either national courts or the CJEU.[114]

Kumm begins by identifying the common principles which underlie the normative foundations of both the national legal systems of EU Member States and the EU legal system itself, namely: liberty, equality, democracy and the rule of law.[115] His argument is that these principles 'will sometimes favour the application of international rules over national – even national constitutional – rules', while, '[a]t other times, they will support the primacy of national rules'.[116] He argues that we should start with the presumption that national courts should not decide on EU law or assess its constitutionality and that national courts should presume that the CJEU is the key institutional authority of the EU legal order.[117] He says that national courts should, therefore, not form an opinion or judgment without the European Court first having decided on the issue.[118] The normative basis for this allocation, Jaklic summarises, 'follows from the principle of the expansion of the rule of law that presupposes the European legal order as an autonomous, supreme body of law within a certain sphere'.[119]

Kumm then argues that this presumption can be rebutted in certain circumstances where the principle of democracy is at stake. He says that where fundamental

[113] Miguel Poiares Maduro, 'Interpreting European Law – Judicial Adjudication in a Context of Constitutional Pluralism' (2007) 2 *European Journal of Legal Studies* 18.

[114] Mattias Kumm, 'The Cosmopolitan Turn in Constitutionalism: On the Relationship between Constitutionalism in and beyond the State' in Jeffrey L Dunoff and Joel P Trachtman (eds), *Ruling the World? Constitutionalism, International Law, and Global Governance* (Cambridge University Press 2009) 274.

[115] Mattias Kumm, 'The Jurisprudence of Constitutional Conflict: Constitutional Supremacy in Europe before and after the Constitutional Treaty' (2005) 11 *European Law Journal* 262, 289.

[116] Kumm, 'The Cosmopolitan Turn in Constitutionalism' (n 114) 274.

[117] Mattias Kumm, 'Who Is the Final Arbiter of Constitutionality in Europe? Three Conceptions of the Relationship Between the German Federal Constitutional Court and the European Court of Justice' (1999) 36 *CML Rev* 351, 378, 381.

[118] ibid 381.

[119] Klemen Jaklic, *Constitutional Pluralism in the EU* (Oxford University Press 2014) 128.

constitutional principles are not being sufficiently protected by European legal practice, then European legislative intervention is justified. It is particularly justified in those areas where such a danger of these constitutional principles not being sufficiently guaranteed persists.[120] By 'sufficient guarantee', as he explains in his later work, Kumm means those circumstances where there are, at the EU level, 'persistent structural deficiencies'.[121] He argues that there are two such areas in which the assertion of jurisdiction by national courts will be normatively justified on the basis of upholding the principle of democratic legitimacy.

The first area where national courts should presumptively exercise jurisdiction over an issue of EU law is where the interpretation of EU law involves fundamental rights or, more accurately, where the national court considers that there has been a breach of the standard of 'sufficient guarantees' with respect to the protection of fundamental rights.[122] The second area is where an issue arises that may violate the state's 'legislative jurisdiction', such as where 'legislation is enacted at the European level concerning subject matters for which there is no reasonable jurisdictional basis' and where 'there are no sufficient safeguards instituted on the European level to prevent an unjustified usurpation of legislative power'.[123] The normative basis for national courts asserting jurisdiction before the CJEU in this area is, Kumm notes, specifically, 'the integrity of the practice of political self-determination on a national level'.[124]

Once one of these two circumstances is present, Kumm suggests, a two-part test should then be applied. The test functions to draw 'the divide between the sphere in which the ECJ should have the final authority and the sphere in which the Member State court should have this sort of authority'.[125] In basic terms, the national court must consider that there has been a breach of both the EU legal order and the national constitutional order before it may assert authority to decide on the legal issue at hand. First, in either area, the Member State court must consider that there: (i) has been a violation of a fundamental aspect of EU law, such as fundamental rights or values, which in effect means that the national court will not form an opinion or pass judgment without the European Court first deciding at the issue;[126] and (ii) that the violation is at the level of being 'manifest and grave'.[127] Second, the national court must consider, as Jaklic summarises it, that the alleged breach 'is severe enough to constitute also a violation, of either basic rights

[120] Kumm, 'Who Is the Final Arbiter of Constitutionality in Europe?' (n 117) 378.

[121] Mattias Kumm and Victor Ferreres Comella, 'The Future of Constitutional Conflict in the European Union: Constitutional Supremacy after the Constitutional Treaty' in Joseph Weiler and Christopher Eisgruber (eds), Jean Monnet Working Paper No 5/04 (2004) 16–17.

[122] Kumm, 'Who Is the Final Arbiter of Constitutionality in Europe?' (n 117) 378.

[123] ibid 379.

[124] ibid.

[125] Jaklic (n 119) 132.

[126] Kumm, 'Who Is the Final Arbiter of Constitutionality in Europe?' (n 117) 381.

[127] ibid. See also Jaklic (n 119) 132.

or the principle of democracy, at the level of the national constitutional order'.[128] With respect to the area of fundamental rights in particular, Kumm argues that the national court will, in this second stage, 'apply the national Constitution and set aside EU law, if necessary':

> When a national community, following the procedure set out in its respective Constitution, decides to entrench a specific rule, the implications of which in a particular case are clear (that is, the constitutional provision does not allow for reasonable interpretive disagreement as applied to a particular case), then national courts should respect that choice.[129]

The CJEU should, according to Kumm, respect the assertion of authority by national courts in these areas and particularly national courts' analysis of the domestic constitutional regime, though he notes that the CJEU can still contribute its views on the interpretation of the national constitution and the shared normative principles.[130]

ii. The EU Constitutional Pluralist Model and Democratic Dialogue

There are similarities between the democratic dialogue model and the EU constitutional pluralist model, specifically with respect to how the models function to allocate normative authority to institutions to decide upon rights issues or legal issues more generally. For instance, both models accept that there is not, and should not be, one institution with definitive final authority or 'the last word' on the issue and, in turn, each model accepts that their function in allocating authority is only provisional or presumptive. There are, however, three key differences between the way the democratic dialogue model allocates normative authority to institutions and the way the EU constitutional pluralist model, applying Kumm's characterisation, allocates normative authority.

First, the institutions in each model are clearly different in that the authority in the domestic democratic dialogue model is being shifted between domestic courts and domestic political branches, while, in the EU constitutional pluralist framework, the shift in allocation is occurring between the CJEU (an international or supranational court) and national constitutional courts. We may, for argument's sake, characterise national courts in the EU constitutional model as being more or less an equivalent institution to domestic legislatures in the dialogue model on the basis that national courts in EU constitutional pluralist theories are the institutions characterised as being 'democratic' or, at least, as institutions which protect democracy. But even if we do so, the two models still function in different ways to allocate presumptive authority to decide on rights issues.

[128] Jaklic (n 119) 133.
[129] Kumm and Comella (n 121) 16.
[130] Kumm, 'The Jurisprudence of Constitutional Conflict' (n 115) 303.

In the democratic dialogue model, the legislature is given greater power to decide on the rights issue in the allocation of authority process. This is demonstrated by the fact that the courts' review is 'weak' in the dialogue process, to be exercised only at the discretion of the court and the legislature, even where the judiciary exercises its review power and retains the power to respond. If the court exercises its power under section 3 of the Human Rights Act, the legislature, although there are of course constraints on its power, may respond and modify or repeal the legislation in question to again pursue its own objectives.

However, insofar as we accept that national courts are a political or democratic institution in the EU constitutional pluralist framework, it appears that the national court is an institution that is given a weak review power, as compared with the CJEU in the allocation process. The guidance proposed by Kumm leaves national courts with very limited opportunities to respond to CJEU decisions. The national court, in line with Kumm's guidance, can only assert its jurisdiction in two areas and, even then, it must only intervene where there is a 'manifest and grave' violation of EU law. The review power of the national court is weak, in the same way as the review power of the judiciary in the democratic dialogue model is weak.

The second difference between the democratic dialogue model and the EU model of constitutional pluralism concerns the reasons *why* the allocation takes place in the above-mentioned way in each model. In the democratic dialogue model, the allocation to either the judiciary or the legislature occurs on the basis of the institutional strengths of each institution vis-a-vis the particular rights issue in question. As discussed, a non-contestable rights issue is more likely to be, at least presumptively, resolved by the courts on the basis that a court – such as via section 3 of the Human Rights Act – can provide a specific remedy to an individual. A contestable rights issue is better resolved by the legislature on the basis that it is a democratic institution and so, on the domestic, democratic dialogue model, is more likely to be allocated to the political branches, again, at least provisionally, for its resolution.

In the EU model of constitutional pluralism, however, the process of allocation of authority, which, as set out above, favours the CJEU, seems to rest not only on arguments with respect to institutional strength, but seemingly also external arguments – such as the coherence of the European legal order. Kumm notes that, when national constitutional courts are exercising their review, they must do so 'in a way that is compatible with other Member States Courts engaging in a comparable practice of review … without undermining the coherence of the European legal order', and that '[c]considerations of [European] unity and coherence generally have greater weight'.[131]

The third key difference between the two models is how the allocation of presumptive normative authority occurs; or, rather, how the allocation is triggered.

[131] Kumm, 'Who Is the Final Arbiter of Constitutionality in Europe?' (n 117) 381–82.

In the democratic dialogue model at domestic law, for instance, the allocation process is largely a matter of constitutional design and structure. Two such mechanisms which trigger the process were discussed by way of sections 3 and 4 of the Human Rights Act, which function to at least provisionally allocate authority based on the nature of particular rights issues and how particular rights issues are best remedied. In the EU model of constitutional pluralism, there are no such mechanisms. Rather, Kumm's theory of institutional allocation is largely a normative analysis as to how he thinks the CJEU and national courts should allocate authority to decide rights issues amongst themselves. Moreover, Kumm's theory relies on the national court itself determining whether particular standards of review have been met for it to assert jurisdiction vis-a-vis the CJEU. No mechanisms guide that allocation.

The democratic dialogue model is accordingly similar but distinguishable from the EU constitutional pluralist model, and so what is proposed in this book represents a new theory and model of provisional institutional allocation on rights issues where rights adjudication is undertaken by an international court. Chapter two demonstrates what this might look like in practice; that is, how democratic dialogue might function to allocate normative authority to decide on rights issues as between the UK Parliament and the ECtHR, and how it functioned to do so between UK Parliament and the CJEU.

For now, we can accept that the application of the democratic dialogue model to the relationship between the UK Parliament and the ECtHR and CJEU should also function to allocate normative authority as between the institutions. Given this, rights issues in respect of which there is 'institutional contestability' (where there is an open question as to which institution should decide upon and resolve the rights issue) should be particularly interesting rights issues with which to test whether a domestic legislature and international court engages in democratic dialogue.

C. Institutional Contestability and a Non-National's Right to Enter and Remain

Insofar as 'institutional contestability' might exist with respect to the resolution of a rights issue, a right to enter and remain as it might apply to non-nationals is clearly a rights issue with respect to which there is institutional contestability. I argue that two factors in particular influence the existence of institutional contestability with respect to this rights issue, namely: (i) the political relationship that exists between citizens and domestic legislatures; and (ii) the relationship between the right to enter and remain in a country and state sovereignty.

The political relationship between a domestic legislature and citizens and the lack of such a relationship between domestic legislatures and non-nationals gives rise to arguments that international courts such as the ECtHR and CJEU have the normative authority to decide on the application to non-nationals of a right to enter and remain in a country.

There is a unique political relationship between citizens and legislatures because legislatures are usually elected by the citizenry of the state. Legislatures therefore remain particularly responsive to, and accountable to, citizens because their continued survival relies on their support. There are, of course, some exceptions to this general rule. In the UK, for example, resident Commonwealth citizens can vote in the British general election.[132] But, as a general matter, voting rights are usually reserved for citizens in national constitutional texts,[133] as well as in certain international treaties,[134] and political rights are the 'typical expression of the relationship between the state and its citizens'.[135] This relationship is often brought up during debates in Parliament to justify immigration measures. See, for example, how in 2022, Priti Patel MP, Home Secretary, justified the Rwanda plan, in part, on the basis that: '[t]he British people have repeatedly voted for controlled immigration and the right to secure borders'.[136] In response to the ECtHR's interim measures decision on the plan, which I touched on in the introductory chapter, Jonathan Gullis MP, stated '[w]e need … to fulfil our promise to the British people by taking back control of our laws and borders' and demonstrate 'that parliament is on the side of the British public'.[137] In 2024, Suella Braverman MP similarly justified the Rwanda plan on the basis that: 'it is what people voted for by a huge majority in 2019: to control our borders and to stop the boats'.[138]

There is no such relationship between the domestic legislature and non-nationals (or rather, there is a relationship of exclusion between them). As Evans says 'none of the rights necessary for [non-nationals] to make a full contribution to the formation of State policy are granted to them'.[139] What this also means is that non-nationals are, as a result, often pushed to the periphery and they are 'often the most powerless and marginalized members of society'.[140] McDougal, Lasswell and Chen describe a 'fear of the stranger' which operates with respect to 'non-members' of the body politic, and the fact that non-nationals may be negatively stigmatised in the country in which they are living.[141] Guiraudon also directly links this marginalisation to non-nationals' lack of political capital

[132] See Representation of the People Act 1983.

[133] Virginie Guiraudon, 'Citizenship Rights for Non-Citizens: France, Germany and the Netherlands' in Christian Joppke (ed), *Challenge to the Nation-State: Immigration in Western Europe and the United States* (Oxford University Press 1998) 297; Henrard (n 21) 285.

[134] See, eg, International Covenant on Civil and Political Rights, adopted 16 December 1966, entered into force 23 March 1976; 999 UNTS 171, art 25.

[135] di Pascale (n 88) 281.

[136] HC deb 15 June 2022, vol 716, col 291.

[137] HC deb 14 December 2022, vol 724, cols 1134, 1136.

[138] HC deb 17 January 2024, vol 743, col 885.

[139] AC Evans, 'The Political Status of Aliens in International Law, Municipal Law and European Community Law' (1981) 30 *ICLQ* 20, 31.

[140] Kanstroom (n 77) 50.

[141] McDougal, Lasswell and Chen (n 28) 468.

with domestic legislatures and she argues that 'since they cannot avail themselves of the rights reserved for citizens, such as rights of political participation, foreigners are more likely to see their human rights usurped and to require their affirmation'.[142]

This lack of a political relationship between the legislature and non-nationals, and the actively negative consequences for non-nationals which result from the lack of such a relationship, seem to tilt arguments about which institution should decide, at least presumptively, on the application to non-nationals of a right to enter and remain, in favour of international courts. This is on the basis of courts' institutional strengths which revolve around courts being institutions 'insulated both from concrete social interests and from political struggle taking place in other state institutions'.[143]

There is evidence of international courts acting in this way with respect to this rights issue, with international courts having provided some legal protection for non-nationals who wish to enter into or remain in a foreign country, in certain circumstances. As discussed earlier, despite there being no textual right of non-nationals to enter and remain in a country in the ECHR, the ECtHR has interpreted the Convention in such a way that refusing to admit a non-national or ordering the expulsion of a non-national may amount to a violation of, among others, Articles 3, 5, 8 or 14 of the Convention.[144]

Taking Article 8 of the ECHR again as one such example: the ECtHR has in effect found, in light of this Convention article, that non-nationals who have family in the territory of a state of which they are not a citizen should be permitted to enter and remain in the country in order to reunite with their family and maintain a family life. Article 8 may even, according to the ECtHR, go as far as to 'impose a positive obligation on states to grant certain long-term residents a residence permit'.[145] As Kesby describes it, the ECtHR has interpreted Article 8 in such a way that:

> [W]ell-established family and social ties may mitigate the effects of a person's status as a non-national and give rise to an intermediate category in which admission and the right to remain may be secured without the formal status of nationality being conferred.[146]

There are, however, in light of the relationship between immigration and state sovereignty, arguments that the application to non-nationals of a right to enter and remain is a rights issue which the domestic legislature should have the authority to resolve, at least presumptively.

[142] Virginie Guiraudon, 'European Courts and Foreigners' Rights: A Comparative Study of Norms Diffusion' (2000) 34 *International Migration Review* 1088, 1092.

[143] Alec Stone Sweet, *The Birth of Judicial Politics in France: The Constitutional Council in Comparative Perspective* (Oxford University Press 1992) 13.

[144] Goodwin-Gill, 'The Limits of the Power of Expulsion in Public International Law' (n 5) 137–38.

[145] See, eg, *Kurić & Ors v Slovenia* App no 26828/06 (ECtHR, 13 July 2010) [359]–[376], [407].

[146] Kesby (n 2) 27–28.

There is a long-standing connection between state sovereignty and the absolute control over who is allowed to enter, and remain on, a state's territory. The exercise of state sovereignty does not just mean the exercise of absolute control over territory. It also relates to control over *who* can be on that territory. As Song writes, 'Absolute control over territory, including control over immigration, is regarded as a defining feature of state sovereignty. It is what makes a state a state'.[147]

What this has meant historically is that questions as to who can enter and remain in a state have been left almost exclusively for their determination to the state.[148] The control of immigration has even been framed as being a 'right' on the part of the state or a 'sovereign right'.[149] Evans has traced the idea that immigration control is a 'sovereign right' held on the part of states to Grotius who wrote in the seventeenth century that states enjoy a sovereign right to expel non-nationals who challenge the political order of the state.[150] Similar assertions can also be found throughout the late nineteenth century. The preamble of the Institute of International Law's 1892 Rules on the Admission and Expulsion of Foreigners provides: 'Considering that, for each State, the right to admit or not admit foreigners to its territory, or to admit them conditionally, or to expel them, is a logical and necessary consequence of its sovereignty and independence'.[151]

This historical position has undergone some change, particularly since the advent of international human rights law.[152] As a reminder, there are some categories of non-nationals, such as refugees and asylum seekers and non-nationals who could face torture or ill-treatment if deported, which have special protection against deportation at international law.

[147] Sarah Song, *Immigration and Democracy* (Oxford University Press 2018) 17. See also Catherine Dauvergne, 'Sovereignty, Migration and the Rule of Law in Global Times' (2004) 67 *MLR* 588, 588; Daniel Thym, 'Residence as De Facto Citizenship? Protection of Long-Term Residence under Article 8 ECHR' in Ruth Rubio Marín (ed), *Human Rights and Immigration* (Oxford University Press 2014) 130; Richard Perruchoud, 'State Sovereignty and Freedom of Movement' in Brian Opeskin, Jillyanne Redpath-Cross and Richard Perruchoud (eds), *Foundations of International Migration Law* (Cambridge University Press 2012) 124.

[148] See generally Frédéric Mégret, 'Transnational Mobility, the International Law of Aliens, and the Origins of Global Migration Law' (2017) 111 *American Journal of International Law Unbound* 13, 13–14. See also Evans (n 139).

[149] The characterisation of states having a 'right' to exclude non-nationals is a matter of some contention: see, eg, International Law Commission, 'Draft Articles on the Expulsion of Aliens, with Commentaries', *Report of the International Law Commission on the Work of its 66th Session* (UN Doc A/69/10 2014) art 3. Kanstroom, however, argues that, specifically with respect to the Draft Articles, the phrasing of this as a 'right' is not entirely accurate and that it would be better described as a 'state sovereign power or, perhaps prerogative': Kanstroom (n 77). Walters (n 62) 279.

[150] Evans (n 139).

[151] Règles internationales sur l'admission et l'expulsion des étrangers', *Revue de Droit International*, vol X, Résolution du 9 septembre 1892, 218-226, preambular [1], cited in International Law Commission, 'Expulsion of Non-Nationals: Memorandum by the Secretariat', *58th Session* (UN Doc A/CN4/565 2006) 131–32.

[152] Peter J Spiro, 'A New International Law of Citizenship' (2011) 105 *American Journal of International Law* 694, 695; Vincent Chetail, 'The Human Rights of Migrants in General International Law: From Minimum Standards to Fundamental Rights International Migrants Bill of Rights: Essay' (2013) 28 *Georgetown Immigration Law Journal* 225, 231.

In addition, there are also now some accepted limits on states' complete discretion to determine who is and is not a national and to determine, therefore, who enjoys a right to enter and to remain on a state's territory. As discussed already, there is some practice and jurisprudence which suggests that to be a 'national' of a state, a person must have an effective and genuine link with that state. Customary international law also prohibits states from arbitrarily or abusively conferring nationality,[153] and the right not to be discriminated against as contained in several international law instruments also functions to constrain a state's discretion in conferring nationality.[154] There are also accepted limits at international law on when a state might deprive its nationals of their citizenship of the state. In this respect, Article 15 of the Universal Declaration of Human Rights prohibits the arbitrary deprivation of nationality (and it also provides for a right to change one's nationality), while the European Convention on Nationality provides that deprivation of nationality is only possible where there is 'a lack of genuine link between the State Party and the national habitually residing abroad'.[155]

On the whole, however, the development of these limitations on the state's discretion to control immigration has been fairly insignificant,[156] and the limitations themselves can be undermined by states. Peters discusses the phenomenon of what she calls 'extra-territorial naturalization' which seems to undermine the requirement at international law described above for there to be a 'genuine link' with a state to be a national of that state. Peters finds that states confer nationality on persons residing abroad as an exercise of sovereignty and a way to actively manifest that sovereignty:

> The bestowment of nationality upon an alien is an official act by the conferring State and an emanation of its sovereignty. The naturalization of a person who was previously a national of another State has internationally relevant legal effects. Through the enlargement of its nation, which is a constituent element of its statehood, a State in a way also enlarges itself. The international effects are even greater when persons residing abroad are involved, because nationality is a basis for the exercise of extraterritorial jurisdiction. The higher the number of a State's nationals abroad, the more often that State will be under international law allowed to apply its laws outside its own territory, even if enforcement of those laws is not permitted.[157]

The control of who can and cannot enter and remain on a state's territory accordingly continues to be a key part of a state's sovereignty,[158] and states still have 'a largely

[153] See Peters (n 10) 678 fn 240.

[154] See, eg, International Convention on the Elimination of All Forms of Racial Discrimination, 7 March 1966, UNTS 660, 195 art 5(d)(iii); Convention on the Reduction of Statelessness, 30 August 1961, UNTS 989, 175 art 9; European Convention on Nationality, 6 November 1997, ETS No 166 art 5(1).

[155] European Convention on Nationality (n 154) art 7(1)(e).

[156] Thym (n 147) 131.

[157] Peters (n 10) 658.

[158] di Pascale (n 88) 203.

unfettered power', to decide the circumstances under which non-nationals can enter, reside and depart from a state's territory.[159] Specifically, in the European context, which is the contextual focus of this book, the ECtHR has consistently confirmed, even as it finds some protection for non-nationals of their right to enter and remain in a country, that 'it is the sovereign prerogative of States to regulate the presence of foreigners in their territory, including their expulsion'.[160]

V. Conclusion

Kanstroom has described how it now seems 'quite jarring from a modern human rights perspective to think of sovereign state power as a "right"'.[161] But it is this exact disjuncture between international human rights law (and its purpose of protecting the people against the state) and the fact that immigration law is still considered 'the last bastion of sovereignty',[162] that makes this rights issue both contestable and institutionally contestable and thus a particularly interesting case study with which to test whether the UK Parliament and the ECtHR engage in democratic dialogue, and whether UK Parliament did so with the CJEU.

[159] Thym (n 147) 130 (emphasis added). See also Kay Hailbronner and Jana Goglin, 'Aliens' in Rüdiger Wolfrum (ed), *The Max Planck Encyclopedia of Public International Law* (Oxford University Press 2013) 14–22; Perruchoud (n 147) 131; Catherine Phuong, 'Minimum Standards for Return Procedures and International Human Rights Law' (2007) 9 *European Journal of Migration and Law* 105, 105–06.

[160] Wojnowska-Radzinska (n 75) 46; *Abdulaziz, Cabales And Balkandali v United Kingdom* App Nos 9214/80; 9473/81; 9474/81 (ECtHR, 28 May 1985) [67]. See also UN HRC (n 8) para 5; Francesca Strumia, 'European Citizenship and EU Immigration: A Demoi-Cratic Bridge between the Third Country Nationals' Right to Belong and the Member States' Power to Exclude: European Citizenship and EU Immigration' (2016) 22 *European Law Journal* 417, 433; T Alexander Aleinikoff, 'International Legal Norms and Migration: A Report' in T Alexander Aleinikoff and Vincent Chetail (eds), *Migration and International Legal Norms* (TMC Asser Press 2003); David Martin, 'The Authority and Responsibility of States' in T Alexander Aleinikoff and Vincent Chetail (eds), *Migration and International Legal Norms* (TMC Asser 2003).

[161] Kanstroom (n 77) 56.

[162] Dauvergne (n 147) 588.

2

Setting Up Transnational Democratic Dialogue

I have thus far established how we might test whether the UK Parliament has engaged in (transnational) democratic dialogue with the ECtHR and CJEU, but the mechanics of how that dialogue might occur, and has occurred, have not yet been explained. The aim of this chapter is to demonstrate that there is a framework in place by which these institutions can engage in democratic dialogue, both in the sense of constitutional collaboration and constitutional counter-balancing. As a reminder, mechanisms that facilitate democratic dialogue in the sense of *constitutional collaboration* are those that enable the institutions to work together in such a way as to 'draw[] on their relative strengths and weaknesses when reasoning about rights'.[1] Mechanisms that facilitate democratic dialogue in the sense of *constitutional counter-balancing* are those that ensure that 'it is not the case that one institution is always able to authoritatively determine the issues, effectively overriding the contribution of the other'.[2]

Before undertaking this analysis, I examine the institutional and constitutional differences between the UK Parliament and, respectively, the ECtHR and CJEU, because these differences illuminate the extent to which democratic dialogue can occur between the institutions. Given that democratic dialogue supports a combination of different ways of reasoning about rights, differences between the institutions influence interactions and thereby facilitate dialogue.[3]

I. Institutional and Constitutional Differences between the UK Parliament and the ECtHR and CJEU

A. Institutional Differences

The ECtHR and the CJEU are both international (albeit regional) courts, set up by international treaties. The ECtHR is established by Article 19 of the ECHR.[4]

[1] Alison L Young, *Democratic Dialogue and the Constitution* (Oxford University Press 2017) 33. See also Sara Jackson, 'Designing Human Rights Legislation: Dialogue, the Commonwealth Model and the Roles of Parliaments and Courts' (2007) 13 *Auckland University Law Review* 89, 92.

[2] Young (n 1) 32–33.

[3] ibid 258.

[4] Art 19 of the European Convention provides that: '[t]o ensure the observance of the engagements undertaken by the High Contracting Parties in the Convention and the Protocols thereto, there shall

The ECtHR's role is to interpret and apply the ECHR and its Protocols,[5] and to do so, in accordance with Article 53 of the Convention, in a way that does not limit or derogate from the guarantees of human rights and fundamental freedoms ensured under a state's domestic law.

The CJEU is established by Article 19 of the Treaty on the European Union (the TEU), which provides that the role of the CJEU is to 'ensure that in the law and application of the Treaties the law is observed'.[6] It is not, accordingly, a specialist human rights court in the same way that the ECtHR is. The CJEU is a generalist court, and protecting fundamental rights and freedoms forms only part of its broader role of interpreting and applying EU law. As O'Leary describes it, the CJEU 'seeks to protect fundamental rights within the confines of a supernational organisation whose principal objective is to harmonise and subject to the principle of conferral'.[7]

The UK Parliament, on the other hand, is established by a series of Acts, coupled with custom and convention.[8] The key role of Parliament is to make, amend and repeal laws, but it also has other roles including scrutinising the work of the British government and holding the government to account through, for instance: (i) debates in the House of Commons about proposed legislation or about other government activity; (ii) parliamentary questions, where specific questions can be asked of government, on the public record; and (iii) parliamentary committees, which examine the government's policy and legislative proposals and which hold government to account through checking and authorising government spending.[9]

These roles impact the relative expertise of each institution in the area of human rights. In light of their differences, we would expect the ECtHR to have institutional knowledge in human rights since it was set up for this purpose, and its main function is to determine human rights issues arising under the ECHR.[10]

be set up a European Court of Human Rights, hereinafter referred to as "the Court". It shall function on a permanent basis'. Note that Slaughter and Helfer refer to the ECtHR as a 'supra-national court': Laurence R Helfer and Anne-Marie Slaughter, 'Toward a Theory of Effective Supranational Adjudication' (1997) 107 *Yale Law Journal* 273.

[5] ECHR, Art 32.

[6] Treaty of the European Union [2012] OJ C 326/13, Art 19(1).

[7] Síofra O'Leary, 'A Tale of Two Cities: Fundamental Rights Protection in Strasbourg and Luxembourg' (2018) 20 *Cambridge Yearbook of European Legal Studies* 3, 13.

[8] See generally Clare Feikert-Ahalt, 'United Kingdom' (2016) 1 National Parliaments – The Law Library of Congress 114, 114. See Stat Wallie 1284, 12 Edw. 1 (repealed); Union with Scotland Act 1706, 6 Ann c. 11, as amended; Union with Ireland Act 1800, 38 & 40 Geo. 3 c. 67; Government of Ireland Act 1920, 10 & 11 Geo. 5 c. 67 (repealed).

[9] Hannah White, 'Parliamentary Scrutiny of Government' (Institute for Government 2015); 'What Is the Role of Parliament?' (UK Parliament): www.parliament.uk/about/how/role/.

[10] The preamble to the European Convention also relevantly provides that the parties to the Convention '[r]eaffirm[] their profound belief in those fundamental freedoms which are the foundation of justice and peace in the world and are best maintained on the one hand by an effective political democracy and on the other by a common understanding and observance of the Human Rights upon which they depend'; and that they 'resolve[], as the governments of European countries which are like-minded and have a common heritage of political traditions, ideals, freedom and the rule of law, to take the first steps for the collective enforcement of certain of the rights states in the Universal Declaration [of Human Rights]'.

The ECtHR's particular institutional competence and knowledge is necessarily in European human rights law and in those specific rights which are set out in the ECHR, although the ECtHR does also in practice often draw on other human rights law and other courts' and bodies' interpretations of that law in its judgments. The ECtHR has, for example, drawn in its case law on Inter-American human rights instruments and on judgments of the Inter-American Court of Human Rights,[11] CJEU judgments,[12] and on the International Covenant on Civil and Political Rights (ICCPR) and United Nations Human Rights Committee (UN HRC) Communications with respect to the ICCPR.[13]

As the CJEU is a generalist court and human rights issues form only one part of its decision-making, we might expect that its institutional knowledge in the area of human rights might be somewhat less than institutions such as the ECtHR.[14] It does, however, consider issues arising under the Charter of Fundamental Rights of the European Union (EU Charter),[15] and the application of EU law entails the application of the Charter.[16] This means it must take into account any implications for human rights guarantees in all its decisions. Moreover, Article 52(3) of the EU Charter provides that where Charter rights correspond to rights protected by the ECHR, 'the meaning of those rights shall be the same as those laid down' in the *EU Charter* and the CJEU has often drawn on, and deferred to, the ECtHR's interpretation of rights.[17] De Búrca's analysis of CJEU jurisprudence between 2009 and 2012 confirms this:

> [T]he Court of Justice has evolved from being a tribunal concerned primarily with economic matters, to one with a much wider range of jurisdiction which is now explicitly tasked with enforcing human rights. As a consequence, the CJEU lacks the kind of

[11] See 'Research Report: References to the Inter-American Court of Human Rights and Inter-American Instruments in the Case-Law of the European Court of Human Rights' (Council of Europe/European Court of Human Rights 2016).

[12] See Sionaidh Douglas-Scott, 'A Tale of Two Courts: Luxembourg, Strasbourg and the Growing European Human Rights Acquis' (2006) 43 *CML Rev* 629, 640–44. Amalie Frese and Henrik Palmer Olsen, 'Spelling It Out – Convergence and Divergence in the Judicial Dialogue between CJEU and ECtHR' (2019) 88 *Nordic Journal of International Law* 429.

[13] See generally Magdalena Forowicz, *The Reception of International Law in the European Court of Human Rights* (Oxford University Press 2010).

[14] Young (n 1) 257.

[15] Charter of Fundamental Rights of the European Union [2010] OJ C 83/389.

[16] Case C-617/10 *Åklagaren v Hans Åkerberg Fransson* [2013] ECR I-9011 (*Åklagaren*). The CJEU also provided in *Åklagaren* that: 'since the fundamental rights guaranteed by the Charter must therefore be complied with, where national legislation falls within the scope of European Union law, situations cannot exist which are covered in that way by European Union law without those fundamental rights being applicable': at [21].

[17] See, eg, Case C-400/10 PPU *JMcB v LE* [2010] ECR 1-8965; Case C-260/89 *ERT v DEP* [1991] ECR 1-2925 [41]; Cases C-402/05 P & C-415/05, P *Kadi and Al Barakaat International Foundation v Council and Commission* [2008] ECR I-6351 [315]–[16]. See generally Guy Harpaz, 'The European Court of Justice and Its Relations with the European Court of Human Rights: The Quest for Enhanced Reliance, Coherence and Legitimacy' (2009) 46 *CML Rev* 105; Sionaidh Douglas-Scott, 'The European Union and Human Rights after the Treaty of Lisbon' (2011) 11 *Human Rights Law Review* 645; Allan Rosas, 'Fundamental Rights in the Luxembourg and Strasbourg Courts' in Carl Baudenbacher, Per Tresselt and Thorgeir Orlygsson (eds), *The EFTA Court: Ten Years On* (Hart Publishing 2005).

> expertise and experience that other human rights courts and treaty-bodies – including the European Court of Human Rights – enjoy.[18]

It is also worth noting that institutional knowledge should not necessarily be conflated with offering a 'better' protection of human rights, in the sense of providing a strong legal protection of rights to an individual. Harpaz, for example, argues that the ECtHR's significant use of the margin of appreciation doctrine in its decisions means that its jurisprudence can sometimes remain 'declaratory, deferential and therefore abstract' and his analysis finds that the CJEU can in fact afford a higher protection of human rights than the ECtHR, in terms of providing a stronger legal protection of rights.[19]

Consideration of human rights issues forms, at least in theory, only a small part of the UK Parliament's role. But this is not to say that that consideration is insignificant. In the UK, the Joint Committee on Human Rights, made up of Members from both the House of Commons and the House of Lords, assesses the human rights implications of all proposed legislation, scrutinises the government's response to court decisions relating to human rights, conducts inquiries, and reports to Parliament on remedial orders made under the Human Rights Act.[20] The presence of this Committee is in part what Anagnostou and Mungiu-Pippidi consider to be why, in their study, the UK was found to be the best performing country in Europe in its domestic implementation of ECtHR judgments.[21] Evans and Evans also point out how domestic legislatures inevitably consider human rights issues, in undertaking their functions beyond that of law-making:

> In established democratic States, legislatures perform several distinct functions. They are representative bodies providing a mechanism by which citizens participate in public affairs and government; they are forums in which governments can be held accountable for their conduct; and they are (more or less) deliberative law-making bodies. In discharging each of these functions they can affect the enjoyment of human rights.[22]

Each institution under consideration here also brings a different perspective to the resolution of rights issues. The ECtHR hears from individuals, given that cases come before it primarily through individual applications, after an individual has exhausted all potential domestic remedies.[23] This, as Flynn describes it, not only

[18] Gráinne de Búrca, 'After the EU Charter of Fundamental Rights: The Court of Justice as a Human Rights Adjudicator?' (2013) 20 *Maastricht Journal of European and Comparative Law* 168, 171.

[19] Harpaz (n 17) 116–17.

[20] See 'Human Rights (Joint Committee)' (UK Parliament): committees.parliament.uk/committee/93/human-rights-joint-committee/. See discussion in Dia Anagnostou and Alina Mungiu-Pippidi, 'Domestic Implementation of Human Rights Judgments in Europe: Legal Infrastructure and Government Effectiveness Matter' (2014) 25 *European Journal of International Law* 205, 222; Samantha Besson, 'The Reception Process in Ireland and the United Kingdom' in Helen Keller and Alec Stone Sweet (eds), *A Europe of Rights: The Impact of the ECHR on National Legal Systems* (Oxford University Press 2008) 74.

[21] Anagnostou and Mungiu-Pippidi (n 20) 221–22.

[22] Carolyn Evans and Simon Evans, 'Evaluating the Human Rights Performance of Legislatures' (2006) 6 *Human Rights Law Review* 545, 548.

[23] European Convention, Art 34. State parties may also refer cases to the ECtHR: see Art 33.

means that a direct link is created between the ECtHR and the citizenry,[24] but also that the ECtHR is able to look at how domestic courts have engaged with the rights issue at hand and the reasons why courts at the national level decided that there was no Convention breach. The ECtHR of course also hears from governments appearing before it, as well as from other signatory states not party to the proceedings, and this further contributes to the ECtHR's comprehensive understanding of how human rights are protected across Europe, at the domestic level.[25] This perspective is consolidated by the ECtHR's use of the margin of appreciation doctrine given the invocation of that doctrine requires the Court to work out the 'European consensus' on the matter.

Cases come before the CJEU, on the other hand, either by direct actions, or usually, by domestic courts referring questions of EU law to it under Article 267 of the Treaty on the Functioning of the European Union (TFEU).[26] This referral mechanism is in practice usually 'used to question the compatibility of domestic legislation with EU law, including EU fundamental rights'.[27] This procedure builds a comprehensive understanding of rights issues across Europe on the part of the CJEU because, when domestic courts refer the case 'upwards', they provide information to the CJEU to give the latter 'a clear understanding of the actual and legal context of the main proceedings',[28] and also often give their own view as to what the answer to the question is and should be.[29] Member States also intervene in proceedings before the CJEU and give their opinion on the rights issue at hand.

Although domestic laws may have extraterritorial effect, the UK Parliament primarily makes laws for the UK, and parliamentarians remain accountable and responsive to the needs of the domestic constituency. The UK Parliament therefore maintains a strongly domestic focus and, we can expect it to seldom take comparative or international perspectives into account. The UK Parliament should have, accordingly, in theory, a better and deeper perspective on human rights matters within the UK, at least with respect to British citizens than, say, either the ECtHR or the CJEU might have. This has been expressly acknowledged by the ECtHR which has stated that 'national authorities have direct democratic legitimation and are … in principle better placed than an international court to evaluate local needs and conditions'.[30]

[24] Tom Flynn, *The Triangular Constitution: Constitutional Pluralism in Ireland, the EU and the ECHR* (Hart Publishing 2019) 18.

[25] Young (n 1) 257–58.

[26] Treaty on the Functioning of the European Union [2016] OJ C 202/1 (TFEU). See Catherine Barnard and Steve Peers (eds), *European Union Law*, 2nd edn (Oxford University Press 2017) 262–309.

[27] Aida Torres Pérez, 'Judicial Dialogue and Fundamental Rights in the European Union: A Quest for Legitimacy' in Gary Jacobsohn and Miguel Schor (eds), *Comparative Constitutional Theory* (Edward Elgar 2018) 117.

[28] Recommendations to National Courts and Tribunals in Relation to the Initiation of Preliminary Ruling Proceedings [2012] OJ C 338/1, para 22.

[29] Information Note on References from National Courts for a Preliminary Ruling [2005] OJ C 143/1, para 24.

[30] *Hatton and Others v United Kingdom* [GC] App no 36022/97 (ECtHR, 8 July 2003) [97].

B. Constitutional Differences

The ECtHR is not a superior court to domestic courts of the signatory states of the ECHR; it does not hear appeals from domestic courts and its judgments stand alone and do not replace domestic court judgments. The ECtHR's judgments are 'binary' in that the Court will find that there either is or is not a violation of the Convention.[31] Once the ECtHR issues a judgment, state parties to the judgment must comply with it.[32] Article 46(2) of the ECHR provides that the execution of a judgment by the Member State is supervised by the Committee of Ministers. As demonstrated by the rights issue of prisoner voting in the UK, however, a Member State's execution of an ECtHR judgment may be slow and not necessarily fully completed,[33] although of course domestic law, such as the UK Human Rights Act, always determines the extent to which international law applies in the domestic legal system of a state and the implementation of human rights courts' judgments relies on the willingness of domestic authorities to do so.[34]

Like the ECtHR, the CJEU similarly does not exercise what might be considered as appellate jurisdiction over national courts. Despite the fact that the CJEU's judgments, in practice, according to Fabbrini and Maduro's analysis, often 'turn into an assessment (even if made in abstract) of the compatibility of national measures and rules with the relevant EU provisions', in theory at least, the CJEU is confined to providing its interpretation of EU law and its opinion on the specific issue arising under EU law before it.[35] Because it is a condition of EU membership that Member States accept that, in circumstances where there is a conflict between domestic law and EU law, the latter prevails,[36] this means that, generally speaking, domestic legislatures must, through national courts, accept CJEU decisions. As Fasone and Lupo describe it:

> According to the CJEU's interpretation of primacy as an absolute principle … EU law supersedes even national constitutional provisions that conflict with it. In this regard, the [national parliament's] law-making authority is seriously jeopardized and

[31] O'Leary (n 7) 11.

[32] ECHR, Art 46(1).

[33] See generally Neil Johnston, 'Prisoners' Voting Rights: Developments since May 2015' (House of Commons Library 2020) Briefing Paper Number 07461.

[34] Colm O'Cinneide, 'Saying "No" to Strasbourg: When Are National Parliaments Justified in Refusing to Give Effect to Judgments of International Human Rights Courts?' in Matthew Saul, Andreas Follesdal and Geir Ulfstein (eds), *The International Human Rights Judiciary and National Parliaments: Europe and Beyond* (Cambridge University Press 2017) 305.

[35] Federico Fabbrini and Miguel Poiares Maduro, 'Supranational Constitutional Courts' (Social Science Research Network 2017) SSRN Scholarly Paper 2990277 11.

[36] ibid 276–77. See, eg, Case C-26/62 *Van Gend & Loos v Netherlands Inland Revenue Administration* [1963] ECR 1; Case C-106/77 *Amminstrazione delle Finanze dello Stato v Simmenthal SpA* [1978] ECR 629 77.

> parliaments can find little assistance in the CJEU, because the latter has significantly contributed to their marginalization in the first place.[37]

Member States choose to be part of the EU and to have EU law apply domestically, and states do ultimately decide on the relationship between domestic law and EU law.[38] A state can always ignore a CJEU decision or refuse to follow it, and leave domestic courts to decide on the application of law.[39] Again, the state can only disregard a decision in this way as a matter of fact and not as a matter of international law.

When the UK Parliament responds to the judgments of international courts, Parliament is not merely implementing (or deciding not to implement) international human rights law. Rather, the UK Parliament contextualises and translates the judgments of these courts to reflect the UK constituency, and its history and culture. The UK Parliament does so both in terms of the duties that attach to the right, and in terms of the content of the right itself.[40] This is precisely why, as Besson argues, international human rights law instruments are 'drafted in minimal and abstract terms'; they are 'calling for domestic reception and specification'.[41]

II. Constitutional Collaboration

A. The UK Parliament and the ECtHR

To identify and explain the operation of the mechanisms that might facilitate democratic dialogue between the UK Parliament and the ECtHR, in the sense of constitutional collaboration, I analogise here with the mechanisms Hogg and Bushell identified in the Canadian Charter as functioning to facilitate dialogue between the Canadian Parliament and the Canadian Supreme Court.

Section 1 of the Canadian Charter provides that rights can be subject to 'reasonable limits prescribed by law as can be demonstrably justified in a free and democratic society'.[42] According to Hogg and Bushell, where a court rules that a law violates the Charter on the basis that a right was not reasonably limited, it

[37] Cristina Fasone and Nicola Lupo, 'Constitutional Review and the Powers of National Parliaments in EU Affairs: Erosion or Protection?' in Davor Jancic (ed), *National Parliaments after the Lisbon Treaty and the Euro Crisis* (Oxford University Press 2017) 63 (citations omitted).

[38] See Young (n 1) 277. Young points to the following to demonstrate this in the UK context: *Thoburn v Sunderland City Council* [2003] QB 151; *R (HS2) v Secretary of State for Transport* [2014] UKSC 3; European Union Act 2011 s 18.

[39] See discussion in Pérez (n 26) 114.

[40] Samantha Besson, 'Human Rights and Democracy in a Global Context: Decoupling and Recoupling' (2011) 4 *Ethics & Global Politics* 19, 29.

[41] ibid.

[42] Peter W Hogg and Allison A Bushell, 'The Charter Dialogue between Courts and Legislatures (Or Perhaps the Charter of Rights Isn't Such a Bad Thing after All)' (1997) 35 *Osgoode Hall Law Journal* 75, 84.

will usually explain why that standard was not met and explain what a less restrictive law would look like. This allows the Canadian Parliament to respond in an appropriate way that would not violate the Charter, but that would still achieve Parliament's original agenda.[43] This is a mechanism that gives rise to constitutional collaboration because it is enables the court and legislature to work together on the rights issue, in such a way that maximises the strengths of each institution.

Similar mechanisms can be found in the ECHR. The Right to Respect for Private and Family Life, in Article 8 of the Convention, provides:

1. Everyone has the right to respect for his private and family life, his home and his correspondence.
2. There shall be no interference by a public authority with the exercise of this right except such as in *accordance with the law* and is *necessary in a democratic society* in the interests of national security, public safety or the economic well-being of the country, for the prevention of disorder or crime, for the protection of health or morals, or for the protection of the rights and freedoms of others (emphasis added).

The Freedom to Manifest One's Religion or Beliefs in Article 9 of the ECHR, the Right to Freedom of Expression in Article 10, the Right to Freedom of Assembly and Association in Article 11, and the Right to Freedom of Movement as set out in Article 2 of Protocol No 4 to the ECHR can similarly be limited where the limitations are: (i) prescribed or are in accordance with law, (ii) necessary in a democratic society; and (iii) in the interests of national security, territorial integrity, public safety, for the prevention of disorder or crime, for the protection of public order, health or morals, or for the protection of the rights and freedoms of others.[44] Mowbray argues that the fact that an interference with these rights needs to be shown as being 'necessary in a democratic society' demonstrated that 'the framers expressly incorporated the idea of democracy into the text of the Convention and gave it a prominent role in the balancing of individual claims against the needs of the community as a whole'.[45]

Hogg and Bushell also identified 'qualified rights' as mechanisms that facilitate dialogue between the Canadian Supreme Court and the Canadian Parliament. This is on the basis that, where a court has found that a law breaches one of these kinds of rights, it can indicate the correct standard of reasonableness or arbitrariness, and the legislature can then take corrective legislative action which satisfies

[43] ibid 85.

[44] The right to freedom of expression can also be limited to protect the reputation or rights of others, to prevent the disclosure of information received in confidence, or to maintain the authority and impartiality of the judiciary.

[45] Alistair Mowbray, 'The Role of the ECtHR in the Promotion of Democracy' [1999] *Public Law* 703, 703, quoted in Conor Gearty, 'Democracy and Human Rights in the ECtHR: A Critical Appraisal' (2000) 51 *Northern Ireland Legal Quarterly* 381, 381.

that standard, while still achieving its own goals.[46] Qualified rights, in the sense described by Hogg and Bushell, can also be found in the ECHR. The Right to Liberty and Security in Article 5 and the Right to a Fair Trial in Article 6 of the Convention, to take two examples, can be limited in various ways, as long as that limitation is 'reasonable'.

The guarantee of equality rights in section 15 of the Canadian Charter and their satisfaction through remedial measures also facilitates dialogue between the Canadian Parliament and Supreme Court. Hogg and Bushell found that the judicial decision usually results in the Parliament needing to accommodate the excluded individual or group, but that this can be achieved in different ways, allowing 'the competent legislative bodies to set their own priorities', while respecting the judicial decision.[47] A similar mechanism to section 15 of the Canadian Charter can be found in Article 14 of the ECHR which prohibits discrimination on various grounds.

The margin of appreciation doctrine, which involves the ECtHR giving to states some latitude to implement their obligations under the ECHR, can also facilitate dialogue between the UK Parliament and the ECtHR. It does so, at least in theory, because the doctrine allows the ECtHR to ensure that the state does not fall below the minimum protection offered by the Convention right, and, at the same time, it gives the state 'a margin' in its response. The ECtHR justifies its use of the doctrine on the following basis:

> By reason of their direct and continuous contact with the vital forces of their countries, State authorities are in principle in a better position than the international judge to give an opinion on the exact content of these requirements as well as on the 'necessity' of a 'restriction' or 'penalty' intended to meet them ... This margin is given both to the domestic legislator ('prescribed by law') and to the bodies, judicial amongst others, that are called upon to interpret and apply the laws in force.[48]

The doctrine facilitates dialogue in the sense of constitutional collaboration because it allows the ECtHR to make sure that the state does not fall below the minimum protection offered by the Convention right, and, at the same time, it gives the state discretion and 'a margin' in its response. This allows the state to respond to the international court with new legislation that can achieve its own goals. The ECtHR is in effect recognising that the legislature might better resolve rights issues in certain circumstances.[49] Judges of the ECtHR speaking and writing extrajudicially with respect to the signing of the 2012 Brighton Declaration confirm that the Court's use of the margin of appreciation doctrine, and the Court's endorsement of the principle of subsidiarity, reflect the

[46] Hogg and Bushell (n 42) 87–88.

[47] ibid 90–91.

[48] *Handyside v United Kingdom* App no 5493/72 (ECtHR, 7 December 1976) [48]. The doctrine has since been given more formal application in Protocol no 15 (2013) to the European Convention.

[49] Young (n 1) 258. See also Mary Arden, *Human Rights and European Law: Building New Legal Orders* (Oxford University Press 2015) 290.

institution's view that national institutions may be better at deciding on aspects of rights issues.[50]

B. The UK Parliament and the CJEU

While EU law applies automatically at domestic law, it is more pluralistic and interactive than it might otherwise appear, and there are mechanisms in the system that facilitated interactions between the CJEU and the UK Parliament.[51] There are mechanisms in the EU Charter, which codifies the CJEU's traditional approach to rights issues,[52] which had the capacity to facilitate dialogue between the UK Parliament and the CJEU. As discussed, the CJEU has held that the EU Charter applies to states when states are applying EU law.[53] I again draw an analogy between those mechanisms identified by Hogg and Bushell in the Canadian Charter and those in the EU Charter:

Article 52(1) of the EU Charter provides:

> Any limitation on the exercise of the rights and freedoms recognised by this Charter must be provided for by law and respect the essence of those rights and freedoms. *Subject to the principle of proportionality*, limitations may be made only if they are *necessary* and *genuinely meet objectives of general interest* recognised by the Union or the need to protect the rights and freedoms of others (emphasis added).

Where the CJEU rules on a point of EU law that engages rights, Article 52(1) can therefore operate to give the state some scope to pursue its own agenda in response, while still implementing EU law and the CJEU's interpretation of that law. In this sense, Article 52(1) of the EU Charter seems analogous to the general limitation provision in section 1 of the Canadian Charter that, for reasons set out earlier, Hogg and Bushell identified as a key dialogic mechanism. Significantly, the CJEU has used Article 51(2) as a more general interpretive tool.[54]

There is also an equality guarantee in Article 21 of the EU Charter, which prohibits discrimination on certain grounds. For those same reasons set out in relation to Article 15 of the Canadian Charter and Article 14 of the ECHR,

[50] See, eg, Sir Nicolas Bratza, Speech given at the High Level Conference, Brighton (18–20 April 2012): www.echr.coe.int/Documents/Speech_20120420_Bratza_Brighton_ENG.pdf; Robert Spano, 'Universality or Diversity of Human Rights?: Strasbourg in the Age of Subsidiarity' (2014) 14 *Human Rights Law Review* 487. The Brighton Declaration declared, among other things, that 'the Convention system is subsidiary to the safeguarding of human rights at the national level and that national authorities are in principle better placed than an international court to evaluate local needs and conditions' and that the Court must have 'due regard to the State's margin of appreciation': at [11].

[51] Young (n 1) 277.

[52] See Margot Horspool, *European Union Law*, 9th edn (Oxford University Press 2016) para [6.60]–[6.125]; Explanations Relating to the Charter of Fundamental Rights [2007] OJ C 303/02 17.

[53] Since the UK's withdrawal from the European Union, the EU Charter no longer applies in the UK: see, European Union (Withdrawal) Act 2018, s 5(4).

[54] Giorgio Monti, *European Union Law: Cases and Materials*, 2nd edn (Cambridge University Press 2010) 248.

Article 21 of the EU Charter would have functioned to facilitate dialogue between the UK Parliament and the CJEU in the sense of constitutional collaboration.

The CJEU can also 'exercise comity' by formulating its decisions in such a way as to provide an opinion on the rights issue at hand, while also leaving space for resolution of the issue at the national level.[55] One way in which the CJEU exercises comity is when it modifies the applicable proportionality standard.[56] Although Young makes this argument with respect to interactions between national courts and the CJEU, it also, arguably, functions to facilitate dialogue in the sense of constitutional collaboration between a legislature such as the UK Parliament and the CJEU.

The CJEU has stated that the principle of proportionality is 'one of the general principles of European Union law' and that it 'requires that measures implemented by acts of the European Union are appropriate for attaining the objective pursued and do not go beyond what is necessary to achieve it'.[57] Martinsen describes the steps involved in undertaking a proportionality assessment as follows:

> When assessing proportionality, the Court carries out a form of balancing inquiry. In this balancing act, the Court examines the weight and justifiability of policy means and ends, often in the light of fundamental Community aims such as the internal market and the constitutive-free movement principles. A proportionality test carried out by the ECJ will normally contain three steps, evaluating (1) the *suitability* of the measure to achieve its stated aim; (2) whether the measure was *necessary* to achieve this aim and (3) whether the measure imposes an *excessive* burden on the individual in the light of the desired aim, i.e., criteria of *reasonableness* and an act of balancing benefits and costs of the measure.[58]

Another way that the CJEU can potentially 'exercise comity' is to answer the question referred to it in a very precise and specific way, while otherwise leaving its views on the application of EU law vague. Ambiguous case law might function to leave space for domestic law-makers and policymakers, as well as, more broadly, for interested litigants, to achieve their own agendas and goals, while respecting the Court's decision on how EU law should be interpreted and applied. Blauberger notes, citing Conant, that, 'legal ambiguity allows national policy-makers to follow ECJ rulings only in concrete cases … [and] to ignore their broader policy impact'.[59] He also, in turn, sets out Schmidt's view that, 'ambiguous case law enables interested litigants to pressure national policy-makers into far-reaching adjustments'.[60]

[55] Young (n 1) 282.

[56] ibid.

[57] Cases C-92/09 & C-93/09, *Volker und Markus Schecke GbRHartmut Eifert v Land Hessen* [2010] ECR I-11063 09.

[58] Dorte Sindbjerg Martinsen, 'Judicial Policy-Making and Europeanization: The Proportionality of National Control and Administrative Discretion' (2011) 18 *Journal of European Public Policy* 944, 947–48 (citations omitted).

[59] Michael Blauberger, 'National Responses to European Court Jurisprudence' (2014) 37 *West European Politics* 457, 457. See generally Lisa J Conant, *Justice Contained: Law and Politics in the European Union* (Cornell University Press 2002).

[60] Blauberger (n 59) 457–58; See Susanne K Schmidt, 'Beyond Compliance: The Europeanization of Member States through Negative Integration and Legal Uncertainty' (2008) 10 *Journal of Comparative Policy Analysis: Research and Practice* 299, 304.

III. Constitutional Counter-Balancing

A. The UK Parliament and the ECtHR

It is also possible to identify several features and characteristics in the European human rights system that should function to facilitate democratic dialogue between the UK Parliament and the ECtHR in the sense of constitutional counter-balancing. These features are similar to those institutional characteristics which Gardbaum identifies in the Commonwealth constitutional model, namely, those which function to allocate provisional institutional normative authority to decide upon rights issues. The fact that the model is allocating normative authority only provisionally (as opposed to definitively) is what functions to ensure that no one institution can always override the contribution of the other. Drawing upon the same mode of analysis as was undertaken earlier for identifying which mechanisms facilitate dialogue in the sense of constitutional collaboration, for ease of understanding, analogies are made here with the institutional features Gardbaum identifies in the Commonwealth constitutional model.

The first condition Gardbaum identifies as being necessary for the provisional allocation of normative authority to occur is that there be in the model either a codified bill of rights or a judicially created charter of rights with legal enforceability. The ECHR is analogous to a codified bill of rights. It sets out rights guarantees and freedoms, and there are consequences for violations of those rights guarantees and freedoms.

The second condition identified by Gardbaum is that the political branches undertake a 'pre-enactment political rights review'. This review 'aims to ensure that the executive thinks and acts in a rights-conscious way when considering and preparing legislative proposals (and so perhaps also more generally), thereby helping to disperse responsibilities for rights review among all three branches of government'.[61]

An analogy can be drawn here between 'pre-enactment review' and the submissions the state must make as part of litigation before the ECtHR. In being a party to the case before the ECtHR, the state must have considered whether, in its view, the relevant legislation is compatible with Convention rights and why it is or is not compatible. It must then, in the formulation of its submissions, which are often themselves recorded in the judgment, have set out its argument as to why it believes the legislation is not incompatible with Convention rights.

Of course, in precisely the same way as occurs at the domestic level in the Commonwealth constitutional model, states may also undertake 'pre-enactment review' of legislation and its compatibility with the ECHR before coming before

[61] Stephen Gardbaum, *The New Commonwealth Model of Constitutionalism: Theory and Practice* (Cambridge University Press 2013) 81.

the ECtHR, by way of parliamentary committee review. The UK's Joint Committee on Human Rights undertakes what Donald and Leach describe as a 'systematic scrutiny of government legislation for compatibility with all the UK's human rights obligations',[62] such as with the ECHR, when human rights-affecting legislation is proposed in the UK Parliament.

The third condition Gardbaum identifies as being necessary for the democratic dialogue model to have this capacity to provisionally allocate institutional authority to decide on the rights issue is that there be weak-form judicial review of the legislation by the judiciary. Gardbaum particularly emphasises that there is a 'weak-form' of judicial review where the judiciary has the power to review the legislation, but where the exercise of that power is not mandatory. That is, there is weak-form review where there is no duty on the court to exercise the power of review.

The power of judicial review of the relevant national law held by the ECtHR is arguably 'weak'. The ECtHR is under no obligation to exercise its review power with respect to national legislation. The margin of appreciation doctrine also, arguably, functions to weaken the potential review power of the Court. The requirement in the application of this doctrine for the Court to consider and in effect yield to the state as part of its judicial review must function to weaken that review.

The fourth condition Gardbaum identifies is that there be a formal power on the part of the legislature to state what the law is. This feature of the democratic dialogue model is necessary in order to ensure that the Court does not simply have the 'last word' to determine the rights issue alone. The mechanisms identified earlier as facilitating dialogue between the UK Parliament and the ECtHR in the sense of constitutional collaboration also function in such a way as to leave the UK Parliament with the power to state what the law is, albeit in a way that is informed by what the ECtHR has said about the law.

With respect to a decision of the ECtHR which finds domestic legislation to be in breach of those rights in the ECHR which can be subjected to reasonable limits, the UK Parliament can respond to the judicial decision by passing new legislation or amending the legislation to be less restrictive of the right in question. In response to a decision of the ECtHR which finds domestic legislation to be in breach of those rights in the Convention which are 'qualified rights', the UK Parliament can similarly pass a new law or amend the existing legislation in such a way as to satisfy appropriate standards of reasonableness or arbitrariness, as would have been set out by the judiciary. If the ECtHR finds that domestic legislation breaches the right to be free from discrimination contained in Article 14 of the Convention, the UK Parliament can respond to the Court's decision by accommodating the excluded group or individual.

[62] Alice Donald and Philip Leach, 'The Role of Parliament Following Judgments of the ECtHR's in Murray Hunt, Hayley Hooper and Paul Yowell (eds), *Parliaments and Human Rights: Redressing the Democratic Deficit* (Hart Publishing 2015) 66.

Of course, these mechanisms are still facilitating the UK Parliament to respond in a way that takes into account what the Court has held the law to be, and Gardbaum emphasises, in the context of the Commonwealth constitutional model, that the legislature must also have the choice to not respond at all. That the model must ensure the legislature *may* (and not *must*) respond, is essential in order to ensure that it is not always the case that the Court is the only institution which sets down the law.

There are, importantly, other mechanisms available to the UK Parliament which allow it to articulate what the law is, in a way that does not reflect what the ECtHR has said about the law and an analogy can be drawn here with section 33 of the Canadian Charter, which Hogg and Bushell identified as facilitating dialogue by conferring on the Canadian Parliament the power to override a judicial decision.

The UK Parliament can respond to the ECtHR by: (i) ignoring the decision of the Court; (ii) openly refusing to follow a decision of the ECtHR based on the view that the decision is incorrect; or (iii) recognising the Court's decision and then not following it for other reasons (as a matter of domestic law). As O'Cinneide summarises:

> [International human rights courts] may as a matter of international law have the final say as to how the provisions of human rights treaties are to be interpreted and applied. However, their authority in this respect co-exists with the potentially competing authority claims of national constitutional actors.[63]

And, ultimately, he notes, the authority of international human rights courts is generally 'contingent upon the willingness of national authorities to give effect to their judgments: [international human rights courts] cannot require national parliaments, executives or courts to defer to their determinations'.[64]

It is worth noting here that the basis on which Gardbaum distinguishes his theory of how the dialogue model allocates provisional normative authority from Young's theory is irrelevant when the democratic dialogue model is applied to the relationship between the ECtHR and UK Parliament. As a reminder, Gardbaum distinguished his theory from Young's on the basis that Young's theory of dialogue allocated provisional normative authority by 'type or nature of the issue' and on 'contestability criterion'.

The distinction between the two theories is irrelevant here because the rights issues arising as the subject matters of dialogue in this context are almost always 'contestable'. The dialogic mechanisms identified within the ECHR, such as those rights which can be limited and qualified, are, by definition, rights about which there can be disagreement. They are not absolute rights. That those rights which can be characterised as contestable are those most likely to arise as the subject of a dialogue between the ECtHR and the UK Parliament is also demonstrated by

[63] O'Cinneide (n 34) 305–06.
[64] ibid 305.

the fact that the margin of appreciation doctrine only usually applies in decisions concerning the interpretation of Articles 8–11 and 14 of the ECHR. This is because these articles are those which are not textually entirely clear and the breach of which may be justified.[65] This argument also applies to the relationship between the CJEU and the UK Parliament.

B. The UK Parliament and the CJEU

Again, the four key institutional characteristics or conditions of the domestic democratic dialogue model, which Gardbaum identifies as giving rise to the process of provisional institutional allocation (and which, accordingly, ensure that no one institution can authoritatively determine the rights issue at hand or override the contribution of the other), can also be identified, when the democratic dialogue model is applied to what was the relationship between the UK Parliament and the CJEU.

With respect to Gardbaum's first condition, like the ECHR, the EU Charter is analogous to a domestic codified bill of rights. However, Gardbaum also notes this condition will be satisfied where there is a judicially created charter of rights with legal enforceability. This first condition is also satisfied on this basis.

As to Gardbaum's second condition, there again appears to be an equivalent 'pre-enactment political rights review' undertaken by the political branches. In the same way as the analogy was drawn with respect to this condition and the dialogic relationship between the UK Parliament and the ECtHR, an analogy can be drawn here between 'pre-enactment political review' and the submissions the state must both prepare and make as part of the litigation before the CJEU.

With respect to the third condition Gardbaum identifies as being necessary for the dialogue model to have this capacity to provisionally allocate institutional authority, as with the ECtHR's power of review, the CJEU's power of judicial review can be characterised as 'weak'. The CJEU is under no obligation to exercise a review of national legislation. Its review power remains discretionary. The ability of the CJEU to also exercise comity in modifying the applicable proportionality standard also functions in such a way as to weaken the potential review power of the CJEU.

[65] Mónika Ambrus, 'The European Court of Human Rights and Standards of Proof: An Evidentiary Approach towards the Margin of Appreciation' in Lukasz Gruszcynski and Werner Wouter (eds), *Deference in International Courts and Tribunals: Standard of Review and Margin of Appreciation* (Oxford University Press 2014) 235, 237; Dean Spielmann, 'Allowing the Right Margin: The European Court of Human Rights and The National Margin of Appreciation Doctrine – Waiver or Subsidiarity of European Review?' (2012) 14 *Cambridge Yearbook of European Legal Studies* 381, 397. See also Steven Greer, 'The Margin of Appreciation: Interpretation and Discretion under the European Convention on Human Rights' (Council of Europe 2000) 15; Oddný Mjöll Arnardóttir, 'The "Procedural Turn" under the European Convention on Human Rights and Presumptions of Convention Compliance' (2017) 15 *International Journal of Constitutional Law* 9, 17.

The yielding to the state in modifying the proportionality standard in the Court's review in effect weakens its review.

With respect to the fourth condition Gardbaum identifies, the mechanisms identified earlier as having facilitated dialogue between the UK Parliament and the CJEU in the sense of constitutional collaboration again would have functioned in such a way as to leave Parliament with the power to state what the law is. The UK Parliament could have modified national legislation or have passed a new law that met the proportionality standard suggested by the court or that was less restrictive in order to satisfy the necessity standard. If the CJEU found that domestic legislation breaches the right to be free from discrimination contained in Article 21 of the EU Charter, the UK Parliament could have responded to the Court's decision by accommodating the excluded group or individual.

Importantly, once again, despite the primacy of EU law, there were mechanisms available to the UK Parliament which allowed it to ignore or otherwise to not follow the view of the CJEU and which, accordingly, functioned to ensure that the CJEU did not always have the authority to set the minimum standard of the law. The UK Parliament could engage in democratic dialogue with the CJEU in the sense of constitutional counter-balancing by: (i) simply ignoring a decision of the CJEU and leaving it to domestic courts to determine how the law should be applied where a specific conflict arises between national law and EU law; and (ii) openly refusing to follow the CJEU's decision based on a belief that the decision is incorrect.

IV. Barriers to Transnational Democratic Dialogue

In the introductory chapter, I discussed briefly the fact that some might view the acknowledgement of a role for the political branch in rights protection with concern, given the potential implications of such recognition for the cohesiveness of the international human rights system and for certain groups of (vulnerable) individuals. For completeness, I mention a limitation that might be placed on transnational democratic dialogue to address those concerns.

Hogg and Bushell themselves acknowledged that there must be some 'barriers to dialogue':

> While it is generally the case that Charter decisions leave some options open to the competent legislative body, and allow a dialogue to take place between courts and legislatures, we must acknowledge that there may be some circumstances where the court will, by necessity, have the last word.[66]

One relevant barrier suggested by Hogg and Bushell in the Canadian context can provide a useful starting point for applicable barriers in our transnational

[66] Hogg and Bushell (n 42) 92.

democratic dialogue framework.[67] They argued that there should be no dialogue on rights guaranteed in the Canadian Charter that 'are framed in such specific terms that there is no room for Parliament or a provincial legislature to impose "reasonable limits" on those rights'.[68] A similar barrier to transnational democratic dialogue might be useful. That is, there should not be transnational democratic dialogue with respect to those rights set out in relevant conventions, or as understood at customary international law, that are in such specific terms that there is no room for their limitation. The right to be free from torture may be such a right, although as discussed, the content of that right and the meaning of the word 'torture' are the subject of debate.

There is some evidence that the ECtHR does ensure that it does not enter into dialogue or discussion with respect to absolute rights and core parts of rights. For example, the Court applies proportionality tests to ensure that the core elements of particular rights are not eroded, and it also appears to change the breadth of the margin of appreciation that it affords to states depending on the particular right and violation in question.[69] The ECtHR in *Evans* held that:

> Where a particularly important facet of an individual's existence or identity is at stake the margin allowed to the State will be restricted … Where, however, there is no consensus within the member States of the Council of Europe … particularly where the case raises sensitive moral or ethical issues, the margin will be wider.[70]

This has resulted in the margin of appreciation doctrine usually being applied in decisions concerning the interpretation of Article 8 to Article 11, and Article 14 of the ECHR, because these articles are those which are not textually entirely clear and the breach of which can be justified.[71]

As I have said, I only note this barrier to transnational democratic dialogue for completeness. This is because it is not directly to this book. There is little, if any, existing international legal protection enjoyed by non-nationals seeking to enter and remain in a country and it is certainly not an absolute right.

[67] ibid 92–94. Hogg and Bushell also suggested that there be barriers to dialogue: (i) where the law's objective is unconstitutional, and (ii) where an issue is so controversial that a legislative response is precluded.

[68] ibid 92.

[69] See, eg, *Obukhova v Russia* App no 34736/03 (ECtHR, 8 January 2009) [22]; *Czarnowski v Poland* App no 28586/03 (ECtHR, 20 January 2009) [32]; *Lautsi v Italy* App no 30814/06 (ECtHR, 18 March 2011) [1] (dissenting opinion of Judge Malinverni), quoting *Buckley v United Kingdom* (1996) 23 EHRR 101, [74].

[70] *Evans v United Kingdom* (2008) 46 EHRR 34, [77].

[71] Ambrus (n 65). See also Spielmann (n 65).

V. Conclusion

There is demonstrably a framework in place which enables the UK Parliament and the ECtHR to engage in democratic dialogue, both in the sense of constitutional collaboration and in the sense of constitutional counter-balancing. There had been such a framework in place with respect to the UK Parliament's relationship with the CJEU. The following chapters will test whether these institutions have in fact engaged in democratic dialogue with one another, specifically about immigration and protection enjoyed by non-nationals to enter and remain in the country.

3

The Relationship between the UK Parliament and the ECtHR

On 14 December 2022, Jonathan Gullis MP, quoting from a Centre for Policy Studies report, stated the following in the House of Commons:

> As long as Britian remains a signatory to the Convention and bound by the jurisdiction of the European Court of Human Rights in Strasbourg, governments will be prevented from adequately enforcing immigration laws.[1]

Is this statement accurate? At this point in the book, we know that the UK Parliament can engage in (transnational) democratic dialogue with the ECtHR and that this is testable by an analysis of the interactions between the institutions concerning the enjoyment by non-nationals of a right to enter and remain in a country. But have these institutions actually, in practice, engaged in democratic dialogue, or has the government been 'prevented from adequately enforcing immigration laws'? This chapter finds out, and it also investigates whether interactions between the UK Parliament and the ECtHR have given rise to the same normative advantages that the dialogue model is said to have at the domestic level.

The chapter is structured around interactions between the UK Parliament and the ECtHR about protection afforded to enter and remain in a country to non-nationals: (i) whose immigration status has been precarious; (ii) who seek to remain in a country where they have committed a criminal offence; (iii) who seek to enter a country for the purpose of family and, specifically, spousal, reunification; and (iv) whose proposed deportation has resulted in, or would result in, the violation of other ECHR rights owed to the non-national. With respect to each circumstance, two questions are addressed in the chapter: (i) have the UK Parliament and the ECtHR engaged in democratic dialogue? and, if so, (ii) were the normative claims of the democratic dialogue model achieved? The answer to each question, with respect to each circumstance, for the most part, is 'yes'.

There are two preliminary points. The first is that this chapter clearly does not look at every instance where an issue has arisen between the institutions about the application to non-nationals of a right to enter and remain in a country. The present analysis is not intended to be a comprehensive empirical account. Rather,

[1] HC deb 14 December 2022, vol 724, col 1135.

the instances examined here are intended to be illustrative and demonstrative of the fact that the UK Parliament and the ECtHR can interact in this way and have in fact done so on many occasions. Some of the cases examined will be fairly well-known to some readers, given their having received significant attention already in the literature. This focus is in part deliberate, given that the proposed application of the democratic dialogue model represents a new approach to how we have previously thought about those cases.

The second preliminary point is that the responses of the UK Parliament almost inevitably always reflect the agenda of the government of the time. The UK government can control the legislative agenda in the UK Parliament through its in-built majority in the House of Commons, or it can respond itself directly through secondary legislation. The latter kind of response is particularly used in the immigration context. In the UK, primary legislation gives the Secretary of State broad powers to make rules:

> For regulating the entry into and stay in the United Kingdom of persons required … to have leave to enter, including any rules as to the period for which leave is to be given and the conditions to be attached in different circumstances.[2]

These rules (the Immigration Rules) are complex. They fall into neither primary nor delegated legislation categories.[3] Rather, they are laid before Parliament and come into force unless Parliament disapproves them by resolution.[4] Rules that provide for a requirement or a condition to be satisfied before a migrant is granted leave to enter the UK, are subject to an affirmative resolution procedure.[5] The Immigration Rules are also supplemented by detailed guidelines, which provide directions as to how the rules should be implemented.[6]

The fact that primary legislation reflects the government's agenda, or that the response to a court decision comes directly from the executive, should not impact the descriptive or normative claims of the (transnational) democratic dialogue model. The government still remains accountable to both Houses of Parliament and it is Parliament which ultimately passes or rejects primary legislation, and which scrutinises the executive.[7]

[2] Immigration Act 1971, s 3(2).

[3] See *Odelola v SSHD* [2009] UKHL 25 [6]–[7] (Lord Hoffmann). Section 3(2) of the Immigration Act 1971 provides that the Secretary of State 'shall from time to time lay before Parliament statements of the rules … to be followed in the administration of th[e] Act'.

[4] ibid. See generally Eric Fripp, Rowena Moffatt and Ellis Wilford, *The Law and Practice of Expulsion and Exclusion from the United Kingdom: Deportation, Removal, Exclusion and Deprivation of Citizenship* (Bloomsbury Publishing 2014) para 7.22–7.34; Megan Addis, Penelope Morrow, and Liberty, *Your Rights: The Liberty Guide to Human Rights* (Pluto Press 2005) 268.

[5] *R (on the application of Alvi) v Secretary of State for the Home Department* [2012] UKSC 33 [94].

[6] See, eg, *ZH (Bangladesh) v Secretary of State for the Home Department* [2009] EWCA Civ 8 [26]; *R (Rashid) v Secretary of State for the Home Department* [2005] EWCA Civ 744.

[7] Of course, another way in which the UK Parliament can respond to an international court decision, in this way, is by responding to use by its executive of Art 10 of the Human Rights Act 1998. Article 10 of the Human Rights Act contains a 'Henry VIII' clause. It provides in effect that a minister can make amendments to primary legislation where the minister considers it necessary to remove an incompatibility between a provision of legislation and a Convention right.

I. Non-Nationals whose Immigration Status is Precarious

In *Rodrigues da Silva and Hoogkamer v the Netherlands*,[8] the ECtHR provided protection to the applicant to remain in the Netherlands, despite the fact that her immigration status in that country had at times been precarious;[9] that is, her residency in the country had not always been lawful.

A. Did the UK Parliament Engage in Democratic Dialogue with the ECtHR?

The applicant in *Rodrigues da Silva* was a Brazilian national who lived in the Netherlands. The applicant's daughter was a Dutch national, by virtue of her father's Dutch nationality. The Dutch authorities refused the applicant's application for leave to remain in the Netherlands in part on the basis that the applicant had not lived legally in the Netherlands, at least for a significant portion of her time residing there.[10]

The issue for the ECtHR to consider was the application of Article 8 of the ECHR to the applicant. The ECtHR determined that it did not have to answer whether the applicant's right to respect for family life had been interfered with by the Dutch government's withdrawal of the applicant's residence status in the Netherlands. Rather, the question was whether the Dutch authorities were in fact under a positive duty to allow the applicant to remain in the Netherlands in order for the applicant to develop a family life in the Netherlands.[11]

The ECtHR concluded that the Netherlands' refusal to grant the applicant leave to remain in the Netherlands was a breach of Article 8 of the ECHR, finding that:

> In the particular circumstances of the case the economic well-being of the country does not outweigh the applicants' rights under Article 8, despite the fact that the first applicant was residing illegally in the Netherlands at the time of [the applicant's daughter's] birth. Indeed, by attaching such paramount importance to this latter element, the authorities may be considered to have indulged in excessive formalism.[12]

Chapter two established that, just as section 1 of the Canadian Charter facilitates dialogue between the Canadian Parliament and the Supreme Court of Canada, so

[8] *Rodrigues da Silva and Hoogkamer v The Netherlands* App no 50435/99 (ECtHR, 31 January 2006) (*Rodrigues da Silva*).

[9] The following cases and commentary set out this understanding of 'precarious' in the immigration context. See *EB Kosovo (FC) v Secretary of State for the Home Department* [2008] UKHL 41 [15]; *Rhuppiah v Secretary of State for the Home Department* [2018] UKSC 58 [44]; *Jeunesse v The Netherlands* [GC] App no 12738/10 (ECtHR, 3 October 2014) 108. See generally Gina Clayton and Georgina Firth, *Immigration and Asylum Law* (Oxford University Press 2021) 186.

[10] *Rodrigues da Silva and Hoogkamer v The Netherlands* (n 8) paras 8–24.

[11] ibid 38.

[12] ibid 44.

too those specific rights set out in the ECHR, which can be subjected to reasonable limits, can function to facilitate dialogue between the UK Parliament and the ECtHR. The ECtHR, when finding a violation of such a right, can indicate to Parliament what a reasonable measure might look like; that is, what might be necessary, or be considered a proportionate response, in a democratic society. By doing so, the ECtHR can give the legislature room to respond to its decision in such a way as to respect and defer to that decision, while still allowing the legislature to achieve its own political goals and to work within the domestic legal framework. The right to respect for private and family life, contained within Article 8 of the ECHR, is identifiably a right of this type, namely, one which can be subjected to reasonable limits.

Chapter two also established that the margin of appreciation doctrine should similarly function to facilitate dialogue between a domestic legislature such as the UK Parliament and the ECtHR and that it is most likely to do so with respect to rights, such as Article 8 of the ECHR, which can be subjected to reasonable limits. These kinds of rights are set out in abstract terms. They require interpretation and development and little European consensus exists around their resolution.

An examination of the nature of the institutional interactions between the UK Parliament and the ECtHR in relation to *Rodrigues da Silva* demonstrates that rights such as Article 8 of the ECHR, and the margin of appreciation doctrine, do function to facilitate dialogue. The ECtHR set out both the minimum standard of reasonableness and, also, the relevant factors to be taken into account in determining what state conduct towards a non-national (ie, the deportation of a non-national) or lack thereof (ie, not granting a non-national a right to remain) would fall below the minimum standard. The Court stated:

> In a case which concerns family life as well as immigration, the extent of a State's obligations to admit to its territory relatives of persons residing there will vary according to the particular circumstances of the persons involved and the general interest.[13]
>
> …
>
> [F]actors to be taken into account in this context are the extent to which family life is effectively ruptured [by the deportation of the non-national], the extent of the ties in the Contracting State, whether there are insurmountable obstacles in the way of the family living in the country of origin of one or more of them, whether there are factors of immigration control (e.g. a history of breaches of immigration law) or considerations of public order weighing in favour of exclusion (see *Solomon v the Netherlands* (dec.), no. 44328/98, 5 September 2000) … whether family life was created at a time when the persons involved were aware that the immigration status of one of them was such that the persistence of that family life within the host state would from the outset be precarious.[14]

[13] ibid 39.
[14] ibid.

With respect to this last factor, the ECtHR also added that:

> The Court has previously held that where this is the case it is likely only to be in the most exceptional circumstances that the removal of the non-national family member will constitute a violation of Article 8 (*Mitchell v. the United Kingdom* (dec.), no. 40447/98, 24 November 1998 [('*Mitchell*')], and *Ajayi and Others v. the United Kingdom* (dec.), no. 27663/95, 22 June 1999) [('*Ajayi and Others*')].[15]

Accordingly, the minimum standard set by the Court can be characterised as follows: whether the deportation of a non-national (ie, the denial to a non-national of a right to remain) violates Article 8 of the ECHR will depend on the particular circumstances of the case and what is found to be in the population's general interest, but a violation of the Convention will usually be found only in exceptional circumstances. The minimum standard is thus formulated in fairly vague terms. What 'particular circumstances' are, is not directly defined. Neither is 'insurmountable obstacles', nor what might be in the 'general interest'. What might be 'exceptional circumstances' is similarly left unclear.

By formulating the standard in fairly vague or undefined terms, the ECtHR left space to the state legislature to pursue its own goals while respecting the minimum standard of rights protection owed to non-nationals with a precarious or illegal immigration status who seek to remain in the country. This is what the UK Parliament did.

In response, at least in part, to the ECtHR's judgment in *Rodrigues da Silva*, the UK's Home Secretary introduced new Immigration Rules on 8 June 2012. The rules took effect on 9 July 2012 (the 2012 Rules),[16] and were claimed to be for the purpose of (among other purposes):

> Provid[ing] a clear basis for considering immigration family and private life cases in compliance with Article 8 of the ECHR on Human Rights (the right to respect for private and family life). In particular, the new Immigration Rules reflect the qualified nature of Article 8, setting requirements which correctly balance the individual right to respect for private or family life with the public interest in safeguarding the economic well-being of the UK by controlling immigration and in protecting the public from foreign criminals.[17]

The 2012 Rules were to provide, 'for the first time', the view of the UK government 'as to how article 8(1) should, as a matter of public policy, be qualified in the public interest under the terms of article 8(2)'.[18] The 2012 Rules relevantly introduced rule 275ADE which set out the requirements a non-national seeking to enter and

[15] ibid. The cases of *Mitchell* and *Ajayi* and others were resolved at the admissibility stage. The Court found that the cases were not admissible because the removal of a non-national family member will only exceptionally amount to a violation of Art 8 of the ECHR.

[16] See 'Archive of Immigration Rules Valid between 9 July to 19 July 2012': assets.publishing.service.gov.uk/government/uploads/system/uploads/attachmentdata/file/257366/18-july-16-aug-2012.pdf.

[17] 'Explanatory Memorandum to the Statement of Changes in Immigration Rules Presented to Parliament on 13 June 2012 (HC 194)' (2012) 1.

[18] Home Office, 'Statement of Intent: Family Migration' (2012) para 10.

remain had to fulfil in order to be granted leave to remain, on the specific ground of the non-national enjoying a 'private life' in the UK. Rule 275ADE provided as follows:

> Private life
>
> Requirements to be met by an applicant for leave to remain on the grounds of private life 276ADE. The requirements to be met by an applicant for leave to remain on the grounds of private life in the UK are that at the date of application, the applicant:
>
> (i) does not fall for refusal under any of the grounds in Section S-LTR 1.2 to S-LTR 1.5 in Appendix FM; and
> (ii) does not fall for refusal under any of the grounds in Section S-LTR 1.6 to 2.3 in Appendix FM; and
> (iii) has lived continuously in the UK for at least 20 years (discounting any period of imprisonment); or
> (iv) is under the age of 18 years and has lived continuously in the UK for at least 7 years (discounting any period of imprisonment); or
> (v) is aged 18 years or above and under 25 years and has spent at least half of his life residing continuously in the UK (discounting any period of imprisonment); or
> (vi) is aged 18 years or above, has lived continuously in the UK for less than 20 years (discounting any period of imprisonment) but has no ties (including social, cultural or family) with the country to which he would have to go if required to leave the UK.[19]
>
> *In considering applications under this paragraph, the Secretary of State shall attach less weight to private life in the UK established following refusal of an earlier application for leave to remain made under paragraph 276ADE* (emphasis added).

The introduction of Rule 276ADE of the 2012 Rules was, it appears,[20] a direct response to the ECtHR's judgment in *Rodrigues da Silva*. There is a provision in the rule that the Secretary of State should afford 'less weight' to any private life an applicant has established, where the applicant's immigration status has been, or is, precarious (ie, where the application has been denied leave to remain in the UK already). This has the same effect as the ECtHR's view set out in *Rodrigues da Silva*. That view is that where a non-national has developed a family or a private life in a country in which the non-national's immigration status is precarious (ie, the non-national is vulnerable to deportation), it is only in 'exceptional circumstances' that the removal of the non-national would violate Article 8 of the ECHR.

[19] The sections in Appendix FM provide for various grounds of 'suitability' for leave to remain. S-LTR 1.1 provides that '[t]he applicant will be refused limited leave to remain on grounds of suitability if any of paragraphs S-LTR.1.2 to 1.7 apply'. To take one example of a ground of suitability, S-LTR 1.6, for instance, provides for the following ground: 'The presence of the applicant in the UK is not conducive to the public good because their conduct (including convictions which do not fall within paragraphs S-LTR.1.3 to 1.5.), character, associations, or other reasons, make it undesirable to allow them to remain in the UK'.

[20] I use the word 'appears' both here and throughout the chapter because it is not usually directly stated that the introduction of rules or legislation is in fact a response to the ECtHR's judgments.

An explanatory document produced by the Home Office, as part of its Statement of Changes document presented to Parliament, which accompanied the 2012 Rules, confirmed this to be the intention behind the Rules. While citing *Rodrigues da Silva* directly, as well as, among others, those admissibility decisions the ECtHR cited in *Rodrigues da Silva* (notably, *Mitchell* and *Ajayi*), the explanatory document provided as follows:

> The new Immigration Rules reflect the approach taken in the relevant jurisprudence as follows:
>
> (a) Where a person establishes a private or family life while they are in the UK illegally or while their immigration status here is precarious, that period of residence in the UK should be accorded less weight as a consequence of it being illegal or precarious in nature. This approach is supported by jurisprudence from the ECtHR in Strasbourg, which also states that where private or family life is established whilst a person does not have lawful status, it is to be given less weight than private or family life established while a person is in the UK lawfully. Further, it is only in the most exceptional circumstances that the removal of the non-national family member will constitute a violation of Article 8 because their removal would be in the interests of the economic well-being of the country, by controlling illegal immigration. Domestic jurisprudence takes a similar approach.[21]

In 2014, the UK Parliament then enacted the Immigration Act 2014 (2014 Act), which, in part, gave the 2012 Rules the force of legislation. Lord Brown of Eaton-under-Heywood specifically noted, during the parliamentary debates on the Immigration Bill 2014, the importance of having primary legislation in place with respect to the application to non-nationals of a right to enter and remain as opposed to simply leaving the legislative response to subsidiary legislation and to the Immigration Rules:

> [I]t is hardly surprising that the Government are intent on clarifying as plainly as possible in primary legislation their policy with regard to Article 8 and the interests that Article 8 furthers. Initially they sought to do this by way of changes to the Immigration Rules back in June 2012, but the courts then said, correctly, in the judgment of the Upper Tribunal in a case called *Izuazu*:
>
>> 'Only the Parliamentary process for primary legislation permits a clause-by-clause discussion of the measures, with opportunity for amendments and revision'.
>
> A little later the judgment quoted from a recognised work on constitutional and administrative law, as follows: 'An Act of Parliament has legal force which the courts are not willing to ascribe to other instruments which for one reason or another fall short of that pre-eminent status'.[22]

[21] 'Immigration Rules on Family and Private Life (HC 194) Grounds of Compatibility with Article 8 of the ECHR on Human Rights' (Home Office 2012) para 88. See also the following cases cited: *Konstatinov v The Netherlands* App no 16351/03 (ECtHR, 26 April 2007); *Y v Russia* App no 20113/07 (ECtHR, 4 December 2008) (citations omitted).

[22] HL deb 5 March 2014, vol 752, col 1395.

In the parliamentary debates, Lord Wallace of Tankerness, who was, at the time, the Lord Advocate and Leader of the House of Lords,[23] also remarked on the importance of an active parliamentary (as opposed to solely an executive) response. His characterisation of the parliamentary response as being a response to 'invitations from the judiciary' confirms that Parliament was using the space around the minimum standard set by the ECtHR. Lord Wallace of Tankerness stated:

> [W]e have sought to put this into statute. The Government have come to Parliament to get Parliament to indicate clearly in primary legislation what it considers to be the matters in the public interest, given that Article 8 is not an absolute right under the European Convention of [sic] Human Rights but, rather, a qualified one. *It is part of our debates that we should not only respond to invitations from the judiciary, but debate what that public interest should be. That is indeed what we are doing in debating these matters.*[24]

The Explanatory Notes to the 2014 Act explained how the Act was intended to give effect to the 2012 Rules as follows:

> In July 2011 the Home Office published a consultation paper on Family Migration. On 11 June 2012 the Government published its response to the consultation setting out that Immigration Rules would be made to reflect the Government's and Parliament's view of how the balance should be struck between the right to respect for private and family life under Article 8 of the ECHR and the public interest, including safeguarding the economic well-being of the UK, enforcing immigration controls and protecting the public from foreign criminals. New Immigration Rules came into force on 9 July 2012. The Act gives the force of primary legislation to the principles reflected in those rules by requiring a court or tribunal, when determining whether a decision is in breach of Article 8 ECHR, to have regard to the public interest considerations as set out in the Act.[25]

The legislative response on the part of the UK to *Rodrigues da Silva* is specifically evidenced by section 19 of the Immigration Act 2014, which inserted new Part 5A into the Nationality, Immigration and Asylum Act 2002 (2002 Immigration Act). Part 5A provides that, in circumstances where either a court or tribunal is required to determine whether a decision by the minister made under the Immigration Acts is in breach of a person's right to respect for private and family life, the factors set out in the Part must be taken into account.[26] As part of the new Part 5A, section 19 of the Immigration Act 2014 relevantly inserted section 117B into the 2002 Immigration Act, which provides as follows:

> 117B Article 8: public interest considerations applicable in all cases
>
> (1) The maintenance of effective immigration controls is in the public interest.

[23] For these purposes, therefore, Lord Wallace of Tankerness was a government minister.
[24] HL deb 5 March 2014, vol 752, col 1398 (emphasis added).
[25] Explanatory Notes to the Immigration Act 2014, c 22, para 21 (citations omitted).
[26] Immigration Act 2014, s 117A.

(2) It is in the public interest, and in particular in the interests of the economic well-being of the United Kingdom, that persons who seek to enter or remain in the United Kingdom are able to speak English, because persons who can speak English –

(a) are less of a burden on taxpayers, and

(b) are better able to integrate into society.

(3) It is in the public interest, and in particular in the interests of the economic well-being of the United Kingdom, that persons who seek to enter or remain in the United Kingdom are financially independent, because such persons –

(a) are not a burden on taxpayers, and

(b) are better able to integrate into society.

(4) Little weight should be given to –

(a) a private life, or

(b) a relationship formed with a qualifying partner, that is established by a person at a time when the person is in the United Kingdom unlawfully.

(5) Little weight should be given to a private life established by a person at a time when the person's immigration status is precarious.

(6) In the case of a person who is not liable to deportation, the public interest does not require the person's removal where –

(a) the person has a genuine and subsisting parental relationship with a qualifying child, and

(b) it would not be reasonable to expect the child to leave the United Kingdom.

Section 117B(4)–(5), like Rule 276ADE of the 2012 Rules, accordingly contains a direction to domestic courts and tribunals to afford 'less weight' to an applicant's private and family life where that 'life' was established while the applicant's immigration status was precarious. This, for the reasons set out earlier with respect to Rule 276ADE, implements and responds to the ECtHR's direction in *Rodrigues da Silva* as to how a non-national with a precarious immigration status might enjoy protection to enter and remain in a foreign country.

The Home Office document entitled 'Immigration Bill ECHR on Human Rights Memorandum by the Home Office' which accompanied the Bill, confirmed that Part 5A was intended as a direct response to the ECtHR's judgment in *Rodrigues da Silva*,[27] as well as being a response to the European Court's subsequent judgment in *Nunez v Norway* (*Nunez*) which affirmed *Rodrigues da Silva* as the correct law.[28]

[27] Home Office, 'Immigration Bill ECHR on Human Rights Memorandum by the Home Office' (2014) para 80.

[28] ibid 73; See *Nunez v Norway* App no 55597/09 (ECtHR, 28 June 2011). The Memorandum sets out in full the following extract from Nunez: 'In Nunez the ECtHR noted "Another important consideration is whether family life was created at a time when the persons involved were aware that the immigration status of one of them was such that the persistence of that family life within the host State would from the outset be precarious. Where this is the case the removal of the non-national family member would be incompatible with Article 8 only in exceptional circumstances"'. The memo also cited *Aponte v Netherlands* App no 28770/05 (ECtHR, 3 November 2011) for this statement.

What brings this interaction beyond being one which can be characterised as Parliament simply implementing the ECtHR's decision (as it is required under the ECHR to do) is the way the legislature used the space left by the Court. The UK Parliament did not passively adopt in the legislation the exact same vague terms used by the Court. It also did not simply take a broad approach to the rights issue, although this is what we might have expected, given that the ultimate outcome in *Rodrigues da Silva* was to grant the applicant, in effect, a right to remain in the Netherlands.

Rather, Parliament used the space left by the ECtHR strategically to achieve its own additional policy goals, which appeared to be to restrict immigration (ie, a right to enter and remain for non-nationals) more generally. The factsheet accompanying the Bill states that the Bill was intended, in part, to make it 'easier to remove and deport illegal immigrants'.[29] The effect of directing the Secretary of State, as well as courts and tribunals, to give 'little weight' to private or family life where the non-national's immigration status is, or has been, precarious is to narrow the circumstances in which non-nationals with a precarious immigration status can benefit from a right to enter and remain. As the Explanatory Note to the 2014 Immigration Act sets out, *Rodrigues da Silva*, along with other ECtHR judgments:

> [P]rovide a basis for arguing that wider measures of immigration control are compatible with article 8 where those who have a legal right to be in the United Kingdom can have their status recognised ... [and] provide the starting point for saying that the United Kingdom can lawfully remove illegal migrants for both crime prevention and wider immigration control reasons.[30]

However, the UK Parliament went further, as the legislative effect of section 117B is to restrict protection against deportation beyond those non-nationals with a precarious status. The legislature achieved this by the way it defines 'public interest' very broadly. Section 117B(1)–(3) defines the maintenance of effective immigration controls to be in the 'public interest'. The admission of those non-nationals who can speak English and who are financially independent is set out in the legislation as being in the 'public interest' and it is significant that 'public interest' is understood as including that which is in the interests of the economic wellbeing of the nation. This seems to reflect the precise concerns raised by the Dutch government before the ECtHR, concerns which the Court summarised as being:

> [E]ven if account was taken of [the daughter's] right to reside in the Netherlands and to be brought up and educated there, the interests of the economic well-being of the country outweighed the interests of the first applicant. Although the first applicant did not claim welfare benefits, she did not pay taxes or social security contributions either, and there were sufficient numbers of nationals of European Union Member States or non-nationals residing lawfully in the Netherlands available to fill the post she was

[29] Home Office, 'Immigration Bill Factsheet: Overview of the Bill' (2013) 2.

[30] Home Office, 'Immigration Bill ECHR on Human Rights Memorandum by the Home Office' (n 27) para 9.

occupying. The general interest also prevailed over Mr Hoogkamer's interest in being able to lead his family life with Rachael in the Netherlands.[31]

That this is what the UK Parliament was doing with respect to using the space left by the ECtHR in its setting down of the minimum standard was made clear by Lord Reed in the UK Supreme Court in the case of *Agyarko*. He stated that the 2012 Rules, which the 2014 Immigration Act reflect, were not intended to be a summary of Strasbourg case law, but were rather 'statements of the practice to be followed, which are approved by Parliament, and are based on the Secretary of State's policy as to how individual rights under Article 8 should be balanced against the competing public interests'.[32]

On Hogg and Bushell's model of democratic dialogue, this interaction between the ECtHR and the UK Parliament would itself amount to 'dialogue'. A court judgment resulted in a legislative response by way of amendment, which achieved the legislature's own policy goals and, furthermore, an ECHR mechanism enabled that interaction. However, as a reminder, the understanding of democratic dialogue as a constitutional model for rights protection has since developed further. Under those more developed theories, an interaction is considered to amount to democratic dialogue where there is recognition by the institutions to the interaction of their own strengths and limitations and of the strengths and limitations of the other institution. The democratic dialogue model is, in light of Young's analysis of the model, better understood as not providing a middle ground between a political protection of rights and a legal protection but, rather, as a model which draws on the strengths of, and minimises the weaknesses of, the institutions to the interaction.[33] There is clear evidence of the UK Parliament and the ECtHR interacting in this way with respect to how non-nationals whose immigration status is precarious might be protected against deportation.

In arriving at its finding, the ECtHR acknowledged what it described as the applicant's 'cavalier attitude to Dutch immigration rules'.[34] It further found that the state's motivation behind the refusal of the applicant's leave to remain was to restrict immigration to the Netherlands on the basis of both social and economic factors, those being areas directly in the state's purview of responsibility. The ECtHR Chamber said:

> The Government pursue a restrictive immigration policy due to the population and employment situation in the Netherlands. Non-nationals are eligible for admission only on the basis of obligations arising out of international agreements, or if their presence serves an essential national interest, or on compelling humanitarian grounds.[35]

[31] *Rodrigues da Silva and Hoogkamer v The Netherlands* (n 8) para 17.
[32] *R (Agyarko and Ikuga) v Secretary of State for the Home Department* [2017] UKSC 11 [46].
[33] Alison L Young, *Democratic Dialogue and the Constitution* (Oxford University Press 2017).
[34] *Rodrigues da Silva and Hoogkamer v The Netherlands* (n 8) para 43.
[35] ibid 27.

The ECtHR also, in explicitly leaving a margin to the state to decide upon the issue, acknowledged that while its role is to set down the minimum standard, states are better placed to determine community (as opposed to individual) interests or at least better placed to strike a balance between those interests and any relevant individual's interests. It also acknowledged that the state's duties towards non-nationals (particularly those whose immigration status is precarious or illegal) are, accordingly, limited:

> The Court reiterates that in the context of both positive and negative obligations the State must strike a fair balance between the competing interests of the individual and of the community as a whole. However, in both contexts the State enjoys a certain margin of appreciation. Moreover, Article 8 does not entail a general obligation for a State to respect immigrants' choice of the country of their residence and to authorise family reunion in its territory.
>
> …
>
> [A] wide margin is usually allowed to the State under the Convention when it comes to general measures of economic or social strategy.[36]

In the parliamentary debates surrounding the passing of the 2014 Immigration Act, the UK Parliament specifically acknowledged, with respect to the 'little weight' test in section 117B of the 2002 Immigration Act, that the Court had given the state this margin in light of the state's competence to control immigration. Lord Wallace of Tankerness noted the following:

> More generally, the Strasbourg court has made clear that the ECHR on Human Rights does not guarantee families a right to reside in a particular country and has consistently recognised that *the Executive enjoy a significant margin of appreciation in determining how most appropriately to control immigration. Clause 14 is framed within the margin of appreciation afforded to states in this respect.*[37]

On the other side of the interaction, there is evidence of the UK Parliament acknowledging the institutional competence and strength of the ECtHR to set down a minimum standard of reasonableness with respect to how a right to remain might apply to a non-national with a precarious immigration status. In the parliamentary debates surrounding the insertion of Part 5A to the 2002 Immigration Act, as contained in section 19 of the 2014 Immigration Act, and, specifically, in response to proposals to remove provisions in the 2014 Bill providing that 'little weight' should be given to a non-national's established private life, Lord Wallace of Tankerness noted in the House of Lords:

> The Human Rights Act requires courts to take into account Strasbourg judgments, but the requirement is not to follow them. However, the clause indicates that, in relation to precarious immigration status, [the House] expect[s] the court to follow the Strasbourg case law.

[36] ibid 39.
[37] HL deb 5 March 2014, vol 752, col 1399 (emphasis added).

> . . .
>
> [Precariousness] is a term that has to be interpreted by the courts, but that is the case whether or not the provision is in the Bill, as it is the correct legal test in determining what weight to give to Article 8 rights. 'Precarious' is difficult to define in a Bill, as there are many different types of immigration status. If one takes the case, for example, of Rodrigues da Silva and Hoogkamer v the Netherlands, the ECtHR found that:
>
>> 'Another important consideration will also be whether family life was created at a time when the persons involved were aware that the immigration status of one of them was such that the persistence of that family life within the host State would from the outset be precarious. The Court has previously held that where this is the case it is likely only to be in the most exceptional circumstances that the removal of the non-national family member will constitute a violation of Article 8.'
>
> *It was to capture that jurisprudence of the ECtHR, which the Government believe is a proper determination of such a situation, that that has been carried through into the provision in the Bill*: that the courts, in taking into account Strasbourg judgments, would give little weight in those circumstances.
>
> . . .
>
> Those who form private or family life while in the UK unlawfully can have even less expectation of being allowed to stay here.[38]

Lord Wallace also later made the following statements during the debates in the House of Lords, where he drew further attention to the competence of the ECtHR to set the standard on this rights issue:

> I sought to try to explain that that expression of little weight was really a way of putting into statutory form what we believe is in fact the practice of courts in the cases which are here. I think it was in the case against the Netherlands; I do not know the first name involved but the other was Hoogkamer. I am sorry not to get that right. *We were seeking to say that we endorse what the position of the ECtHR has been on that. Whereas under the Human Rights Act the court is asked to consider and have regard to the Strasbourg jurisprudence, what we are seeking in this is to say that we agree that the court should follow the Strasbourg jurisprudence.* This has not suddenly been conjured up; it is based on what we believe the courts would do.[39]

The UK Parliament's awareness of the institutional competence of the ECtHR (as well as its own competence) is further encapsulated in the following passage of Lord Wallace in the House of Lords, who acknowledged the Court's role, but also pushed back on that role while asserting the legislature's own significance:

> It is right that Parliament should make clear its view that little weight in terms of the public interest should be given to family life with a partner, or to private life which was formed when the person was in the UK unlawfully or to private life formed with precarious immigration status. *We do not believe that that encroaches on the proper judicial function. It will remain a matter for the court to decide whether the weight to be accorded*

[38] HL deb 5 March 2014, vol 752, cols 1398–99 (emphasis added).
[39] HL deb 5 March 2014, vol 752, col 1403 (emphasis added).

> *to the public interest as set out by Parliament in Clause 14 outweighs the individual's right to respect for private and family life, and therefore whether the decision is proportionate in Article 8 terms.*[40]

B. Was this Dialogue Normatively Advantageous?

I suggested in the introductory chapter that if the UK Parliament and the ECtHR engage in democratic dialogue, then the normative claims of the democratic dialogue model at the domestic level should also be realised. The first such claim in this respect was that a 'better' protection should be produced when the institutions engage in dialogue. As a reminder, 'better' denotes a protection of rights that draws on accounts of both political constitutionalism and legal constitutionalism.

There is evidence that the ECtHR did reason in *Rodrigues da Silva* in a way that reflected its status as an impartial forum of principle, focusing on the individual's situation or on the minority's interests. In *Rodrigues da Silva*, the ECtHR focused on the individual's particular circumstances and on how the applicant would be affected by her deportation from the Netherlands. An example of the ECtHR scrutinising how the individual applicant would be affected is demonstrated by the way in which it directly pointed to the Dutch domestic court's decision that custody of the applicant's daughter should lie with the daughter's father. That domestic court decision made the argument that the applicant could reunite with her daughter in Brazil unworkable. The Chamber of the ECtHR reasoned as follows:

> In these circumstances, the Court considers that the Government's claim that the first applicant and Mr Hoogkamer might have agreed that [the applicant's daughter] would move to Brazil with her mother is untenable, bearing in mind that it was the Dutch courts, following the advice of the Dutch child-care authorities, who concluded that it was in Rachael's best interests to stay in the Netherlands.[41]

The UK Parliament, on the other hand, also reasoned in the way that reflects a legislature's institutional strengths; that is, in a way that balances competing interests and groups, and in such a way that reflects the nature of the legislature as a democratically representative and accountable body. In this example, we can, significantly, see instrumental reasoning with the electorate clearly in mind in the legislature's emphasis on the wellbeing of the economy (as opposed to the wellbeing of non-nationals seeking to remain in the UK) and in its emphasis on only admitting those non-nationals who can successfully integrate into society and who will not be a burden on *other* taxpayers. The explanatory material to the 2014 Immigration Act explicitly sets out how the state has a 'right' 'to

[40] HL deb 5 March 2014, vol 752, col 1399 (emphasis added).
[41] *Rodrigues da Silva and Hoogkamer v The Netherlands* (n 8) para 41.

maintain immigration and border controls' and notes that control of immigration is 'a means of protecting the economic well-being of a country'.[42]

An extension of the normative claim that the democratic dialogue model produces a 'better protection' of rights is that the model should also allocate authority to decide on the rights issue to the institution that is normatively the most desirable one to decide on the issue. As a reminder, this function of the democratic dialogue model was set out in chapter two in the context of justifying the choice, as a case study, of the application to non-nationals of a right to enter and remain in a country.

It appears, from this example, that the democratic dialogue model, when applied to the relationship between the UK Parliament and the ECtHR did, as the framework set up in chapter two predicted, function to allocate normative authority to the best institution to decide upon the rights issue. In the interaction under scrutiny here, we can see that the framework of Article 8 of the ECHR functions to allocate normative authority first to the ECtHR to set a minimum standard of rights protection. The ECtHR then, in turn, defers to Parliament to determine: (i) when it would be in the 'public interest' for a non-national to remain; (ii) what 'insurmountable obstacles' a non-national would need to show exist; or (iii) what would qualify as 'exceptional circumstances'. The UK executive and then the Parliament subsequently give direction to the domestic courts to decide on the issue and undertake the necessary balancing act and proportionality analysis, having considered both the ECtHR position (ie, individual rights) and what Parliament considers to be in the public interest (ie, the rights of the majority). The Home Office Report on the 2012 Immigration Rules envisioned this allocation of normative authority taking place following the ECtHR judgment:

> The new Immigration Rules are intended to fill this public policy vacuum by setting out the Secretary of State's position on proportionality and to meet the democratic deficit by seeking Parliament's agreement to her policy. The rules will state how the balance should be struck between the public interest and individual rights, taking into account relevant case law, and thereby provide for a consistent and fair decision-making process. Therefore, if the rules are proportionate, a decision taken in accordance with the Rules will, other than in exceptional cases, be compatible with Article 8.
>
> This does not mean that the Secretary of State and Parliament have the only say on what is proportionate. The Courts have a very clear role in determining the proportionality of the requirements in the Immigration Rules. It is for the State to demonstrate that measures that interfere with private and family life are proportionate. But a system of rules setting out what is or is not proportionate, outside of exceptional circumstances, is compatible with individual rights, as has been accepted by the Courts in other spheres, e.g., housing law. Where the rules have explicitly taken into account proportionality, the role of the Courts should shift from reviewing the proportionality of individual administrative decisions to reviewing the proportionality of the rules.[43]

[42] Home Office, 'Immigration Bill ECHR on Human Rights Memorandum by the Home Office' (n 27) paras 4, 8.

[43] ibid paras 38–39.

It was also suggested that the second normative claim of the democratic dialogue model at the domestic level, namely, that the model increases and leads to greater deliberation, including in the wider community, should also translate across to the relationship between the ECtHR and the UK Parliament. There is evidence of this suggestion being accurate here. In *Rodrigues da Silva*, the ECtHR in its judgment set out the views on the rights issue of the Amsterdam regional court,[44] the Supreme Court,[45] the regional court of the Hague,[46] the Amsterdam Court of Appeal[47] and the various arguments of different government departments, such as the Dutch Ministry of Justice.[48] Further, the explanatory material that was produced alongside the 2014 Act also set out the views and judgments of various domestic courts.[49] Accordingly, the dialogic interaction had the effect of bringing diverse and various voices to the rights discourse around the interaction and specifically to the UK Parliament, voices with which Parliament might not otherwise have engaged.

II. Non-Nationals who have Committed Criminal Offences

Utilising the same structure as the first case study, I now examine the interactions surrounding *Boultif v Switzerland* (*Boultif*), *Üner v Netherlands* (*Üner*),[50] *Maslov v Austria* (*Maslov*)[51] and *Unuane v United Kingdom* (*Unuane*),[52] which all concern non-nationals who have faced deportation given their committal of a criminal offence or offences. The first three cases are considered together and the case of *Unuane* is considered separately.

A. Did the UK Parliament Engage in Democratic Dialogue with the ECtHR?

i. Boultif, Üner *and* Maslov

The applicant in *Boultif* was an Algerian national who initially entered Switzerland on a tourist visa. In Switzerland, the applicant committed a number of serious

[44] *Rodrigues da Silva and Hoogkamer v The Netherlands* (n 8) para 15.
[45] ibid 19.
[46] ibid 20.
[47] ibid 21.
[48] ibid 16–17.
[49] See, eg, Home Office, 'Immigration Bill ECHR on Human Rights Memorandum by the Home Office' (n 27) para 8.
[50] *Üner v The Netherlands* [GC] App no 46410/99 (ECtHR, 18 October 2006).
[51] *Maslov v Austria* App no 1638/03 (ECtHR, 23 June 2008).
[52] *Unuane v United Kingdom* App no 80343/17 (ECtHR, 24 November 2020).

offences, including robbery, damage to property and attacking a man, and it was on this basis that he was ultimately deported from Switzerland.[53] The ECtHR held that there had been a violation of Article 8 of the ECHR on the basis that the deportation of the application was not proportionate to the aim of preventing disorder and crime.[54]

The applicant in *Üner* was a Turkish national who was in the Netherlands on a residency permit, having come to the Netherlands when he was 12 years old for family reunification purposes. The applicant committed a number of violent offences, following which the Dutch authorities withdrew the applicant's permanent residence permit and the applicant was deported to Turkey.[55] The Grand Chamber of the ECtHR held that the withdrawal of the applicant's residency permit did not amount to a violation of the applicant's Article 8 Convention right to respect for private and family life.[56]

Maslov is another relevant case which affirmed this approach. The applicant in *Maslov* was a Bulgarian national who was a lawful resident in Austria from the age of six. The applicant committed a number of offences at the ages of 14 and 15, including aggravated burglary, extortion and assault, and was subsequently deported to Bulgaria at the age of 17.[57] The Grand Chamber held that the exclusion order given to the applicant was not necessary in a democratic society and was therefore an unlawful interference with the applicant's rights under Article 8 of the ECHR.[58]

Turning to analyse the nature of the institutional interactions between the UK Parliament and the ECtHR, it appears again that the framework set out in chapter two was accurate; that is, that dialogic mechanisms, such as Article 8 of the ECHR and the margin of appreciation, function to facilitate democratic dialogue between these institutions.

In reaching its conclusions in the above-mentioned cases, the ECtHR again appears to set out the minimum standard of reasonableness and the relevant factors to be taken into account to determine what state conduct toward a non-national (ie, again the deportation of a non-national), or lack thereof in not granting a non-national a right to remain in these circumstances, would fall below the minimum standard of an interference with an individual's Article 8 rights. The ECtHR in both *Boultif and Üner*, relevantly stated:

> [The state's] decisions in this field must, in so far as they may interfere with a right protected under paragraph 1 of Article 8, be necessary in a democratic society, that is to say justified by a pressing social need and, in particular, proportionate to the

[53] *Boultif v Switzerland* App no 54273/00 (ECtHR, 2 August 2001) [7]–[22].
[54] ibid 55–56.
[55] *Üner v The Netherlands* [GC] (n 50) paras 12–29.
[56] ibid 67.
[57] *Maslov v Austria* (n 51) paras 10–29.
[58] ibid 100–01.

> legitimate aim pursued (see *Dalia*, cited above, p. 91, §52, and *Mehemi v. France*, judgment of 26 September 1997, *Reports* 1997-VI, p. 1971, §34).[59]

In both cases, the ECtHR recognised that the relevant measures (ie, revoking residence permits) pursued the legitimate aim of preventing disorder or crime.[60] The concurring opinion in *Boultif* similarly noted:

> [T]heir decisions comply with the requirements of Article 8 only if they are justified by a pressing social need and, in particular, proportionate to the legitimate aim pursued. Accordingly, there must be a fair balance between the relevant interests, namely the applicant's right to respect for his private and family life, on the one hand, and the prevention of disorder and crime, on the other.[61]

In coming to its respective conclusions in *Boultif* and *Üner*, the ECtHR held that the following factors should be taken into account when assessing whether an interference with an applicant's Article 8 right, by way of deportation, amounts to an unjustifiable interference with that right. That is, when assessing whether or not it is reasonable to remove from non-nationals the right to remain in a country where a non-national has committed a criminal offence. The first nine factors to be considered were arrived at in *Boultif* and the Grand Chamber in *Üner* added the final two:

1. The nature and seriousness of the offence;
2. Duration of the applicant's stay in the country from which he is going to be expelled;
3. Time which has elapsed since the commission of the offence and the applicant's conduct during that period;
4. Nationalities of the various persons concerned;
5. Applicant's family situation, such as the length of the marriage;
6. Other factors revealing whether the couple lead a real and genuine family life;
7. Whether the spouse knew about the offence at the time when he or she entered into a family relationship;
8. Whether there are children in the marriage and, if so, their age;
9. The seriousness of the difficulties which the spouse would be likely to encounter in the applicant's country or origin, although the mere fact that a person may face certain difficulties in accompanying her or his spouse cannot in itself preclude expulsion;
10. Best interests and well-being of the children, in particular the seriousness of the difficulties which any children of the applicant are likely to encounter in the country to which the applicant is to be expelled; and
11. Solidity of social, cultural and family ties with the host country and with the country of destination.

[59] *Boultif v Switzerland* (n 53) para 46; *Üner v The Netherlands* [GC] (n 50) para 56.
[60] *Boultif v Switzerland* (n 53) para 45; *Üner v The Netherlands* [GC] (n 50) para 61.
[61] *Boultif v Switzerland* (n 53) (Concurring Opinion of Baka, Wildhaber and Lorenzen JJ).

In *Maslov*, the ECtHR stated that the following factor (being age) must also be considered when working out whether an interference with a non-national's Article 8 rights would breach a minimum standard of reasonableness:

> [F]or a settled migrant who has lawfully spent all, or the major part, of his or her childhood in the host country very serious reasons are required to justify expulsion. This is all the more so where the person concerned committed the offences underlying the expulsion measure as a juvenile.[62]

Accordingly, the minimum standard set by the ECtHR across these cases can be characterised as follows: a non-national's Article 8 right should only be interfered with by way of deportation where such an interference is, considering various factors, necessary in a democratic society and proportionate to the (legitimate) aim of preventing disorder and crime. Again, the minimum standard set down by the ECtHR across these cases seems to be formulated in vague terms. Guidance is given to the legislature by the Court as to when an interference with a non-national's Article 8 rights in these circumstances would be (or not be) considered necessary or proportionate in the form of a list of factors (those set out above) to be considered. But these factors need to be given practical effect: the ECtHR sets down that the duration of the applicant's time in the host country should be considered, but not as to what length of duration would result in a breach of the minimum standard.

By formulating the standard in this way across cases, the ECtHR left space for state legislatures to determine and then to legislate or otherwise respond in such a way as to respect that minimum standard, while achieving its own goals. The UK executive, and subsequently the UK Parliament, did appear to respond in this way.

The Immigration Rules which came into effect on 9 July 2012, also included several rules which, at least in part, responded to *Boultif*, *Üner* and *Maslov*. As a reminder, one of the key purposes of the introduction of the 2012 Rules was to protect the community from foreign criminals.

In that vein, the 2012 Rules relevantly introduced Rules 390A–399A which provided the following with respect to applications to revoke deportation orders:

> 390A. Where paragraph 398 applies the Secretary of State or Entry Clearance Officer assessing the application will consider whether paragraph 399 or 399A applies and, if it does not, it will only be in exceptional circumstances that the public interest in maintaining the deportation order will be outweighed by other factors.
>
> …
>
> 396. Where a person is liable to deportation the presumption shall be that the public interest requires deportation. It is in the public interest to deport where the Secretary of State must make a deportation order in accordance with section 32 of the UK Borders Act 2007.
>
> …

[62] *Maslov v Austria* (n 51) para 75.

398. Where a person claims that their deportation would be contrary to the UK's obligations under Article 8 of the Human Rights Convention, and

(a) the deportation of the person from the UK is conducive to the public good because they have been convicted of an offence for which they have been sentenced to a period of imprisonment of at least 4 years;
(b) the deportation of the person from the UK is conducive to the public good because they have been convicted of an offence for which they have been sentenced to a period of imprisonment of less than 4 years but at least 12 months; or
(c) the deportation of the person from the UK is conducive to the public good because, in the view of the Secretary of State, their offending has caused serious harm or they are a persistent offender who shows a particular disregard for the law,

the Secretary of State in assessing that claim will consider whether paragraph 399 or 399A applies and, if it does not, it will only be in exceptional circumstances that the public interest in deportation will be outweighed by other factors.

399. This paragraph applies where paragraph 398 (b) or (c) applies if –

(a) the person has a genuine and subsisting parental relationship with a child under the age of 18 years who is in the UK, and
    (i) the child is a British Citizen; or
    (ii) the child has lived in the UK continuously for at least the 7 years immediately preceding the date of the immigration decision; and in either case
        (a) it would not be reasonable to expect the child to leave the UK; and
        (b) there is no other family member who is able to care for the child in the UK; or
(b) the person has a genuine and subsisting relationship with a partner who is in the UK and is a British Citizen, settled in the UK, or in the UK with refugee leave or humanitarian protection, and
    (i) the person has lived in the UK with valid leave continuously for at least the 15 years immediately preceding the date of the immigration decision (discounting any period of imprisonment); and
    (ii) there are insurmountable obstacles to family life with that partner continuing outside the UK.

399A. This paragraph applies where paragraph 398(b) or (c) applies if –

(a) the person has lived continuously in the UK for at least 20 years immediately preceding the date of the immigration decision (discounting any period of imprisonment) and he has no ties (including social, cultural or family) with the country to which he would have to go if required to leave the UK; or
(b) the person is aged under 25 years, he has spent at least half of his life living continuously in the UK immediately preceding the date of the immigration decision (discounting any period of imprisonment) and he has no ties (including social, cultural or family) with the country to which he would have to go if required to leave the UK.

The factors set out in *Boultif* and *Üner* appear to be directly translated into the Rules. For instance, consideration of the nature and seriousness of the offence, set out as being relevant in *Boultif* and *Üner*, is reflected in how the rules apply differently depending on the length of the sentence of imprisonment given to a non-national whose deportation is proposed. The emphasis in *Maslov* on the need to particularly consider the age of the non-national at the time when the crime was committed and the non-national's attachment to their country of nationality is also directly reflected in rule 399A.

The explanatory document produced by the Home Office as part of its Statement of Changes document, which accompanied the 2012 Rules, confirmed that the 2012 Rules were intended to be a response to the ECtHR's judgments in these cases. In citing *Boultif*, *Üner* and *Maslov*, the document provided:

> This approach reflects the case law of the ECtHR that makes it clear that a foreign national's criminality can justify deportation. The leading case of *Üner v Netherlands* (2006) sets out the factors to be taken into consideration in a criminal deportation case. They include those relating to family life (as opposed to the individual's personal position), namely the applicant's family situation (e.g., length of marriage, effectiveness of family life), whether there are children and if so what age, seriousness of difficulties which any spouse is likely to encounter on deportation, and the best interests and well-being of children, in particular seriousness of difficulties they are likely to encounter on deportation. These factors can be seen in the criteria set out above.[63]

And: 'The new Rules reflect that it may not be proportionate to deport a young person who has lived in the UK for a significant period of time falling short of 20 years.'[64] As well as:

> The new Immigration Rules reflect the approach taken in the relevant jurisprudence as follows:
>
> ...
>
> b) Where both parties were legally present in the UK at the time the relationship started but a subsequent event (most frequently the commission of a criminal offence) means that the removal of one party is pursued, different circumstances at the beginning of the relationship that forms the basis of the A8 claim mean that Strasbourg jurisprudence does not require the application of the exceptional circumstances test that it does in respect of relationships established while one party's status in the UK is illegal or precarious. But it does take account of the gravity of the crime, amongst other factors, in considering whether the removal of the individual is in pursuit of the legitimate aims of public safety or the prevention of disorder or crime.[65]

In a similar pattern to the response of the UK Parliament to *Rodrigues da Silva*, Parliament then responded to *Boultif*, *Üner* and *Maslov* by way of primary legislation in the 2014 Immigration Act. Section 19 of the Immigration Act 2014 also inserted section 117C into the 2002 Immigration Act. Section 117C relevantly

[63] 'Immigration Rules on Family and Private Life (HC 194) Grounds of Compatibility with Article 8 of the ECHR on Human Rights' (n 21) para 41.

[64] ibid 78.

[65] ibid 88 (citations omitted).

provides additional considerations that a court or tribunal must take into account in determining whether a decision by the minister made under the Immigration Acts is in breach of a person's right to respect for private and family life:

> 117C Article 8: additional considerations in cases involving foreign criminals
>
> (1) The deportation of foreign criminals is in the public interest.
> (2) The more serious the offence committed by a foreign criminal, the greater is the public interest in deportation of the criminal.
> (3) In the case of a foreign criminal ('C') who has not been sentenced to a period of imprisonment of four years or more, the public interest requires C's deportation unless Exception 1 or Exception 2 applies.
> (4) *Exception 1 applies where –*
>   (a) C has been lawfully resident in the United Kingdom for most of C's life,
>   (b) C is socially and culturally integrated in the United Kingdom, and
>   (c) there would be very significant obstacles to C's integration into the country to which C is proposed to be deported.
> (5) *Exception 2 applies where C has a genuine and subsisting relationship with a qualifying partner, or a genuine and subsisting parental relationship with a qualifying child, and the effect of C's deportation on the partner or child would be unduly harsh.*
> (6) In the case of a foreign criminal who has been sentenced to a period of imprisonment of at least four years, the public interest requires deportation unless there are very compelling circumstances, over and above those described in Exceptions 1 and 2.
> (7) The considerations in subsections (1) to (6) are to be taken into account where a court or tribunal is considering a decision to deport a foreign criminal only to the extent that the reason for the decision was the offence or offences for which the criminal has been convicted (emphasis added).

Section 117C of the 2002 Immigration Act, like Rules 390–399A of the 2012 Rules, sets out guidance to domestic courts and tribunals considering a decision to deport a foreign criminal. The guidance draws on the criteria put forward in *Boultif*, *Üner* and *Maslov*. It instructs domestic courts as to the importance of considering the nature and seriousness of the offence and that, where that offence is not 'serious', factors such as the social integration of the non-national in the UK, the non-national's family life in the UK and the age of the non-national, should be considered.

The Home Office document entitled 'Immigration Bill ECHR on Human Rights Memorandum by the Home Office' which accompanied the Immigration Act 2014, confirmed the new Part 5A of the 2002 Immigration Act as being specifically a response to the ECtHR's judgments in *Boultif*, *Üner* and *Maslov*. The Memorandum noted that section 117C(1) and (2) was intended to reflect the ECtHR's opinion in *Boultif* and *Üner* that non-nationals could be deported under Article 8(2) of the ECHR for the 'prevention of disorder and crime'.[66] The

[66] Home Office, 'Immigration Bill ECHR on Human Rights Memorandum by the Home Office' (n 27) para 8.

Memorandum also provided that exceptions 1 and 2 in section 117C(4)–(5) were intended to specifically reflect *Maslov* and the principle therein that it is necessary for the state to have regard to the person's age in coming to the host country and that serious reasons would be needed to remove the person in circumstances where the person is a settled migrant:

> The Exceptions 1 and 2 have been formulated with these principles in mind. Exception 1 seeks to provide for the *Maslov* 'settled migrant'. It is consistent with this approach to state that private life established or developed when immigration status is precarious should be given very little weight and, where there is in addition the public interest in deporting a foreign criminal, the public interest will be in deportation unless there are very significant obstacles to the person relocating.[67]

There is again evidence that Parliament did not implement the judgment or, specifically, the minimum standard of rights protection, passively. Rather, it strategically used the space left by the Court to achieve its own goals which, again, were to restrict how non-nationals who have committed criminal offences in the host country might enjoy a right to enter and remain in the country specifically and, also, to restrict how non-nationals more generally might enjoy such a right. As the explanatory material to the Immigration Act 2014 indicates below, Exception 1 in section 117C of the 2002 Immigration Act (as inserted by section 19 of the 2014 Act) functions not only to respond to the ECtHR's judgments in *Boultif*, *Üner* and *Maslov*, but to allow Parliament to push back on domestic case law it disagrees with, and specifically case law in which domestic tribunals and courts have broadly interpreted how a right to enter and remain should apply to non-nationals who have an established private life in the UK but who have committed criminal offences. The overall effect of this is to further restrict how the right to remain is owed to non-nationals in these circumstances:

> The current Rules seek to deal with this category of person through a 'no ties' test and the person having spent a significant amount of time in the United Kingdom. However, the recent Tribunal case law of *Ogundimu* [2013] UKUT 60 (IAC) has diluted this test, by saying a 'tie' means something more than remote or abstract links to the country – rather that it involves there being a continued connection to life in that country; something which ties an applicant to his or her country of origin. *This is fairly vague and open to interpretation, and it is considered goes further than the ECtHR case law requires. Instead therefore the more precise language about integration is used in Exception 1 together with the requirement that the person has been in the United Kingdom for most of their life* (emphasis added).

That the UK Parliament consciously used the space left to it is further demonstrated by secton117C(6). In relation to section 117C(6), the Explanatory Memorandum to the 2014 Act provides that the periods of imprisonment set out as the basis for deciding what considerations should be taken into account with respect to a

[67] ibid 84.

foreign criminal's deportation (ie, whether the period of imprisonment is more or less than four years) are based on judgments of the ECtHR, including 'the lead cases of *Üner* and *Maslov*'.[68] The Explanatory Memorandum does, however, note that this provision is intended to implement the general approach of the ECtHR and not *every* approach of the European Court. The Memorandum states:

> It is considered the approach is not out of kilter with the general tenor of these cases, but it is accepted that some ECtHR decisions are more generous than others and therefore it is recognised in the statement that there may be some exceptions.[69]

The UK Parliament, in fact, appeared, in effect, to argue that it could have gone further in restricting immigration in light of the space left to it by the Court. Lord Wallace of Tankerness said the following in the House of Lords:

> I reassure the Committee that the clause will impact only on a very small cohort of cases – those whose actions and behaviour is non-conducive to the public good – and that in limiting the power to deportation cases, the Government are acting in a proportionate way, and not going as far as ECtHR cases allow.
>
> …
>
> Equally, the drafting of the Bill means that this power will not be available for those whom the Government are seeking administratively to remove for the purposes of immigration control – such as illegal entry or overstaying a visa, although ECHR case law would in fact have allowed such an approach.[70]

There is also evidence of understanding on the part of each party to the interaction as to the institutional competence and strength of the other. In reaching these findings, both the Chamber and Grand Chamber respectively acknowledged that the state's motivation for the deportation of the applicants was the maintenance and protection of public order. In *Boultif*, the ECtHR noted in its discussion of whether the deportation of the applicant was, in the words of Article 8(2) of the ECHR, 'necessary in a democratic society':

> The Court recalls that it is for the Contracting States to maintain public order, in particular by exercising their right, as a matter of well-established international law and subject to their treaty obligations, to control the entry and residence of non-nationals. To that end they have the power to deport non-nationals convicted of criminal offences.[71]

In *Üner*, the Grand Chamber similarly noted the competence of the state to expel non-nationals, stating that:

> [t]he Convention does not guarantee the right of a non-national to enter or to reside in a particular country and, in pursuance of their task of maintaining public order,

[68] ibid 86.

[69] ibid.

[70] HL deb 5 March 2014, vol 752, col 1366.

[71] *Boultif v Switzerland* (n 53) para 46. The Concurring Opinion of Baka, Wildhaber and Lorenzen JJ similarly noted: 'The majority has rightly stressed that according to the constant case-law of the Court, it is for the Contracting States to maintain public order, and to that end they have the power to deport non-nationals convicted of criminal offences'.

> Contracting States have the power to expel a non-national convicted of criminal offences.[72]

The ECtHR also, in explicitly leaving a margin to the state to decide upon the issue, acknowledged that, while its own role is to set down the minimum standard of reasonableness, states are better placed to determine community interests. In *Üner*, the Grand Chamber affirmed that the state is afforded a margin of appreciation with respect to the application to non-nationals of a right to enter and remain in a foreign country:

> The Government submitted that no support could be found, either in the Convention or in the Court's case-law, for the idea that the expulsion of non-nationals belonging to the category of second-generation or long-term immigrants was always disproportionate and discriminatory. Such a premise would entirely eliminate the margin of appreciation enjoyed by the State when assessing individual immigration cases.[73]

In coming to its conclusion, the ECtHR further acknowledged that the national authorities should 'enjoy a certain margin of appreciation when assessing whether an interference with a right protected by Article 8 was necessary in a democratic society and proportionate to the legitimate aim being pursued', the legitimate aim being the prevention of further disorder and crime.[74] In the explanatory material to the 2014 Immigration Act, the UK Parliament also set out its own interpretation of the ECtHR's view that a margin should be afforded to states on this rights issue: 'The margin of appreciation granted to contracting states means that the United Kingdom is entitled to reach its own view on where the public interest lies in deportation'.[75]

There is evidence of this awareness on the part of the UK Parliament as to its own institutional competence in the parliamentary debates surrounding section 117C. Lord Wallace of Tankerness reaffirmed Parliament's role and institutional strength in deciding these questions and, specifically, in balancing individual rights and community interest vis-a-vis the courts:

> We believe that the benefits of a framework set out by Parliament in primary legislation are clear. *It is right that Parliament's view of the public interest should be given proper weight in immigration and deportation decisions engaging Article 8. Such a framework will also bring greater efficiency, consistency, fairness and transparency of decision-making.*
>
> Parliament has not previously provided a full and clear statement in legislation on where the public interest lies in considering family and private life claims. As I said before, the 2007 Act requires the Secretary of State to make a deportation order against a foreign criminal sentenced to at least 12 months' imprisonment, unless one of the several specified exceptions applies, including where deportation would breach the criminal's human rights. Although an indication of the public interest, it is a limited

[72] *Üner v The Netherlands* [GC] (n 50) para 54.
[73] ibid 48.
[74] *Maslov v Austria* (n 51) para 76.
[75] Home Office, 'Immigration Bill ECHR on Human Rights Memorandum by the Home Office' (n 27) para 85.

> view, and does not assist the courts in determining how to balance an individual's right to family and private life against that public interest.
>
> Inevitably, therefore, the courts have had to reach their own view on public policy imperatives. In other words, it has been left to the court in an individual case to determine how best to balance relevant factors, based on the decision-maker's individual perception of public policy considerations. *I am sure we all agree that it is right and proper for the Government to make decisions about public policy, subject to the views of Parliament, and ensure that the public interest is given proper weight.*[76]

The Attorney General similarly acknowledged Parliament's policy expertise and its institutional strength in balancing different and diverse interests, noting in a public speech with respect to the 2012 Rules that: 'Parliament, before whom these changes to the Immigration Rules will be laid, is best placed to decide on difficult policy questions such as where the balance should be struck in relation to the deportation of foreign criminals'.[77]

There is again evidence of the UK Parliament acknowledging the institutional competence and strength of the ECtHR to set down a minimum standard of reasonableness with respect to how the right to remain should apply to a non-national who has committed criminal offences. While recognising that the Court gives it a margin of appreciation to decide upon the rights issue, the UK Parliament acknowledged in explanatory material to the 2014 Immigration Act that it is the ECtHR through its case law that first sets down the standard and establishes the margin owed:

> ECtHR case law is clear that the Convention does not guarantee a person/couple a right to reside in a particular country, and in respect of criminality in particular, there is a margin of appreciation afforded to states in setting the right balance.[78]

There is also evidence of the UK Parliament's appreciation that the ECHR (and therefore the ECtHR as the adjudicator of the Convention) sets the minimum standard of reasonableness with respect to non-nationals in this circumstance, and that the legislature must not (particularly in certain circumstances, such as where the right to life or the right to be free from torture are at risk) cross that minimum standard. Lord Wallace commented:

> I assure the Committee that by framing the provision in this way, an arguable asylum claim would never qualify for certification under the power. The Secretary of State *cannot use the new power where there is an arguable risk of a breach of Article 2 or Article 3 of the ECHR.*[79]

Further evidence of the UK Parliament's understanding of this role of the ECtHR is also, albeit more implicitly, found in then Home Secretary Theresa

[76] HL deb 5 March 2014, vol 752, col 1400 (emphasis added).

[77] Dominic Grieve QC, 'Speech on Understanding the Human Rights Act and ECHR on Human Rights' (London, Common Law and Commercial Bar Lecture, 2012).

[78] Home Office, 'Immigration Bill ECHR on Human Rights Memorandum by the Home Office' (n 27) para 80.

[79] HL deb 5 March 2014, vol 752, col 1366 (emphasis added).

May MP's declaration in the year following the passage of the 2014 Immigration Bill that:

> *[The] ECtHR has led to rulings that have prevented us from removing dangerous foreign criminals from Britain.* That has been the case in too many other instances, helping rapists, murderers and illegal immigrants rather than their victims or the law-abiding majority. Where we can, we have taken action. Even under the coalition, we legislated to deal with abuse of article 8 of the ECHR on human rights – the right to a family life – by requiring the courts to have regard to Parliament's view of the public interest in such cases, as set out in the Immigration Act 2014 (emphasis added).[80]

ii. Unuane

So far we have examined how the UK Parliament and the ECtHR engaged in transnational democratic dialogue on this topic by way of constitutional collaboration. The case of *Unuane* similarly concerned a situation of a non-national seeking to remain in a host country despite having committed criminal offences, but it is considered separately here because the legislative response to the ECtHR's judgment is better characterised as an example of constitutional counter-balancing.

The applicant in *Unuane* was a Nigerian national who had lived in the UK for 20 years. He was convicted of several criminal offences and was subsequently deported. The applicant's family remained in the UK, having successfully challenged their own deportation orders.[81] The specific issue before the ECtHR was whether the Immigration Rules prevented the courts from looking at Article 8 arguments, as those Rules provided, as we know, that the applicant had to have 'very compelling circumstances' in order to successfully appeal his deportation order and to remain in the UK. The ECtHR held that the Immigration Rules did not prevent domestic courts from applying Article 8 of the ECHR and, specifically, from applying the *Boultif* criteria in order to assess whether the deportation was proportionate and necessary.[82] The ECtHR held that the applicant's deportation had been disproportionate.[83]

As a reminder, the following characteristics of the dialogue model at the domestic level, as identified by Gardbaum, should also function to facilitate democratic dialogue in the sense of constitutional counter-balancing between the UK Parliament and the ECtHR: (i) a codified bill of rights or a judicially created charter of rights with legal enforceability; (ii) pre-enactment political review; (iii) weak-form judicial review of the legislation by the judiciary, which is framed as a 'power' of the courts which *can* be exercised, as opposed to a 'duty' which *must*

[80] HC deb 28 May 2015, vol 596, col 210.
[81] *Unuane v United Kingdom* (n 52) paras 5–10.
[82] ibid 83.
[83] ibid 89.

be; and (iv) a formal power, again not a duty, held by the legislature to articulate what the law is.

The last feature of the democratic dialogue model listed was identified as a particularly important mechanism for facilitating transnational democratic dialogue as it ensures that the ECtHR does not always have the final, authoritative say on what the law is. Chapter two also identified that the UK Parliament and the ECtHR could engage in democratic dialogue by way of constitutional counter-balancing given the capacity of Parliament: (i) to ignore a judgment of the ECtHR; (ii) to openly refuse to follow a judgment of the ECtHR on the basis that it is incorrect; and (iii) to recognise an ECtHR judgment and then not follow it for other reasons.

It is also useful to re-state in summary form some of the points made in the introductory chapter with respect to these kinds of interactions. Constitutional counter-balancing ensures that both the legislature and court contribute to determining rights issues, while making sure that one institution's analysis does not always dominate or override the contribution of the other. Constitutional counter-balancing should be used when one institution believes that the other has overstepped its competence or the proper scope of its powers. These mechanisms keep the model stable, but they should only be used rarely if they are to facilitate dialogue.

Turning back to *Unuane*: the ECtHR, in setting down the minimum standard of reasonableness stated:

> [The states'] decisions in this field must, in so far as they may interfere with a right protected under paragraph 1 of Article 8, be in accordance with the law and necessary in a democratic society, that is to say, justified by a pressing social need and, in particular, proportionate to the legitimate aim pursued.[84]

In coming to its finding in *Unuane*, the ECtHR acknowledged the state's competence in determining how a right to enter and remain applies to non-nationals, noting that '[t]he State is entitled, as a matter of international law and subject to its treaty obligations, to control the entry of non-nationals into its territory and their residence there'.[85] It also acknowledged the state's motivation and desire to 'maintain public order':

> The Convention does not guarantee the right of a non-national to enter or to reside in a particular country and, in pursuance of their task of maintaining public order, Contracting States have the power to expel a non-national convicted of criminal offences.[86]

In addition, the ECtHR set out how, in determining whether an interference with Article 8 of the ECHR was necessary and proportionate, states enjoy 'a certain

[84] ibid 70 (citations omitted).
[85] ibid (citations omitted).
[86] ibid.

margin of appreciation'.[87] The Court went on to explain the function of this margin, in some detail, and the process of applying it:

> In Article 8 cases the Court has generally understood the margin of appreciation to mean that, where the independent and impartial domestic courts have carefully examined the facts, applying the relevant human rights standards consistently with the Convention and its case-law, and adequately balanced the applicant's personal interests against the more general public interest in the case, it is not for it to substitute its own assessment of the merits (including, in particular, its own assessment of the factual details of proportionality) for that of the competent national authorities.[88]

However, the ECtHR then noted that the margin afforded to states with respect to this specific rights issue goes 'hand in hand with European Supervision' and that the Court has the power to 'give the final ruling on whether an expulsion measure is reconcilable with article 8'.[89]

The UK Parliament could have responded in such a way as to accommodate the Court's minimum standard, while achieving its own public policy goals of maintaining public order. It could have passed legislation which articulated more fully in rules or primary legislation what it understood to be 'very compelling circumstances'.

Instead, the UK Parliament responded by acknowledging the decision but signalled that it intended to ignore the judgment. The following exchange in Parliament between Sir Christopher Chope MP and Jacob Rees-Mogg MP, who was, at the time Leader of the House of Commons and Lord President of the Council, illustrates this:

> [Sir Christopher Chope]:
>
> May I remind him that there is an organisation still *frustrating our power to control our own borders and laws? I am referring to the ECtHR.* Can we have a debate about that Court, particularly in light of its judgment, reported in The Times law reports yesterday, in the case of Unuane? That is a case where we deported a foreign national offender who had been sentenced to five and a half years' imprisonment for very serious immigration offences – facilitating other people to break our immigration laws. The Court has said that deportation was unlawful. *Can we have a debate to discuss judge-made law, which the Court itself referred to? It said that it was interpreting the law itself, although it is not spelt out in article 8.*
>
> [Jacob Rees-Mogg]:
>
> The official Home Office line is that the Home Office is disappointed with the judgment of the ECtHR, as it has a duty to protect the public by removing foreign criminals who violate our laws, and that is obviously right, but I would say to my hon. Friend that there is one fundamental difference between the ECJ and the ECtHR: ECJ judgments became our law automatically, but judgments of the ECtHR have to come through *Parliament at*

[87] ibid 75 (citations omitted).
[88] ibid 76 (citations omitted).
[89] ibid 75 (citations omitted).

> *some point to make our law compatible, but that ultimately is a choice. He will remember that was a choice we were very reluctant to make over voting rights for prisoners. The ECtHR has a different status – a lesser status – and the great protector of human rights in this nation is this House of Commons, not any court outside the country.*[90]

From this exchange, we can see that the UK Parliament intended to ignore the ECtHR's judgment not simply because it disagreed with the decision, but because (significantly for the purposes of defining the interaction as one of democratic dialogue in the sense of constitutional counter-balancing): (i) it considered that the ECtHR had overstepped its institutional authority, by stepping into and 'frustrating' the legislature's own competence in this area; and (ii) it considered that the Parliament is the institution which should be deciding on this rights issue, or be the institution which should at least have the 'last word' (and 'choice') on how the issue is resolved.

B. Was this Dialogue Normatively Advantageous?

The normative claim of the democratic dialogue model, that it produces a 'better protection' of rights, in the sense of drawing on both legal constitutionalism and political constitutionalism, was realised, at least to some extent, in these interactions.

The ECtHR reasoned in a way that reflects a focus on the particular situation of the individual and the minority. In each judgment discussed, the ECtHR examined the personal circumstances of the applicant and asked questions such as how long each applicant had been in the country where the offence had been committed and the age of the applicant. For example, in *Boultif*, the Court took into account the Swiss domestic court's decision as to the appropriate punishments for the relevant crimes committed by the applicant. The ECtHR looked at the fact that the domestic court had already found that the applicant had received adequate punishment for the offence and thus should not be punished further by the revocation of residency. The ECtHR reasoned as follows:

> It is true that the applicant committed a serious offence and was sentenced to a prison sentence which he has served in the meantime. The Court further notes that the Zürich District Court in its judgment of 17 May 1995 had considered that a mere conditional sentence of eighteen months' imprisonment, suspended on probation, was adequate punishment for the offence committed by the applicant. The Zürich Court of Appeal later pronounced an unconditional sentence of two years' imprisonment.[91]

The UK Parliament, on the other hand, reasoned in a way that reflects its ability to balance competing groups and interests, and thereby reflected its democratically representative and accountable nature. Parliament's focus and motivation in

[90] HC deb 30 December 2020, vol 686, col 655 (emphasis added).
[91] *Boultif v Switzerland* (n 53) para 51.

its responses to the ECtHR were the prevention of disorder and crime for the society as a whole. That Parliament reasoned with the voting majority in mind is not just reflected in those extracts from *Hansard* and from the parliamentary material already set out, but is demonstrable in the very structure of section 117C itself. Section 117C makes it more difficult to prevent the deportation of a non-national who has committed criminal offences on the basis of the non-national having a family or private life in the UK. But the section is structured in a way that presents the deportation of non-nationals as being in the public interest and the particular circumstances of non-nationals, such as the presence of a relevant family or private life, as 'exceptions'. Section 117C begins from the standpoint of the majority's interests, not the individual's.

There is also evidence that the dialogue between the two institutions led to increased and more diverse deliberation. In *Boultif*, the ECtHR raised the views and decisions of the Directorate for social matters and security (Canton of Zurich), the Federal Court and the Federal Aliens' office.[92] In *Üner*, the Court brought up the laws of various other Member States to demonstrate its point that, in the majority of Council of Europe Member States, 'second-generation immigrants may be deported by the authorities on the ground that they have been convicted of a criminal offence'.[93] It reasoned:

> [E]ight member States have provided in their laws that second-generation immigrants cannot be deported on the basis of their criminal record or activities: Austria, Belgium, France, Hungary, Iceland, Norway, Portugal and Sweden. Apart from Iceland and Norway, this protection is not confined to those who were actually born in the host country but also applies to foreigners who arrived during childhood (varying from before the age of three in Austria to before the age of fifteen in Sweden).[94]

The German government also intervened in *Üner*, and the Court stated the following with respect to that intervention:

> [The Government of Germany] ... pointed out in the first place that the possibility for a State to expel individual non-nationals – on whom the Convention did not confer a right not to be expelled – was a necessary means by which a State could effectively fulfil its core tasks, namely maintaining and guaranteeing public safety and the protection of its nationals and other non-nationals residing on its territory. The fact that a non-national had been living on the State's territory for a long time, had perhaps even been born there, and had started a family there did not put him or her on a par with the State's nationals in terms of rights of residence.[95]

Similarly, in *Maslov*, the ECtHR referred to the judgment and finding of the Vienna Juvenile Court, and to the Vienna Federal Policy Authority's decision under the

[92] ibid paras 19–21.
[93] *Üner v The Netherlands* [GC] (n 50) para 39.
[94] ibid.
[95] ibid 52.

Aliens Act (the exclusion order).[96] In setting out these different voices in its judgments, and then interacting with the state legislature, the ECtHR in effect brought these views to the attention of the legislature, which might not have otherwise engaged with them.

As I discussed in the introductory chapter, instances of constitutional counterbalancing are more likely to give rise to the third normative claim of the dialogue model: that it produces a system of checks and balances. We can see this to be the case here. In *Unuane*, the UK's response (or lack thereof) demonstrated the UK Parliament's view that the ECtHR had not stayed within its mandate and had overstepped its competence. The UK Parliament in its legislative response, by providing direction to domestic courts, also kept 'in check' domestic courts with respect to how they interpret Article 8 of the ECHR and how they balance different factors, such as the public interest, in that interpretation.[97]

III. Non-Nationals who Seek Family Reunification

In *Abdulaziz, Cabales and Balkandali v United Kingdom* ('*Abdulaziz*'),[98] the ECtHR provided protection to the applicants to enter the UK on the basis of family and, specifically, spousal, reunification.

A. Did the UK Parliament Engage in Democratic Dialogue with the ECtHR?

In *Abdulaziz*, the applicants were three women who were settled lawfully and permanently in the UK. Their husbands and fiancées were trying to enter (and remain in) the UK for the purposes of family reunification.[99] The relevant law, the Immigration Act 1971 read with the Immigration Rules, provided that wives could enter and remain in the UK in order to join their husbands and fiancés, but husbands and male fiancés could not join their wives and fiancées. In light of the law only applying to husbands and male fiancés, the ECtHR held that the legislation and scheme was discriminatory and accordingly was in breach of Article 14 of the ECHR (when read with Article 8). Article 14 provides in full:

> The enjoyment of the rights and freedoms set forth in this Convention shall be secured without discrimination on any ground such as sex, race, colour, language, religion,

[96] *Maslov v Austria* (n 51) paras 10, 17.

[97] This concern, with respect to how domestic courts interpret Art 8 of the ECHR in this context and in how domestic courts balance the different factors, was also reflected in the UK government's proposed 'modern' Bill of Rights, which, in effect, instructed domestic courts, when undertaking the balancing exercise, to give greater weight to the public interest and less weight to any established private or family life of a 'foreign criminal': see Bill of Rights Bill (2022–23) 117, ss 8 and 20.

[98] *Abdulaziz, Cabales And Balkandali v United Kingdom* App nos 9214/80; 9473/81; 9474/81 (ECtHR, 28 May 1985).

[99] ibid 10.

> political or other opinion, national or social origin, association with a national minority, property, birth or other status.

Chapter two established that equality rights, such as Article 14 of the ECHR, can facilitate democratic dialogue between the UK Parliament and the ECtHR because, where the ECtHR finds a piece of legislation is discriminatory, and in breach of Article 14 of the ECHR, then the UK Parliament can respond to a judgment by passing a new law that can accommodate the excluded individual or group, by either: (i) including the excluded group within the policy; or (ii) by applying the policy to everyone.

The ECtHR first rejected various arguments made by the UK. While the Court accepted that the relevant legislation had been intended to protect the domestic labour market, it was:

> [n]ot convinced that the difference that may nevertheless exist between the respective impact of men and of women on the domestic labour market is sufficiently important to justify the difference of treatment … as to the possibility for a person settled in the United Kingdom to be joined by, as the case may be, his wife or her husband.[100]

The ECtHR acknowledged that the law's aim was to maintain 'public tranquillity', but it concluded that the aim was not achieved by differentiating between husbands and wives. The Court also rejected the UK government's argument that no violation of Article 14 should be found given its approach was more generous than the Convention strictly required as it permitted the entry of men's non-national wives and fiancées.[101] The Court then set down the minimum standard of reasonableness, namely that:

> Article 14 (art. 14) is concerned with the avoidance of discrimination in the enjoyment of the Convention rights in so far as the requirements of the Convention as to those rights can be complied with in different ways. The notion of discrimination within the meaning of Article 14 (art. 14) includes in general cases where a person or group is treated, without proper justification, less favourably than another, even though the more favourable treatment is not called for by the Convention.[102]

The ECtHR also invoked its margin of appreciation doctrine, and emphasised that the usually wide margin given in immigration matters does still 'vary according to the circumstances, the subject-matter and its background'.[103] The Court found that in light of there being a European consensus on the need to advance 'the equality of the sexes', 'very weighty reasons would have to be advanced before a difference of treatment on the ground of sex could be regarded as compatible with the Convention',[104] and the UK had not provided such reasons.

[100] ibid 79.
[101] ibid 82.
[102] ibid.
[103] ibid 78.
[104] ibid.

The minimum standard set by the Court could be characterised as: rules on family reunification must not differentiate between different types of non-nationals unless there are 'very weighty reasons' justifying the different treatment.

The ECtHR left space for the UK Parliament to legislate or otherwise respond pursuant to its own goals, but in such a way as to respect the minimum standard of rights protection owed to non-nationals seeking to enter the UK on the basis of family and, specifically spousal, reunification. The Court left a choice for Parliament: either it could legislate to allow entry to both foreign husbands and wives; or it could legislate to bring the rules for non-national wives in line with the rules for non-national husbands, thus making it more difficult for them to enter the UK.

The UK Parliament took the latter approach, with the UK initially amending the Immigration Rules in 1985 'to put[] the provisions under which husbands and wives are allowed permanent residence here on the basis of marriage on a common footing',[105] and then by repealing section 1(5) of the 1971 Immigration Act through the introduction of the 1988 Immigration Act (the 1988 Act). Section 1(5) of the 1971 Immigration Act had provided as follows:

> The rules shall be so framed that Commonwealth citizens settled in the United Kingdom at the coming into force of this Act and their wives and children are not, by virtue of anything in the rules, any less free to come into and go from the United Kingdom than if this Act had not passed.

The effect of this amendment was to remove the differential treatment that existed between types of spouses seeking entry into the UK. A review of the debates around the amendment of the Rules and the introduction of the Act demonstrate the amendment was in response to *Abdulaziz*.

Lord Glenarthur, Parliamentary Under-Secretary of State for Home Affairs, stated the following in the debates on the amendments to the Immigration Rules in the House of Commons in 1985:

> The Government of course accept the judgment of the European Court. The changes we have made to the immigration rules conform with our obligations under the ECHR. They reflect the spirit of the court judgment, not just its letter, and are not the grudging response which I think the noble Lord seems to think they are, to our obligations. Indeed our response has actually involved a relaxation of the provisions for admitting husbands.[106]

The Home Secretary, Douglas Hurd MP, set out the following in the Second Reading Speech for the Immigration Bill 1987:

> Fourteen years have passed since section 1(5) came into effect. It is not confined to adult men living here before 1972, their wives at that time and their children at that time. I want to emphasise that. If section 1(5) continues in force, it will have effect well into

[105] HC deb 23 July 1985, vol 83, col 893.
[106] HL deb 23 October 1985, vol 467, col 1183.

the next century on those who were settled here as boys before 1973 when they marry and have children. It has also been objected to on the ground that it confers benefits on wives and not on husbands. *Following the Abdulaziz case at the ECtHR, the Government gave a commitment to end that element of sex discrimination.*[107]

And Lord Ferrers, Minister of State for Home Affairs at the time, stated in the House of Lords:

> Since Section 1(5) benefits only the wives of Commonwealth citizen men, and not the husbands of Commonwealth citizen women, the prospect would be of the continuation of what is in fact a sexually discriminatory provision for possibly decades to come. The Government do not believe that it is right that that element of sexual discrimination should remain. *It gave a commitment to the ECtHR following the case of Abdulaziz that it would be removed.* That we are seeking to do.[108]

There is again evidence that the legislature was not simply passively implementing the judgment because of its status as an international court decision. Rather, the UK Parliament was using the space left by the ECtHR strategically to achieve its own policy goals and agenda, which here were to enforce strict immigration control. Recognition that this space had been left to Parliament, and there were options left to it, is evidenced by the then Home Secretary's statement in the House of Commons:

> The essential choice that had to be made, therefore, was whether to provide that from now on wives could join their husbands here only if their husbands were British citizens, and not merely settled here; or whether to allow husbands to join wives here, even if the wives were only settled here, and not British citizens. In other words, we had to choose between narrowing the basic rule to which the admission of wives is subject, or widening the rule applying to the admission of husbands.[109]

That the executive chose to narrow the Immigration Rules, and that the effect of amending the Rules and repealing section 1(5) was to make it more difficult for immigrants to enter into the UK on the basis of family reunification is evidenced by the following statement of Leon Brittan MP during the debates around the amendments to the Rules:

> The Government intend, as part of their response to the European Court judgment, to introduce legislation in due course to put an end to the sexually discriminatory features of this provision in a way *that preserves the Government's commitment to firm immigration control.*[110]

He later added:

> [I]t is entirely reasonable that, if we are to comply with the principle of the judgment while maintaining strict immigration control, we should admit husbands of women

[107] HC deb 16 November 1987, vol 122, col 784 (emphasis added).
[108] HL deb 4 March 1988, vol 494, col 365 (emphasis added).
[109] HC deb 23 July 1985, vol 83, col 895.
[110] HC deb 23 July 1985, vol 83, col 896.

> who are settled here, but not British citizens, but should retain the marriage tests applying to the admission of husbands, and extend them to apply on the same basis to the admission of wives. This is what the new rules do. The tests are perfectly proper requirements for people seeking admission on the basis of marriage. The existing rules applying to the admission of husbands are legitimate. They will be equally legitimate when applied to the admission of wives. The rules are directed at establishing that the marriage through which a man is claiming the right to settle in this country is not one which has been entered into with the primary aim of securing admission. It would not be right to allow firm immigration control to be circumvented by the use of marriage. That is what the rules are directed towards. It is an objective which, on grounds of non-discrimination, has to be applied to the admission of wives.
>
> …
>
> We came to office committed to take a firm grip of immigration. We have done so. Primary immigration has fallen. *It is against that background that our balanced response to the European Court judgment is justified both in policy and effect.* The new rules as a whole will fully uphold the firm policy to which we are committed. Accordingly, I commend them to the House.[111]

The need to respond to the ECtHR's judgment was also used as an opportunity to make other changes to the Rules, some of which were noted by Lord Glenarthur:

> Let me now turn to the three aspects of the marriage rules affected directly or indirectly by the European Court judgment: the nationality requirement, the marriage tests and the maintenance and accommodation requirement. The issue arising directly out of the court's judgment was whether to extend the nationality restriction to which the admission of husbands was subject, so that it applied to the admission of wives; or to relax the provisions for the admission of husbands.[112]

Both institutions in this interaction again demonstrated an appreciation of the other's particular strengths and competence. The ECtHR acknowledged the right on the part of states to control the entry of immigrants onto its territory,[113] and the Court noted the long history in the UK of the state doing just that. The Court recognised as legitimate the state's aim to limit immigration, in order to protect the job market in light of ongoing unemployment rates and 'to advance public tranquillity and, by exercising firm and fair immigration control, to assist in securing good community relations',[114] and justified its giving the state a margin of appreciation on this basis.[115]

On the other side of the interaction, the UK Parliament recognised the competence of the ECtHR to set the minimum standard of international law. Lord

[111] HC deb 23 July 1985, vol 83, cols 989, 900 (emphasis added).
[112] HC deb 23 October 1985, vol 467, col 1183.
[113] *Abdulaziz, Cabales And Balkandali v United Kingdom* (n 98) para 67.
[114] ibid 21, 75, 78.
[115] ibid 72.

Glenarthur first affirmed the UK Parliament's competence, and then recognised the Court's role in setting the standard of rights protection:

> It is a fundamental aim of the Government's immigration policy to protect the domestic labour market. The European Court explicitly endorsed the objective of immigration policy to protect that domestic labour market. But it expressed the firm view that the advancement of equality of the sexes is today a major goal in the member states of the Council of Europe. This means that the court did not hold that the goal of sex equality must in every case be overriding.[116]

As Leon Brittan stated in the House of Commons in the debates around the Immigration Rules:

> *We are therefore duty bound to make the changes required to comply with the convention as interpreted by the court.*
>
> In the context of cases before it, the court said that the advancement of equality of the sexes is today a major goal in the member states of the Council of Europe. According to the court, therefore, very weighty reasons would have to be advanced before a difference of treatment on the ground of sex could be regarded as compatible with the convention. The court did not hold that the goal of sexual equality must always be paramount, but it found that the Government's arguments for treating wives more favourably than husbands in this case did not provide sufficient justification for this distinction in treatment. Thus, while the court accepted the aim of the rules in restricting primary immigration, the effect of its judgment is to require a change removing the differences in the rules between the admission of husbands and wives of those permanently resident here.
>
> …
>
> *We are duty bound to give effect to the Court's interpretation of the convention. The rules give effect to that* … We are giving effect to the convention as interpreted. It would not be compatible with the court decision to continue to frame the provisions relating to settlement through marriage in the immigration rules on the basis that men were regarded as heads of households and wives as dependants.[117]

Recognition and understanding of the Court's competence to set the minimum standard of rights protection did not mean that parliamentarians necessarily agreed with that standard. See Alex Carlile MP's view:

> The new rules represent the most grudging adoption possible of the ECtHR rulings. They clearly demonstrate the British Government's lack of will to adhere to the principle of the ECHR. The new rules fail to rectify many anomalies. One of the many anomalies which will still exist is that sex discrimination against women will continue in relation to work permits. Women work permit holders will not be able to bring in a foreign husband, but male work permit holders will be able to bring in their foreign wives. How on earth can the Government say that such discrimination is fair or just and accords with the principles that British Governments have ratified in article 8 of the convention?[118]

[116] HC deb 23 October 1985, vol 467, col 1182.
[117] HC deb 23 July 1985, vol 83, col 895 (emphasis added).
[118] HC deb 23 July 1985, vol 83, col 927.

Alf Dubs MP similarly indicated that:

> The changes in the immigration rules are a consequence of what the Government and the country must have seen as a major defeat for the Government's immigration policies at the hands of the ECtHR.
>
> ....
>
> I fully understand how embarrassing all this must be for the Government. It is an embarrassment that other people predicted as the European Court made its decision.[119]

It is also worth noting that one argument that was made was that the very restrictive approach on the part of the UK Parliament in response to the ECtHR, meant that the judgment was in fact not being implemented at all. Clare Short MP stated:

> The changes in rule that we are debating have been introduced to comply with a ruling of the ECtHR. In fact, the Government are failing to comply with the court's ruling and are showing quite serious disrespect for the convention.[120]

B. Was this Dialogue Normatively Advantageous?

The interaction produced a 'better' protection of rights by drawing on arguments for both legal constitutionalism and political constitutionalism. In *Abdulaziz*, the ECtHR once again seemed to reason in the way that we would expect and hope from an international human rights court; that is, with a focus on the protection of an individual's rights. The Court provided a minimum standard of the right, namely, that it cannot be discriminatory. The ECtHR focused intensely on how the law directly impacted the specific applicants in the case, initially setting out each applicant's particular circumstances in detail over 15 paragraphs.[121]

The UK Parliament, on the other hand, overtly balanced the needs of competing groups and interests, reflecting its status as a democratically representative and accountable body. As Leon Brittan reasoned, the Parliament considered issues such as the burdens placed on the nation's resources and services by immigration, and the UK's economic wellbeing more generally, rather than focusing on, say, the economic circumstances of individual non-nationals:

> The current immigration rules reflect the commitment of this Government to apply a tight immigration control, a control to be exercised firmly and fairly. That is a policy for which I make no apology. It is based on a recognition of the strain that the admission of a substantial number of immigrants can place on existing resources and services in this country. We have therefore reduced fresh primary immigration to a minimum.[122]

[119] HC deb 23 July 1985, vol 83, col 947.
[120] HC deb 23 July 1985, vol 83, col 942.
[121] *Abdulaziz, Cabales And Balkandali v United Kingdom* (n 98) paras 39–54.
[122] HC deb 23 July 1985, vol 83, col 893.

See further the following passage from Lord Glenarthur in the House of Lords:

> The rules concerning the admission of men for marriage are a necessary part of firm immigration control. The need for firm immigration control has of course been accepted by successive Governments. At a time of high unemployment – to which the noble Baroness particularly referred – and economic recession firm immigration control is essential to protect the domestic labour market. It would make no sense to tighten the provisions for admission for employment but to continue to allow men to use marriage to gain admission. The European court specifically acknowledged that the main and essential purpose of the 1980 rules was to curtail primary immigration.[123]

This is not to say that Parliament's response was of no benefit to some individuals in the protection of their rights. Lord Glenarthur in the House of Lords did not characterise the legislative response as having restricted the legal protection of rights owed to individuals and non-nationals at all. Rather, he openly characterised the response as being inclusive, noting that:

> As my right honourable friend, the then Home Secretary said in another place, a restrictive approach, narrowing the rules for the admission of wives, would have raised formidable difficulties. It would have meant that men settled here who were not British citizens would not have been able to bring in their wives when successive Governments have acknowledged the importance of allowing men who have come here to work and have settled here to be joined by their families. The new rules accordingly allow women as well as men who are settled here to bring in their spouses, whether or not the husband or wife here is a British citizen, provided they meet the other provisions of the rules. I believe that this is a generous response to the European Court judgment.[124]

Lord Glenarthur later that year, in October 1985, usefully summarised the balance struck between what he perceived to be the way Parliament reasoned about rights with respect to non-nationals seeking to enter the UK on the basis of family reunification and the way the Court reasoned about the same issue. He acknowledged the UK Parliament's role and institutional strength in its ability to understand community interests and to subsequently, appropriately, balance those community interests against the protection of an individual's rights:

> The changes we have made strike a balance. They preserve the Government's policy of firm control over immigration. The rules preserve the protection of the labour market and the protection of public funds. But the rules also respect the important principles of family unity – indeed, respect for family life … enjoined in the ECHR … [t]hey are the right response to the issues raised by the European Court.[125]

It is, however, worth noting that not all members of Parliament considered that the appropriate balance had been struck as Lord Glenarthur did. Some members considered that the ECtHR had wrongfully engaged in reasoning more suited to

[123] HL deb 14 June 1985, vol 464, col 1548.
[124] HL deb 23 October 1985, vol 467, cols 1184–85.
[125] HL deb 23 October 1985, vol 467, cols 1187–88.

the legislature and that it had, accordingly, overstepped its institutional authority. Shortly after the judgment in *Abdulaziz*, Ivor Stanbrook MP asked in the House of Commons: 'On the question of the judgment by the ECtHR, are the Government content that a group of unelected foreigners should legislate for this country on matters of political and social importance?'[126]

A similar statement was made by Enoch Powell MP in the House of Commons, suggesting that the ECtHR had overstepped its institutional authority with respect to this rights issue:

> The whole basis of the right and claim of the House to legislate is destroyed if we can be obliged to legislate as a result of an interpretation placed by foreign judges upon a document of extreme vagueness in its formulation. There is no reason why such interpretation of such a document should be acceptable to the opinion or the wishes of our people, or that it should be workable and compatible with the rest of our law and with the circumstances of the people of this country. The obligation is an affront to the whole process of parliamentary government and legislation.[127]

Once again the interaction produced greater deliberation, with views brought to the attention of the legislature when they may not otherwise have been if the institutions were deciding on the rights issue alone. The ECtHR set out the views of domestic tribunals and courts, such as the Immigration Appeal Tribunal's decisions on the applicants' cases, and, among others, Lord Denning's views on the status of the Immigration Rules in *R v Secretary of State for the Home Department, ex parte Hosenball* [1977] 3 All ER 452.[128]

Various views, including those of the wider community, were also brought into the public fora and to the attention of the institutions through Parliament's response. David Waddington MP, in his capacity as Minister of State at the Home Office, explained how the proposed amendments to be made in response to the ECtHR judgment had engaged hundreds of wide-ranging written representations. In response to a question from Teddy Taylor MP, Waddington said:

> We had received at 2 July about 125 written representations arising out of the Court's decision, the great majority in favour of maintaining firm immigration control. The Government are urgently reviewing the options for amending the immigration rules to comply with the court's judgment and will announce their decision as soon as possible.[129]

The interactions between the UK Parliament and the ECtHR on this issue also produced a system of checks and balances. The ECtHR provided a 'check' on Parliament to ensure that rights protection did not go below a minimum standard, namely, a right to enter should not operate differently or in a discriminatory way depending on the type of non-national. The UK Parliament, in turn, 'checked' that the ECtHR stayed within its mandate. While some members of the legislature appreciated the ECtHR setting down the minimum standard of rights protection

[126] HC deb 6 June 1985, vol 80, col 427.
[127] HC deb 23 July 1985, vol 83, col 914.
[128] See, eg, *Abdulaziz, Cabales And Balkandali v United Kingdom* (n 98) paras 18, 41.
[129] HC deb 4 July 1985, vol 82, col 235.

with respect to the issue, others felt it had overstepped that mandate and expressed that view. With respect to this case study, there also appears to have been a constant 'threat' felt by the UK Parliament of needing to go back to Strasbourg should the legislation fall below that minimum standard. This also functioned to keep Parliament in 'check'. As Clare Short stated in the House of Commons with respect to the fact that the executive decided to narrow the rules, rather than broaden them:

> That means that all the palaver and levelling down, and all the hurt that will flow from these changes in the rules, will not comply with the judgment and 70 or 80 per cent of the men of marriageable age living in Britain are covered by that undertaking. *Therefore, cases will go back immediately to the ECtHR, which will find that the Government have failed to comply with the judgment because the bulk of men are treated differently from women in their right to marry a foreigner.*[130]

The fact that future litigation can function as a 'check' on the legislature to not fall below the minimum standard of rights protection set by the Court is also evidenced by Nicholas Budgen MP's statement and subsequent question:

> My right hon. and learned Friend is *dealing with the constraints of the law*. Is he absolutely satisfied that if individuals petition the European Court of Human Rights against the new rules, *there will not be further successful litigation and the need once again for the House to conform to foreign supervision?*[131]

IV. Non-Nationals whose Proposed Deportation has Resulted in, or would Result in, the Violation of Other ECHR Rights

In *Chahal v United Kingdom* (*Chahal*),[132] and *(Othman) Abu Qatada v The United Kingdom* (*Abu Qatada*),[133] the ECtHR provided protection to non-nationals to remain in a foreign country so long as the proposed deportation had resulted in, or would result in, the violation of other ECHR rights.

A. Did the UK Parliament Engage in Democratic Dialogue with the ECtHR?

i. Chahal

The facts in *Chahal* are lengthy and complicated: the four applicants were all members of the same family. The first applicant (Mr Karamjit Singh Chahal) came

[130] HC deb 23 July 1985, vol 83, cols 944–45 (emphasis added).
[131] HC deb 23 July 1985, vol 83, col 896 (emphasis added).
[132] *Chahal v United Kingdom* App no 22414/93 (ECtHR, Grand Chamber, 15 November 1996).
[133] *Othman (Abu Qatada) v The United Kingdom* App no 8139/09 (ECtHR, 17 January 2012).

to the UK in 1971 from India. The second applicant (Darshan Kaur Chahal) came to the UK following her marriage to Mr Chahal, and the children of the first and second applicant, who were British nationals, were the third and fourth applicants. The UK government suspected Mr Chahal was engaged in criminal activity, and he was accused of supporting a group which allegedly conspired to murder Sikhs living in the UK. While in the UK, he was charged with several criminal offences, although his convictions were subsequently quashed.[134]

On the basis of these charges, the Home Secretary decided to deport Mr Chahal, finding that his being in the UK 'was unconducive to the public good for reasons of national security and other reasons of a political nature, namely the international fight against terrorism'.[135] Mr Chahal, in response, sought asylum in the UK, arguing that he would be tortured on his return to India. That argument was dismissed by the Home Secretary,[136] and given that national security was invoked in part as the reason for that dismissal, Mr Chahal could not appeal the deportation order. The only review available of the order was by an advisory panel, the advice of which did not have to be followed by the Home Secretary.[137] The judicial review of the Home Secretary's decision – both in terms of the asylum decision and the deportation decision – was dismissed.[138]

The ECtHR held that there would be a violation of art 3 of the Convention (the right to be free from torture and ill-treatment) if the applicant was deported.[139] In doing so, it rejected the UK's claims that Article 3 was not an absolute right and was one that could be subjected to a balancing exercise,[140] as well as the UK's argument that national security concerns could be taken into account where any doubt surrounded the Article 3 claim.[141] The Court also found that the UK had breached Mr Chahal's right to liberty and security of person contained in Article 5(4) of the ECHR during his period of detention for the purpose of deportation. Article 5(4) provides:

> Everyone who is deprived of his liberty by arrest or detention shall be entitled to take proceedings by which the lawfulness of his detention shall be decided speedily by a court and his release ordered if the detention is not lawful.

Chapter two argued that 'qualified rights' (ie, those rights which 'admit of the possibility of corrective legislative action') set out in the ECHR can function to facilitate democratic dialogue between the UK Parliament and the ECtHR. This was on the basis that the legislature can pass a new law that satisfies the judiciary's standard of reasonableness or arbitrariness, while still achieving its own goals. The

[134] *Chahal v United Kingdom* (n 132) paras 12–24.
[135] ibid 25.
[136] ibid 27.
[137] ibid 32–33.
[138] ibid 34–43.
[139] ibid 107.
[140] ibid 79–80.
[141] ibid 76, 79–80.

argument identified the right to liberty and security in Article 5 of the ECHR as one such 'qualified' right and, based on the nature of the institutional interactions between the UK Parliament and the ECtHR surrounding *Chahal*, it appears that this identification was correct.

In its judgment, the Grand Chamber again set out the minimum standard of reasonableness. It also set out the factors to be taken into account to determine what conduct on the part of the state towards a non-national would fall below the minimum standard.

The ECtHR relevantly stated that proceedings for judicial review and habeas corpus with respect to a decision to detain a person for reasons of national security did not adequately place the person in a position to challenge the lawfulness or appropriateness of that detention, as required by the Convention.[142] The way to put a person in that position, as required by Article 5, was to have a court, which the advisory panel was not, undertake the review of detention and determine whether it was justified for reasons of national security. The advisory panel had no actual decision-making power, and it did not allow applicants to have legal representation nor for applicants to see relevant material.[143]

The Grand Chamber further stated that the notion of lawfulness in Article 5(1)(f), which provides in effect that a person may be detained for the purpose of deportation in accordance with a procedure prescribed by law, 'does not refer solely to the obligation to conform to the substantive and procedural rules of national law. It requires in addition that any deprivation of liberty should be in keeping with the purpose of article 5'.[144]

The Grand Chamber referred to Canada as an example of how to set up a system which accommodates security concerns, but also accords individuals procedural justice:

> A Judge holds an in camera hearing of all the evidence, at which the applicant is provided with a statement summarising, as far as possible, the case against him or her and has the right to be represented and to call evidence. The confidentiality of the security material is maintained by requiring such evidence to be examined in the absence of both the applicant and his or her representative. However, in these circumstances, their place is taken by a security-cleared counsel instructed by the court, who cross-examine the witnesses and generally assists the court to test the strength of the State's case. A summary of the evidence obtained by this procedure, with necessary deletions, is given to the applicant.[145]

While acknowledging the importance of national security concerns to states, however, the Court went on to state that taking such concerns into account 'does not mean … that the national authorities can be free from effective control by the

[142] ibid 132–33.
[143] ibid 130.
[144] ibid 129.
[145] ibid 131–44.

domestic courts whenever they choose to assert that national security and terrorism are involved'.[146]

The minimum standard set by the Court could be characterised as follows: a non-national who is detained must be afforded substantial procedural justice with respect to that decision to detain, but this right can be restricted in a way that is proportionate to legitimate security concerns. The minimum standard is formulated in fairly vague terms. It is clear that there is an irreducible minimum to the right, namely, that a decision to detain must be reviewable. But, apart from referring to the Canadian system as an example, the Court otherwise simply noted that there are 'techniques' available, which were not defined, and those techniques can address both 'national security' concerns, also not defined, and the need to afford procedural justice to an individual.

The UK Parliament used the space left to it by the Court to respond to *Chahal*, and in 1997 it passed the Special Immigration Appeals Commission Act 1997 (SIAC Act).[147] This Act set up the Special Immigration Appeals Commission to hear asylum and immigration appeals, involving some national security element. The Act required that the membership of the Commission include one judge (or someone who has held high judicial office) and either a chief adjudicator in accordance with paragraph (1) of schedule 5 to the Immigration Act 1971 or a member of the Immigration Appeals Tribunal.[148]

The 'special advocate' regime was also set up by the Act. A special advocate is someone who 'represent[s] the interests of an appellant in any proceedings before the Special Immigration Appeals Commission from which the appellant and any legal representative of his are excluded'.[149] Lord Goldsmith, the Attorney General, summarised it in 2001:

> First, and most importantly, the legislation creating SIAC provides a mechanism by which both SIAC and a person working on behalf of the appellant – called a 'special advocate' – can have full access to the security information which the Secretary of State has seen and relied on in forming his view about the national threat posed by the appellant. That is something that is not possible under traditional judicial review.
>
> Secondly, the membership of SIAC includes a High Court judge to give it the appropriate judicial standing. It also has a senior immigration judge and a lay member. It thus brings a range of relevant expertise to bear on any case.
>
> Thirdly, the Bill provides that when hearing an appeal or review, SIAC will be required to take account of all relevant information, including information which comes to light after the date of the Secretary of State's decision. This ability to take account of new information does not apply to judicial review.[150]

[146] ibid 131.
[147] Special Immigration Appeals Commission Act 1997.
[148] ibid sch 1(5).
[149] ibid s 6.
[150] HL deb 13 December 2001, vol 629, col 1436.

These legislative amendments and specifically the setting up of the SIAC regime, meant that persons detained for the purpose of deportation, like Mr Chahal, would be able to challenge their immigration detention – beyond means of habeas corpus and judicial review – and would be able to access representation through the special advocate regime. The setting up of this regime was clearly based on the Canadian model and was in clear response to *Chahal*. As Mike O'Brien MP, the Parliamentary Under-Secretary of State for Immigration, said on the passing of the SIAC Bill in the House of Commons:

> The introduction of a right of appeal to an independent commission in these cases means that the commission will be in a position to overturn decisions made personally by the Secretary of State. Of course, any such decisions taken by the commission will be unwelcome to the Secretary of State, but it is an essential aspect of complying with the Chahal judgment that the commission should be able to take decisions, rather than only make non-binding recommendations in the manner of the three advisers who formerly acted in such cases.[151]

In another debate, a year later, Jack Straw MP, the Home Secretary, confirmed this:

> The Special Immigration Appeals Commission Act has provided a remedy to the mischief identified by the European Court in the Chahal case. That is a very good example. Since the original Chahal decision was made under the Government of whom he was a member, it is fair to point out that, quite quickly after the Chahal judgment, the previous Administration said what they needed to do, and got on with it.[152]

Statements along similar lines were also made by the Attorney General Lord Goldsmith during the debates on the Anti-Terrorism, Crime and Security Bill 2001:

> The reason for setting up SIAC was, following the *Chahal* case, to deal with cases where the Secretary of State had formed a view that it was not conducive to the public interest that someone should stay here but, rather, that that person should be deported. Such a view would be based on intelligence information. That is why SIAC was set up.[153]
>
> …
>
> SIAC was invented because our existing 'Judicial Review' with a capital 'j' and a capital 'r' is inadequate to deal with that situation. That is why we lost the *Chahal* case. We cannot show the information to the traditional standard court because that court has no method by which it can examine that information without also revealing it to the individual.[154]

Again, there is evidence that the legislature was not simply implementing the judgment of an international court, and the minimum standard of rights protections set out therein, passively. Rather, it used the space left by the ECtHR to fulfil its own agenda and intentions, which were to restrict the usual procedural

[151] HC deb 26 November 1997, vol 301, cols 1032–33.
[152] HC deb 21 October 1998, vol 317, col 1305 (Mr Straw).
[153] HL deb 29 November 2001, vol 629, col 551 (Lord Goldsmith).
[154] HL deb 6 December 2001, vol 629, col 1008 (Lord Goldsmith).

justice measures afforded to those in detention where there were national security concerns. The SIAC Act importantly retained closed material procedures for immigration cases involving some national security element. As James Clappison MP, who was at the time a Shadow Home Office Minister, noted in the House of Commons in the debates surrounding the SIAC Bill:

> [The Bill] ensures compliance with the judgment of the ECtHR in the case of Chahal and it sustains our proud record of complying with that court's judgments. *The Bill also does justice to the important considerations of national security and it has our support.*[155]

There is also evidence of understanding on the part of each party to the interaction as to the institutional competence and strength of the other. The ECtHR appeared to recognise that the state was best placed to decide on matters of national security, acknowledging that 'the use of confidential material may be unavoidable where national security is at stake'.[156] On the other side of the interaction, there is also evidence of the UK Parliament acknowledging the institutional competence and strength of the ECtHR to set down a minimum standard of reasonableness with respect to what procedural rights should apply to a non-national who seeks to remain in circumstances such as Mr Chahal's. Mike O'Brien recognised the Court's role in, in effect, setting down the content of the legislation,[157] while Richard Allan MP added:

> The Bill represents a most sensible response to the judgment of the ECtHR in the Chahal case and we look forward to a process whereby human rights will be placed at the heart of all our immigration and asylum legislation.[158]

The fact that the SIAC model was based on the Canadian model endorses this proposition – that the Parliament respects the Court's competence to give it direction as to what kind of system will respect rights. Attorney General Lord Goldsmith noted:

> As I mentioned in my winding-up speech on Second Reading, the ECtHR drew attention to the existence of a Canadian model that it thought would solve the United Kingdom Government's problems. The Canadian model is the SIAC model. That is what was introduced as a result of the ECtHR saying that we could at least have something involving a special advocate procedure and a means of ensuring that material was considered.[159]

The Attorney General subsequently added in 2005:

> One has to remember that the Special Advocate procedure is a procedure which was actually promoted by the ECtHR; attention was drawn to it based on a Canadian model

[155] HC deb 26 November 1997, vol 301, col 1034 (emphasis added).
[156] *Chahal v United Kingdom* (n 132) para 131.
[157] HC deb 26 November 1997, vol 301, col 1032.
[158] HC deb 26 November 1997, vol 301, col 1034.
[159] HL deb 29 November 2001, vol 629, col 493 (Lord Goldsmith).

by Human Rights organisations. The ECtHR has subsequently expressed approval of the system.[160]

Mike O'Brien in the House of Commons usefully set out what he perceived to be the ECtHR's understanding of the competence of Parliament with respect to national security issues and, also, what Parliament understood to be the role of the Court, with its providing of guidance as to what might meet the demands of natural justice. He said:

> The Government accept that those provisions fall short of the normal demands of natural justice under the law, but they have introduced the provisions having taken account of the views expressed by the ECtHR in its judgment in Chahal and in other cases involving national security considerations. The court has explicitly acknowledged that, when national security issues are at stake, consideration will almost inevitably have to be given to confidential material and that, when that is the case, safeguards – such as the ones included in the Bill – may be essential. In such cases, the court has said that what is needed is a remedy that is 'as effective as can be', given the threat to national security.[161]

ii. Abu Qatada

The applicant in *Abu Qatada* was a recognised refugee living in the UK, with an application for indefinite leave to remain outstanding at the time of the case. The applicant had been convicted of several terrorist-related offences in absentia in Jordan and, the day after the UK and Jordan signed a memorandum of understanding on the deportation of terrorist suspects to Jordan, the Secretary of State served a deportation notice on the applicant.[162]

SIAC and the House of Lords found that there would be no 'flagrant denial of justice' if the applicant was deported to Jordan in the circumstances.[163] The ECtHR found that the applicant's deportation to Jordan would be in violation of the applicant's right to a fair trial in Article 6 of the ECHR on the basis that there was a real risk at the applicant's retrial of those offences of which he was convicted in absentia of the admission of evidence obtained by torture of third persons.[164] Article 6 of the ECHR in relevant part provides:

> 1. *In the determination of his civil rights and obligations or of any criminal charge against him, everyone is entitled to a fair and public hearing within a reasonable time by an independent and impartial tribunal established by law.* Judgment shall be pronounced publicly but the press and public may be excluded from all or part of the trial in the interests of morals, public order or national security in a democratic society, where the interests of juveniles or the protection of the private life of the parties so require, or to

[160] Select Committee on Constitutional Affairs, Minutes of Evidence, Lord Goldsmith (8 March 2005) Q 251.
[161] HC deb 30 October 1997, vol 299, col 1056.
[162] *Othman (Abu Qatada) v The United Kingdom* (n 133) paras 7–25.
[163] ibid 42–47, 59–66.
[164] ibid 285, 287.

> the extent strictly necessary in the opinion of the court in special circumstances where publicity would prejudice the interests of justice.

Article 6(2) then sets out the minimum rights to be afforded to someone charged with a criminal offence, such as, among others, the right to legal assistance and to an interpreter.

Like Article 5 of the ECHR, Article 6 is a qualified right. It can also be reasonably limited, though in a different way from Article 5 of the ECHR. Article 6 also contains the concept of 'reasonable time', and the term 'fair hearing' itself is contestable. Article 6 of the Convention should therefore facilitate dialogue between the ECtHR and the UK Parliament.

The ECtHR, in coming to its finding, set down the minimum standard of rights to be applied. The ECtHR held that a non-national could not be deported where that non-national might face a criminal trial in their country of nationality in which evidence obtained by torture could be used and admitted. The Court stated that the use of such evidence would amount to a 'flagrant denial of justice' in violation of Article 6 of the ECHR, and rejected the UK's submission that the applicant needed to show on the balance of probabilities, or beyond reasonable doubt, that evidence would not be used at trial that had been obtained by torture. Rather, what needed to be shown was that there was a 'real risk' that such evidence would be used.[165]

Unlike the previous cases examined in this chapter, the minimum standard of rights protection here leaves less space to Parliament, although some space is still left in the form of what a 'real risk' might amount to. In formulating the minimum standard in this way, the ECtHR in effect left Parliament with two options. The first option was to use Article 6 of the ECHR to collaborate with the Court, such as by passing legislation stipulating that non-nationals would not face deportation (or the removal of their right to remain) if, on deportation, the non-national could face a criminal trial in which there would be a real risk of evidence obtained by torture being admitted and used. The second option was to take a counter-balancing approach: namely, the legislature could (i) ignore the judgment; (ii) refuse to follow the judgment; or (iii) recognise the judgment but otherwise not follow it.

The government did not pursue a legislative response. Rather, what it did was sign a treaty (the UK–Jordan Treaty on Mutual Legal Assistance).[166] Theresa May, the then Home Secretary, said that ratifying the Treaty would put 'the answer to that final question beyond any doubt' and guarantee 'a fair trial for anyone deported from either of our countries'.[167] Relevantly, Article 27 of the Treaty appears to be in direct response to the *Abu Qatada* judgment:

> 3. Where there are serious and credible allegations that a statement from a person has been obtained by torture or ill-treatment by the authorities of the receiving State and it

[165] ibid 274–75.
[166] HC deb 8 July 2013, vol 566, col 23.
[167] HC deb 8 Jul 2013, vol 566, col 23.

might be used in a criminal trial in the receiving State referred to in paragraph 1 of this Article, then the statement shall not be submitted by the prosecution nor admitted by the Court in the receiving State, unless the prosecution submits evidence on the conditions in which the statement was obtained, *and the Court is satisfied to a high standard that such statement has been provided out of free-will and choice and was not obtained by torture or ill-treatment by the authorities of the receiving State.*

4. Where, before the date of signature of this Treaty, a Court in the sending State has found that there is a real risk that a statement from a person has been obtained by torture or ill-treatment by the authorities of the receiving State, and might be used in a criminal trial in the receiving State referred to in paragraph 1 of this Article, this statement shall not be submitted by the prosecution nor admitted by the Court in the receiving State, *unless the prosecution in the receiving State proves beyond any doubt that the statement has been provided out of free-will and choice and was not obtained by torture or ill-treatment by the authorities of the receiving State, and the Court in the receiving State is so satisfied* (emphasis added).

Characterising the response to the ECtHR here as constitutional collaboration, as the other case studies have, is possible, but it is not an entirely straightforward example of such collaboration given that the response here takes the form of signing a treaty. While the text of a treaty is put before Parliament,[168] there is a question as to whether this is a truly legislative response in the sense of democratic dialogue, given that Parliament cannot amend, approve, or reject the text of the treaty. This seems to undermine the descriptive claims, and subsequently, the normative claims, of the democratic dialogue model, a model which relies for its power and persuasiveness on a democratically elected body weighing in on the interaction.

The interaction may, however, be better characterised as an example of constitutional counter-balancing. This is because, while the treaty appeared on the surface to implement the ECtHR's judgment,[169] it did not necessarily do so in substance. The two paragraphs extracted from the treaty reflect the minimum standard of rights protection set down by the ECtHR because they provide domestic courts with the responsibility of examining whether evidence may or may not have been obtained by torture or ill-treatment and put the ultimate decision with respect to that evidence on the prosecution of the receiving state. Why this does not necessarily seem, in substance, to implement or follow the judgment is the fact that, in the judgment, the ECtHR points out that there are some countries the criminal justice system of which will never be able to provide the proper guarantees with respect to procedural fairness in accordance with Article 6 of the ECHR. The

[168] Constitutional Reform and Governance Act 2010 (UK), s 20(1)(c).

[169] See, eg, Theresa May's statement that: 'British courts have found that Abu Qatada is a dangerous man, that he is a risk to our national security and that he should be deported to Jordan. We have now obtained from the Jordanian Government the material that we need to comply with the ruling of the European Court. I believe that the assurances and the information that we have gathered will mean that we can soon put Qatada on a plane and get him out of our country for good': HC deb 17 April 2012, vol 543, col 175.

ECtHR made this point specifically with respect to Jordan, and Jordan's criminal justice system, when it explained that:

> The Court recognises that Jordanian law provides a number of guarantees to defendants in State Security Court cases. The use of evidence obtained by torture is prohibited. The burden is on the prosecution to establish that confessions made to the GID have not been procured by the use of torture and it is only in relation to confessions made before the Public Prosecutor that the burden of proof of torture is imposed on the defendant. However, in the light of the evidence summarised in the preceding paragraph, the Court is unconvinced that these legal guarantees have any real practical value. For instance, if a defendant fails to prove that the prosecution was implicated in obtaining an involuntary confession, that confession is admissible under Jordanian law regardless of any prior acts of ill-treatment or other misconduct by the GID. This is a troubling distinction for Jordanian law to make, given the closeness of the Public Prosecutor and the GID. Furthermore, while the State Security Court may have the power to exclude evidence obtained by torture, it has shown little readiness to use that power. Instead, the thoroughness of investigations by the State Security Court into the allegations of torture is at best questionable.
>
> …
>
> [The applicant has] … shown that the Jordanian State Security Court has proved itself to be incapable of properly investigating allegations of torture and excluding torture evidence, as Article 15 of UNCAT requires it to do. His is not the general and unspecific complaint that was made in *Mamatkulov and Askarov*; instead, it is a sustained and well-founded attack on a State Security Court system that will try him in breach of one of the most fundamental norms of international criminal justice, the prohibition on the use of evidence obtained by torture. In those circumstances … the present applicant has met the burden of proof required to demonstrate a real risk of a flagrant denial of justice if he were deported to Jordan.[170]

Accordingly, while the UK said that it was complying with the judgment, in light of this passage, it seems unlikely that a treaty being signed with Jordan on the issue and the subsequent deportation of the applicant could ever really follow the judgment.

Once again, there is evidence that this interaction between the ECtHR and the UK government was dynamic and conscious. In coming to its finding, the ECtHR acknowledged the state's motivation of protecting its populations from terrorist violence and its competence, which, it noted, the state has enjoyed throughout history, to deport non-nationals who pose a threat to national security:

> First, the Court wishes to emphasise that, throughout its history, it has been acutely conscious of the difficulties faced by States in protecting their populations from terrorist violence, which constitutes, in itself, a grave threat to human rights … Faced with such a threat, the Court considers it legitimate for Contracting States to take a firm stand against those who contribute to terrorist acts, which it cannot condone in any circumstances

[170] *Othman (Abu Qatada) v The United Kingdom* (n 133) 278, 285 (citations omitted).

> …
>
> Second, as part of the fight against terrorism, States must be allowed to deport non-nationals whom they consider to be threats to national security. It is no part of this Court's function to review whether an individual is in fact such a threat; its only task is to consider whether that individual's deportation would be compatible with his or her rights under the Convention.[171]

The UK government again demonstrated an understanding of the role and competence of the ECtHR. But, rather than demonstrating an appreciation of that role, as was the case in the other case studies, the language of the ECtHR having 'moved the goalposts' was prevalent in the discourse surrounding *Abu Qatada*. The confined, treaty-based response to the decision itself reflected a view held on the part of several MPs that the ECtHR had overstepped its institutional authority. Following the judgment and prior to agreeing to the UK–Jordan Treaty, Theresa May said in the House of Commons:

> We are also talking to the Jordanian Government about what other avenues might be open to us. *Ultimately, however, the problem is that the bar has now been set extremely high by the European Court, and it was that decision, which moved the goalposts*, that made it harder for decisions to be made in the British courts.[172]

And, following Abu Qatada's deportation, which took place on 7 July 2013:

> The problems caused by the Human Rights Act and the European Court in Strasbourg remain, and we should remember that Qatada would have been deported long ago had the European Court not *moved the goalposts by establishing new, unprecedented legal grounds* on which it blocked his deportation. I have made clear my view that in the end the Human Rights Act must be scrapped. We must also consider our relationship with the European Court very carefully, and I believe that all options – including withdrawing from the convention altogether – should remain on the table, but those are issues that will have to wait for the general election. Today we should take quiet satisfaction from the fact that a dangerous man has been deported to face justice in his home country.[173]

And:

> It is important to remember that the UK Government already had assurances about Qatada's treatment in Jordan – assurances that have been upheld in the courts – *but in February last year the ECtHR moved the goalposts and declared that his deportation would be unlawful because of the risk that evidence obtained through the mistreatment of others might be used against him*. That was the first time ever Strasbourg had blocked a deportation on that basis.[174]

That Parliament considered the ECtHR's judgment in *Abu Qatada* to be such a significant intrusion into its competence is evidenced by the fact that Parliament

[171] ibid 183–84 (citations omitted).
[172] HC deb 12 November 2012, vol 553, 42.
[173] HC deb 8 July 2013, vol 566, col 24.
[174] HC deb 16 July 2013, vol 566, col 6MC (emphasis added).

seemed to call into question the entire relationship between the two institutions, beyond this particular case study. There were suggestions that the UK needed to withdraw from the European Human Rights project more generally. Theresa May called the entire system into question shortly after the ECtHR's judgment was handed down:

> It is simply not acceptable that after the Jordanians have guaranteed his treatment, after British courts have found that he is dangerous and after his removal has been approved by the highest courts in our land, we still cannot deport such a dangerous foreign national. We continue to consider the case for a British Bill of Rights, and the Prime Minister is leading the Government's attempts to reform the ECtHR.
>
> The right place for a terrorist is a prison cell. The right place for a foreign terrorist is a foreign prison cell, far away from Britain. That is why we will do everything that we can within the existing legal regime to deport Qatada, and we are doing everything that we can to reform that regime to avoid such cases in future.[175]
>
> …
>
> Of course everybody in this country – everybody who wants to ensure that we can deport those who are a danger to us here in the United Kingdom – will be appalled by the decision that was taken by the Strasbourg Court. As I have said, we are doing everything we can to examine the legal options available to us. I continue to say that I believe it is right that we should be working to reform the ECtHR, and to do that we need to get the support of all of the other 46 countries involved.[176]

More directly, perhaps, Bob Stewart MP stated the following in the House of Commons:

> Surely this international law is an ass. It is clear that this man is a terrorist and he laughs at our weakness. He considers that he is at war with us – that is what he thinks. In wartime conditions, our Government can take extraordinary actions, so surely he should not come out of prison. If we cannot send him to Jordan now, he should stay in prison until we can send him there.[177]

Of course, this might just be political reasoning; Parliament may not agree with the decision of the ECtHR and point to institutional factors and arguments to be making its argument. Some statements seem to indicate this might be the case:

> I hardly need tell the House that the Government disagree vehemently with Strasbourg's ruling. We believe that Abu Qatada should be deported. We are considering all the legal options available, including whether to refer the case to the Grand Chamber. As we do so, we will continue to negotiate with the Jordanians to see what assurances they can give us about the evidence used against Qatada in their courts.[178]
>
> …

[175] HC deb 7 February 2012, vol 540, col 165.
[176] HC deb 7 February 2012, vol 540, col 176.
[177] HC deb 7 February 2012, vol 540, col 176.
[178] HC deb 12 November 2012, vol 553, col 37.

> Notwithstanding the fact that I still believe that the European Court's ruling was wrong, I also believe that we have obtained from the Jordanian Government the information and assurances that would allow us to deport Qatada in compliance with that ruling and the law … The Government have been doing everything we can to get rid of Abu Qatada, and we will continue to do so.[179]
>
> …
>
> The noble Lord then asked what we are doing to ensure that Qatada will in due course be deported. I assure him that we will do everything we can, in terms of the negotiations that have taken place and the negotiations that will take place, to make sure that we can deport him to Jordan, and that he will be entitled to a fair trial that is compliant under Article 6. We believe that the ECtHR got that wrong and that our own courts got it right in that what he was going to face was compliant under Article 6, but that is another matter which is for discussion on future occasions. We will continue to discuss it with the Jordanian Government and I hope that in due course my right honourable friend or myself or both of us will be able to let the House know how we are managing on that. But as regards a timescale, I cannot give the noble Lord one at this stage, and nor do I suspect he would expect to have one from me on this occasion.[180]

Political expediency demanded and rewarded an attack on the ECtHR and a distinction drawn between it as a 'European Court' and 'our own courts'. This was despite a protection of rights being produced, which did achieve the UK government's original and desired policy objective and which, importantly, reflected the minimum standard of rights protection set down by the Court.

B. Was this Dialogue Normatively Advantageous?

There is evidence that a 'better protection' of rights, in the sense of drawing on both legal constitutionalism and political constitutionalism, was again realised here. The ECtHR reasoned in a way that reflects it being an institution which we would expect to uphold the individual's rights, where those rights conflict with majority interests. We can see this by the focus of the Court on the particular situation of and ultimately findings in favour of the applicants in both *Chahal* and *Abu Qatada* vis-a-vis the security and welfare interests of the majority. For instance, in the *Abu Qatada* judgment, the Court considered the particular difficulties in proving allegations of torture that would be faced by the applicant in Jordan specifically, where the criminal justice system may itself be 'complicit in the very practices which it exists to prevent'.[181] Instead of focusing more generally on the deportation of a non-national to a country where the non-national could face a trial involving evidence obtained by torture, the Court looked at the specific individual before it and, as part of that, the particular situation that could be faced by the applicant.

[179] HC deb 12 November 2012, vol 553, col 38.
[180] HC deb 12 November 2012, vol 553, cols 42–43.
[181] *Othman (Abu Qatada) v The United Kingdom* (n 133) 278, 285 (citations omitted).

The UK Parliament, on the other hand, reasoned in such a way as to balance the needs and desires of competing groups and interests and to reflect the voting majority's views. We saw this in the extracts set out earlier where the UK Parliament focused in on national security issues and on the need to protect its population. A further example of this kind of reasoning is also found in the following statement of Theresa May in the House of Commons, which drew specific attention to the fact that Parliament is an elected place, representing the views of 'millions of people':

> I do not believe that millions of people are losing confidence in our legal system. I believe that they are concerned about the ability of the European Court to come to decisions that we do not believe to be in the best interests of the United Kingdom. This decision on Abu Qatada is clearly a case in point. That is why it is important for the Government to pursue the work that we are doing, not only in looking into the possibility of a British Bill of Rights but in trying to make changes to the way in which the European Court operates, so that in future we will be able to deport people who present a danger to us.[182]

Lord Goldsmith in 2001 articulated a view that a desirable 'balance' between the provision of a political protection of rights and a legal protection of rights was reached as a result of the interaction between the UK Parliament and the ECtHR that arose out of the *Chahal* case. He said, with respect to amendments made in light of *Chahal*:

> I recognise that that may be a second best approach, but it is the best that can be done in order to balance the need to protect sensitive security information against the need for SIAC to be given the best possible means of being able to judge whether the grounds on which the Secretary of State reached a decision were justified.[183]

Lord Goldsmith also described the result of the interaction as a 'fair compromise' and one which was 'taken from the Canadian experience'.[184]

A similar argument was not, however, made about an appropriate balance being achieved between a political protection of rights and a legal protection of rights with respect to the interaction between the two institutions arising out of *Abu Qatada*. The nature of the UK Parliament's response to *Abu Qatada* indicated its perception that the ECtHR had overstepped its competence. However, this does not mean that a 'better' protection of rights was not produced. As we know, the availability of constitutional counter-balancing to the institutions is important for the stability of the dialogue model and in that sense indirectly facilitates this normative claim.

It is again possible to see how democratic dialogue between the UK Parliament and the ECtHR can function to facilitate greater democratic deliberation than would otherwise occur if only the Court or the legislature were separately deciding

[182] HC deb 7 February 2012, vol 540, col 170.
[183] HL deb 29 November 2001, vol 629, col 499.
[184] HL deb 29 November 2001, vol 629, cols 493, 499.

the issue. Once again, the ECtHR in *Chahal* set out: (i) the opinions of the Indian National Human Rights Commission in its reports and quoted directly from it (from their visits to the Punjab in 1994);[185] (ii) Special Rapporteur reports, as well as other reports, on torture and other cruel, inhuman and degrading treatment or punishment and on extrajudicial, summary or arbitrary executions;[186] (iii) US Department of State reports on India which set out human rights abuses;[187] (iv) the UK Immigration Appeal Tribunal's decisions;[188] and (v) reports of Amnesty International.[189] This meant that these institutions' voices and views were brought to the attention of the legislature when they otherwise would not have been. This is demonstrated in the following statements subsequently made, years later, in the UK Parliament:

> Indeed, in the Chahal case, to which reference has been made – I have the judgment here – bodies such as Amnesty International, Liberty and the Air Centre drew the court's attention to a similar procedure in Canada from which the SIAC procedure was drawn.[190]
>
> …
>
> SIAC was set up because English judicial review and Northern Irish judicial review proved to be a wholly ineffective remedy. That is why Amnesty, Liberty, the AIRE Centre and the Joint Council for the Welfare of Immigrants proposed to the ECtHR in the case of Chahal that the Canadian procedure along the lines of SIAC should be introduced.[191]

The interactions also appear to produce a system of checks and balances. This is particularly the case with respect to those interactions around *Abu Qatada*, which we would expect from an instance of constitutional counterbalancing. Again, the ECtHR in both decisions provided a 'check' on Parliament to ensure that rights protection did not go below a minimum standard, namely, that non-nationals whose deportation, or proposed deportation, would result in a violation of other ECHR rights should not be deported. The UK Parliament, in turn, 'checked' that the ECtHR stayed within its mandate. As discussed, several members of the legislature, particularly with respect to *Abu Qatada* did not feel that the ECtHR had stayed within its mandate, and they responded accordingly, through expressing a desire for the UK to leave the European human rights project.

The constant 'threat' felt by the state legislature, or at least as perceived to exist by the state legislature, of needing to go back to Strasbourg should Parliament's

[185] *Chahal v United Kingdom* (n 132) paras 49–50.
[186] ibid 51.
[187] ibid 52–53.
[188] ibid 54.
[189] ibid 55–56.
[190] HL deb 27 November 2001, vol 629, col 282 (Lord Goldsmith).
[191] HL deb 6 December 2001, vol 629, col 988 (Lord Lester of Herne Hill).

response fall below that minimum standard again functioned to keep Parliament in 'check'. As Jack Straw stated with respect to *Chahal*:

> The other point to be made about the Chahal judgment was that it was made by the ECtHR in Strasbourg and not by the Judicial Committee of the House of Lords. Had it been a judgment of the Judicial Committee and had the Bill been in force, it would have been open to the Government to say, 'We do not accept this, and we shall simply run the procedures of the Immigration Act 1971 as we always have.' *They would have been very unwise to do that in that circumstance, because it would have been obvious that, since the matter was one of the liberty of a subject, there would be an appeal to Strasbourg, which almost certainly the Government would have lost.* The Government may have decided – such considerations must be borne in mind – that it was worth taking such a risk for other reasons of state (emphasis added).[192]

Theresa May similarly argued with respect to the legislative response to *Abu Qatada*:

> The other option available to us, which is to refer the case to the Grand Chamber of the ECtHR, could take even longer and would risk reopening our wider policy of seeking assurances about the treatment of terror suspects in their home countries. That policy was upheld by the European Court's judgment in January, and it is crucial if we want to be able to deport terror suspects to countries where the courts have concerns about their treatment. There are 15 other such cases pending. I confirm that the Government have therefore not referred the Abu Qatada case to the Grand Chamber.[193]

V. Conclusion

The UK Parliament and the ECtHR have engaged in democratic dialogue, in the sense of both constitutional collaboration and constitutional counter-balancing. The normative claims of the dialogue model also seemed to be achieved when the institutions engaged in dialogue.

[192] HC deb 21 October 1998, vol 317, col 1305.
[193] HC deb 17 April 2012, vol 543, col 175.

4

The Relationship between the UK Parliament and the CJEU

Chapter three began with a statement by Jonathan Gullis MP in the House of Commons, made in the context of his introducing the Asylum Seekers (Removal to Safe Countries) Bill. The purpose of this Bill was 'to provide that certain provisions of the Nationality and Borders Act 2022 relating to the removal of asylum seekers to safe countries shall have effect notwithstanding inconsistency or incompatibility with international or other domestic law'.[1] His intention in presenting the Bill was to respond to the ECtHR's interim measures decision I discussed in the introductory chapter, which had the effect of temporarily stopping flights taking off pursuant to the government's plan to relocate asylum seekers to Rwanda. As part of his presentation Gullis also stated the following:

> When we as a country voted to leave the European Union in 2016 – the largest mandate in British political history – we did so to restore our ability to control our laws, money and borders. The people of this great country felt that too much power wrongly lay in Europe and that their voices were ignored. Leaving the European Union and restoring parliamentary sovereignty represented transferring power back to the people who elect their Members of Parliament to represent their views.[2]

How accurate is this statement? Did Parliament really have no control over 'laws, money and borders' when the UK was subject to EU law and to the jurisdiction of the CJEU? This chapter investigates this, and it follows much the same structure as chapter three to do so. It looks at whether the UK Parliament and the CJEU engaged in democratic dialogue with one another, and whether those interactions were normatively advantageous, as the dialogue model promises. The chapter looks at the interaction between the UK Parliament and the CJEU with respect to two specific situations: (i) the situation of a non-European Economic Area (EEA) national who seeks to enter and remain in a country for the purpose of family reunification with, or maintenance of family life with, a Member State national spouse; and (ii) the situation of a third-country national who, not having previously been a lawful resident in a Member State, seeks to enter and remain in that state with a their EU national spouse.

[1] HC deb 14 December 2022, vol 724, col 1134.
[2] ibid.

The chapter again addresses two questions: (i) did the UK Parliament and the CJEU engage in democratic dialogue? if so, (ii) were the normative claims of the model achieved? The chapter argues that the answer to each question, for the most part, is 'yes', noting, however, that, as predicted, because of the primacy of EU law, democratic dialogue between the UK Parliament and the CJEU did not necessarily occur to the same extent as it does between the ECtHR and the UK Parliament.

I. Non-Nationals who Seek to Maintain a Family Life

A. Did the UK Parliament Engage in Democratic Dialogue with the CJEU?

i. Case C-370/90 Surinder Singh

In *Surinder Singh*, the CJEU provided protection against deportation to a non-EEA national, who had initially come to the UK for the purpose of family reunification with a non-EEA spouse.[3] The applicant in *Singh* (Mr Singh) was an Indian national who married a British citizen who lived in Germany. The applicant and his wife subsequently returned to the UK and the applicant was granted limited leave to remain in the UK, on the basis that he was married to a British national. Following the applicant's divorce from his wife, the UK government cancelled the applicant's leave to remain in the UK and, later, made an order for his deportation.[4]

The CJEU (then called the European Court of Justice (ECJ) and referred to as such in this section when discussing the *Singh* case) held that deportation in Mr Singh's circumstances would be unlawful. The Court held specifically that deportation in the circumstances would be in violation of: (i) Article 52 of the EEC Treaty which, in brief, provides that EU Member States should progressively abolish restrictions on the freedom of movement for nationals of Member States; and (ii) EEC Directive 73/148 on the abolition of restrictions on movement and residence within the Community for nationals of Member States with regard to the establishment and provision of services.

Chapter two established that an exercise of comity on the part of the CJEU might have functioned to facilitate dialogue between the UK Parliament and the CJEU in the sense of constitutional collaboration. This was on the basis that the CJEU can provide an opinion on the rights issue at hand, while also leaving space for resolution of the issue at the national level. The modification of the proportionality standard was one way in which the CJEU was identified as exercising comity vis-a-vis domestic legislatures. Various other mechanisms which could potentially facilitate dialogue between the CJEU and the UK Parliament in the sense of constitutional counter-balancing

[3] Case C-370/90 *Surinder Singh* [1992] ECR I-4265 (*Singh*).
[4] ibid 3–6.

were also identified: the UK Parliament could have openly refused to amend relevant domestic legislation to reflect a CJEU decision or simply have ignored a CJEU decision and leave it to domestic courts to determine how the law should be applied, where a specific conflict arises between national law and EU law.

The nature of the institutional interactions between the UK Parliament and the ECJ surrounding *Singh* indicates that these initial hypotheses were correct. The UK Parliament, in response to *Singh*, appears to have engaged in dialogue with the ECJ. The ECJ, in reaching its finding, set out the minimum standard that states owe to non-nationals in these circumstances. The Court held that:

> [Rights of movement and establishment] cannot be fully effective if such a person may be deterred from exercising them by obstacles raised in his or her country of origin to the entry and residence of his or her spouse. Accordingly, when a Community national who has availed himself or herself of those rights returns to his or her country of origin, his or her spouse must enjoy at least the same rights of entry and residence as would be granted to him or her under Community law if his or her spouse chose to enter and reside in another Member State. Nevertheless, Articles 48 and 52 of the Treaty do not prevent Member States from applying to foreign spouses of their own nationals rules on entry and residence more favourable than those provided for by Community law.[5]

Significantly, the Advocate General, Giuseppe Tesauro had proposed that the Court reach its conclusion on this basis. His Opinion set out guidance as to how a state may comply with the minimum standard, but still use the space left by that standard, specifically, if the state wished (as the UK did) to prevent the evasion of immigration conditions set out in national legislation. While the Advocate General's Opinion is not formally part of the judgment, it functions to shed light on the reasoning behind the CJEU's decision.[6] He said:

> However, I should point out again in that regard that Directive 73/148/EEC allows Member States, under Article 8, to derogate from its provisions on grounds of public policy, public security or public health.
>
> Moreover, the Court's case-law to the effect that in order to be regarded as such an occupational activity must be effective and genuine, and not purely marginal and ancillary, may provide a useful point of reference for the national authorities in seeking to prevent abuses.
>
> Indeed, the Court has recently held that a national court may, in assessing the genuine and effective nature of an activity, take into account the irregular nature and *limited duration of work done* under a contract for occasional work (my emphasis).
>
> Furthermore, the continued ability of the national authorities to take measures to prevent abuses is attested by the fact that even in this case the Immigration Appeal Tribunal, in upholding the appeal, expressly reserved the possibility of examining any factual issue of evasion of national law.[7]

[5] ibid 23.

[6] See generally Laure Clément-Wilz, 'The Advocate General: A Key Actor of the Court of Justice of the European Union' (2012) 14 *Cambridge Yearbook of European Legal Studies* 587.

[7] Case C-370/90 *Surinder Singh* Advocate General Tesauro (20 May 1992) I–4286, I–4287 (citations omitted).

The minimum standard set by the ECJ could be characterised as follows: at a minimum, Member States are required under EU law to grant leave to enter and remain to a spouse, of whatever nationality, of an EU national in circumstances where the EU national and the non-national spouse have gone to another Member State to work before returning (here, to the UK). Where a British citizen returned to the UK after having worked in another EU Member State, the UK would be obliged, according to this judgment, to grant a non-national spouse of that national a right to enter and reside in the UK.

The UK initially responded to *Singh*, a year after the judgment, by acknowledging the ECJ's judgment, but by choosing not to amend the relevant immigration legislation or the Immigration Rules. As Charles Wardle MP, Parliamentary Under-Secretary at the Home Office at the time, stated with respect to *Singh* in the House of Commons:

> The case of Mr. Surinder Singh will now be considered by the High Court in the light of the decision by the European Court of Justice on the relevant point of Community law. It would not be appropriate for me to comment in detail on this particular case in advance of the High Court's judgment. I will carefully study the judgments of both Courts and consider their wider implications, *but at present I see no need to amend the immigration rules in the light of the case.*[8]

About a year later, Wardle again stated that there was no need, in his view, to amend the relevant secondary legislation in order to respond to the judgment:

> There is no need to amend the immigration rules. The effect of the European Court of Justice's judgment in the particular circumstances of this case is that, where a British citizen has been exercising rights under the treaty of Rome to work in another member state and has a spouse who is not a European Community national, on their return to the United Kingdom the entry of the spouse is governed by European Community law rather than by the United Kingdom immigration rules.[9]

Ann Widdecombe MP, Home Secretary, similarly argued, a few years later, that the ECJ's judgment in *Singh* did not require any domestic legislative response, on the basis that domestic legislation already accommodated the judgment:

> Nationals of the other member states of the European Economic Area are free to come to the United Kingdom with their close family members to exercise rights conferred under the provisions of the treaty of Rome relating to the free movement of workers and rights of residence.
>
> *Those rights were not affected by the Surinder Singh judgment, delivered by the European Court of Justice in July 1992.* The effect of that judgment is that where a British citizen returns to the United Kingdom after exercising treaty rights in an economic capacity in another member state, his or her third-country national spouse and other close family

[8] HC deb 13 July 1992, vol 211, col 491 (emphasis added).
[9] HC deb 20 July 1993, vol 229, col 141.

> members are entitled to enter and reside in the United Kingdom under European Community law.
>
> In giving effect to the judgment, we require that the British citizen must have exercised substantive treaty rights in another member state, normally for a period of at least six months, as a worker or in another economically active capacity; those who resided abroad as tourists or students, for example, do not qualify. The primary purpose rule does not apply but the application is refused if the marriage is one of convenience. If the marriage ends in divorce, or if the British citizen goes abroad, the third-country spouse will no longer have a right to reside here under European Community law.[10]

Despite this initial response on the part of the UK Parliament, the executive did, subsequently in 2000 (eight years after the ECJ's judgment in *Singh*) respond to the judgment, in making the Immigration (European Economic Area) Regulations (2000 Regulations).[11] Regulation 11 of the 2000 Regulations, when read with Regulation 12, set out the conditions that needed to be satisfied for a non-EEA national to be granted admission to the UK. Regulation 11 provided as follows:

> Family members of United Kingdom nationals
>
> 11. – (1) If the conditions in paragraph (2) are satisfied, these Regulations apply to a person who is the family member of a United Kingdom national returning to the United Kingdom as if that person were the family member of an EEA national.
>
> (2) The conditions are that –
>
> (a) after leaving the United Kingdom, the United Kingdom national resided in an EEA State and –
>
> (i) was employed there (other than on a transient or casual basis); or
> (ii) established himself there as a self-employed person;
>
> (b) the United Kingdom national did not leave the United Kingdom in order to enable his family member to acquire rights under these Regulations and thereby to evade the application of United Kingdom immigration law;
> (c) on his return to the United Kingdom, the United Kingdom national would, if he were an EEA national, be a qualified person; and
> (d) *if the family member of the United Kingdom national is his spouse, the marriage took place, and the parties lived together in an EEA State, before the United Kingdom national returned to the United Kingdom* (emphasis added).

Regulation 12 of the 2000 Regulations relevantly provided as follows:

> Right of admission to the United Kingdom
>
> 12. – (1) Subject to regulation 21(1), an EEA national must be admitted to the United Kingdom if he produces, on arrival, a valid national identity card or passport issued by an EEA State.

[10] HC deb 11 January 1996, vol 269, col 276 (emphasis added).
[11] Immigration (European Economic Area) Regulations 2000, SI 2000/2326.

(2) Subject to regulation 21(1) and (2), a family member of an EEA national who is not himself an EEA national must be admitted to the United Kingdom if he produces, on arrival –

(a) a valid national identity card issued by an EEA State, or a valid passport; and
(b) either –
   (i) where the family member is a visa national or a person who seeks to be admitted to install himself with a qualified person, a valid EEA family permit or residence document; or
   (ii) in all other cases (but only where required by an immigration officer) a document proving that he is a family member of a qualified person.

As Regulation 11 of the 2000 Regulations, read with Regulation 12, in effect provided that a spouse of a UK national who has worked in another Member State has the right to enter and reside in the UK, it appears to be a direct response to the CJEU's judgment in *Singh*. The Explanatory Note to the 2000 Regulations confirms this:

> Regulation 11 implements the judgment of the European Court of Justice in *Case C-370/90 R v Immigration Appeal Tribunal and Surinder Singh, ex parte Secretary of State for the Home Department* [1992] ECR I-4265, by extending Community rights (in certain circumstances) to family members of a United Kingdom national.[12]

Significantly, in responding to *Singh* in this way in Regulation 11, the Regulations reflected the minimum standard set down by the ECJ in its judgment. The amendments to the Regulations permitted a spouse of an EEA national who has lived with that national in another Member State to enter and reside in the UK.

The way that the executive used the space left by the Court brings this interaction beyond being one which can be characterised as the state simply implementing the CJEU's judgment (as it is required to do). It did not simply implement the minimum standard nor passively implement the judgment. The UK executive, as permitted by Parliament, rather, used the space left by the CJEU for resolution of the issue at the national level to achieve its own objectives, here being to avoid evasion of national immigration legislation. The effect of Regulation 11 was in fact to make it more difficult for some non-nationals to remain in the UK, and to evade national immigration law. Regulation 11 implemented a requirement that for an EEA national spouse to join a UK national spouse in the UK, in circumstances such as those of Mr Singh, the UK national must have been employed in the EEA State, other than on a 'transient or casual' basis, or have been established as a self-employed person in the EEA. The UK executive also implemented a requirement that the UK national show that he or she did not leave the UK with the intention of enabling a family member to acquire a right to remain.

[12] 2000 Regulations, Explanatory Note, [3].

There is, significantly, also evidence of understanding on the part of each party to the interaction as to the institutional competence and strength of the other. Although the ECJ noted that the case 'is not concerned with a right under national law but with rights of movement and establishment granted to a Community national' by the EC Treaty,[13] in coming to its finding, the ECJ acknowledged both the state's competence with respect to this rights issue and the relationship that exists between a citizen and a citizen's particular state of nationality. The Court held:

> Admittedly, as the United Kingdom submits, a national of a Member State enters and resides in the territory of that State by virtue of the rights attendant upon his nationality and not by virtue of those conferred on him by Community law. In particular, as is provided, moreover, by Article 3 of the Fourth Protocol to the European Convention on Human Rights, a State may not expel one of its own nationals or deny him entry to its territory.[14]

The Advocate General, Tesauro, also acknowledged the state's motivation of stopping its own nationals from evading immigration conditions as enacted in domestic legislation. The Advocate General set out the following in his Opinion:

> [T]he United Kingdom states that every Member State has a legitimate interest in preventing its own nationals and their spouses from relying on Community law in order to evade the conditions laid down in national legislation.
>
> *Those concerns certainly reflect a real need and merit the greatest attention.* The Court itself, referring in particular to legislation concerning occupational training, has acknowledged that it is not possible to disregard the *legitimate interest* which a Member State may have in preventing certain of its nationals, by means of facilities created under the Treaty, from attempting to evade the application of national legislation.[15]

On the other side of the interaction, there is also evidence of the UK executive acknowledging the institutional competence and strength of the CJEU to set down a minimum standard of reasonableness with respect to a non-national in Mr Singh's position. Those additional aspects of Regulation 11 which the UK executive implemented to achieve its own goals are based almost directly on those suggestions of the Advocate General and this clearly lends weight to the idea that the UK Parliament acknowledged the competence and strength of the Court in its guidance to it. The Advocate General had suggested, in effect, that the state could comply with the relevant international (European) law, while achieving its own objective to prevent evasion of national legislation by: (i) requiring that the activity of the national and the national's spouse in another EEA Member State have been 'effective and genuine, and not purely marginal and ancillary'; (ii) considering any irregularity with respect to that stay; or (iii) imposing some minimum time-limit with respect to the stay. As discussed, these two first suggestions are directly reflected in Regulation 11.

[13] Case C-370/90 *Surinder Singh* (n 3) para 23.
[14] ibid 22.
[15] Case C-370/90 *Surinder Singh* (n 7) I–4286 (citations omitted) (emphasis added).

ii. Case C127/08 Metock and Others

In *Metock and Others*,[16] the CJEU provided protection to remain in a country to a non-national who was a third-party national and who, having not previously been a lawful resident in a Member State, sought to remain in that state, with a Member State national spouse.

The first applicant (who was one of three applicants) in *Metock* was a third-country national who claimed asylum on his arrival in Ireland. The asylum claim was refused by the Irish authorities, but the applicant subsequently married an EU citizen who was residing in Ireland. The applicant then applied for a residency permit to remain in Ireland,[17] on the basis that EU Directive 2004/38EC (2004 Directive) provided for the right of Union citizens and their families to move and reside freely within Member State territories. Specifically, the Directive provided that a family member of a Union citizen had to demonstrate that they were lawfully resident in another Member State prior to their entry into the Member State in which they sought to remain, in order to have the right to reside there. That is, the family members of Union citizens needed to show that they were lawfully within the Community before being able to benefit from free movement rights.[18] The applicant was subsequently refused the right to remain in Ireland, despite being married to an EU citizen, on the basis that the applicant had entered Ireland from a third country and had thus not been a lawful resident in a Member State prior to their entry into Ireland.

The issue before the CJEU was, accordingly, whether the relevant national legislation was compatible with the Directive. The CJEU held that all family members who seek to reunify with a citizen of the Union fall under the Directive and, therefore, that national legislation requiring lawful residence of the family member prior to entry into a Member State in the Community is unlawful.[19]

The CJEU, in reaching the finding in *Metock*, set out the minimum standard that states owe to non-nationals in these circumstances. The CJEU held that the 2004 EU Directive is about granting rights of entry and residence without condition. On that basis, the Court found that if Member States regulated the entry into the Community of third-country nationals who were family members of Union citizens and imposed additional requirements on entry for such non-nationals, then the free movement of persons, which is essential to the objective of an internal market as set out under Article 3(1)(c) of the Treaty on European Union, would be impeded. The Court held that:

> To allow the Member States exclusive competence to grant or refuse entry into and residence in their territory to nationals of non-member countries who are family members of Union citizens and have not already resided lawfully in another Member State would

[16] Case C-127/08 *Metock and Others* [2008] ECR I-6241 (*Metock*).
[17] ibid 18–37.
[18] ibid 39–42, 47.
[19] ibid 80.

> have the effect that the freedom of movement of Union citizens in a Member State whose nationality they do not possess would vary from one Member State to another, according to the provisions of national law concerning immigration, with some Member States permitting entry and residence of family members of a Union citizen and other Member States refusing them.[20]

Significantly, the CJEU, in coming to this finding, set out guidance as to how a state may comply with the minimum standard but still use the space left by that standard to achieve its own legislative agenda and goals. Specifically, if the state wished, as Ireland did in this case, to restrict immigration and tighten border control, it could do so within the boundary set by the minimum standard. The Court explained that

> the answer must be, first, that it is not all nationals of non-member countries who derive rights of entry into and residence in a Member State from Directive 2004/38, but only those who are family members, within the meaning of point 2 of Article 2 of that directive, of a Union citizen who has exercised his right of freedom of movement by becoming established in a Member State other than the Member State of which he is a national.
>
> Second, Directive 2004/38 does not deprive the Member States of all possibility of controlling the entry into their territory of family members of Union citizens. Under Chapter VI of that directive, Member States may, where this is justified, refuse entry and residence on grounds of public policy, public security or public health. Such a refusal will be based on an individual examination of the particular case.
>
> Moreover, in accordance with Article 35 of Directive 2004/38, Member States may adopt the necessary measures to refuse, terminate or withdraw any right conferred by that directive in the case of abuse of rights or fraud, such as marriages of convenience, it being understood that any such measure must be proportionate and subject to the procedural safeguards provided for in the directive.[21]

The minimum standard set by the CJEU could be characterised as follows: at a minimum, Member States must not regulate the entry of third-country nationals into a Member State where that entry is for the purpose of family reunification with a Union citizen. In other words, the state must grant leave to enter and remain into a Member State, to a third-country national, even where that third-country national had not been lawfully resident in a Member State.

The UK executive's initial response to *Metock* appears to have been similar to how it first responded to the ECJ's judgment in *Singh*. As Reynolds described it, the UK government's response was 'extremely slow',[22] and the executive's eventual response in 2011, discussed further below, was described by Shaw, Miller

[20] ibid 67.

[21] ibid 75.

[22] See Stephanie Reynolds, 'Obstacles to the Right of Free Movement and Residence for EU Citizens and Their Families: Country Report for the United Kingdom' (Directorate-General for Internal Policies, European Parliament 2016) 17.

and Fletcher as evidence of the UK government's 'heel dragging'.[23] While ignoring the CJEU's judgment in *Metock*, the domestic courts were left to act on the issue. Soon after the CJEU delivered the judgment in *Metock*, the Court of Appeal in *ZH (Afghanistan) v Secretary of State for the Home Department* [2009] EWCA Civ 1060, for instance, disapplied the prior residency requirement as it had been contained within the UK's Immigration (European Economic Area) Regulations 2006 (2006 Regulations),[24] while the UK's High Court, on the other hand, labelled the UK government's continued application of the prior lawful residency test as 'flagrantly unlawful'.[25]

Evidence that the UK executive was consciously and deliberately ignoring the CJEU's judgment is also demonstrated by the fact that it acted and responded very differently to the other judgments of the CJEU, on the same rights issue around the same time. It appeared to respond to those judgments the conclusion of which it agreed with, or at least those judgments it did not consider were infringing upon its parliamentary sovereignty.

In *Akrich*,[26] for example, the CJEU limited the application of *Singh* (though *Metock* later overturned *Akrich*) by finding that third-country nationals who are spouses of EU nationals must have legally resided in an EU Member State before coming to the UK in order to benefit from Community law. With respect to that case, Baroness Scotland of Asthal, a Minister of State at the Home Office at the time, stated in the House of Lords that 'the United Kingdom's sovereignty over its immigration policy remains unchanged' and that the ECJ's ruling in *Akrich* 'supports the UK's view that third country nationals who are illegally in the UK and marry British citizens, should not be able to use EC law to remain here'.[27] She added that the judgment 'will allow the UK to continue to be able to apply its national immigration legislation in such cases'.[28] The UK Parliament, in its initial ignoring of the judgment and its eventual, long-delayed response, clearly did not respond to *Metock* in the same way as it did to the CJEU's judgment in *Akrich*.

Despite this initial reaction, three years after the CJEU's judgment in *Metock*, the UK Parliament's response to the judgment appeared to shift to one of democratic dialogue in the sense of constitutional collaboration with the CJEU. In 2011, the UK executive proposed the Immigration (European Economic Area) (Amendment) Regulations (2011 Amendment Regulations),[29] which amended the 2006 Regulations, in order to give effect to *Metock*. The 2006 Regulations

[23] See, eg, the extracts from interviews conducted by Jo Shaw, Nina Miller and Maria Fletcher in Jo Shaw and others, 'Getting to Grips with EU Citizenship: Understanding the Friction between UK Immigration Law and EU Free Movement Law' (Edinburgh Law School Citizenship Studies 2013) 50, 52.

[24] Immigration (European Economic Area) Regulations 2006, SI 2006/1003.

[25] *R (on the application of Owusu) v Secretary of State* [2009] EWHC 593 (Admin) [8].

[26] Case C-109/01 *Akrich* [2003] ECR I-9607 (*Akrich*).

[27] HL deb 17 November 2003, vol 654, cols 252WA–253WA.

[28] ibid 253WA.

[29] Immigration (European Economic Area) (Amendment) Regulations 2011, SI 2011/1247.

had relevantly, prior to this amendment, defined an 'extended family member' in Regulation 8(2)(a) as being, a person who 'is a relative of an EEA national, his spouse or his civil partner' and who 'is residing in an EEA State in which the EEA national also resides and [who] is dependent upon the EEA national or is a member of his household'. Regulation 12(1)(b) of the 2006 Regulations had also provided that an EEA family permit must be given to an applicant who is a family member of an EEA national who is

> (b) .... accompanying the EEA national to the United Kingdom or joining him there and –
>
> (i) is lawfully resident in an EEA State; or
>
> (ii) would meet the requirements in the immigration rules (other than those relating to entry clearance) for leave to enter the United Kingdom as the family member of the EEA national or, in the case of direct descendants or dependent direct relatives in the ascending line of his spouse of his civil partner, as the family member of his spouse or his civil partner, were the EEA national or the spouse or civil partner a person present and settled in the United Kingdom.

The 2011 Amendment Regulations amended these two sections, substituting the words 'an EEA State' in Regulation 8(2)(a) for 'a country other than the United Kingdom', and substituting paragraph (1)(b) of the 2006 Regulations for '(b) the family member will be accompanying the EEA national to the United Kingdom or joining the EEA national there'.[30] These amendments in effect removed the prior lawful residency requirement to entering and remaining in the UK. This reflects the CJEU's judgment in *Metock*. That this was indeed a direct response to *Metock* is evidenced, in part, by the Explanatory Note accompanying the 2011 Amendment Regulations, which provided as follows:

> Article 3(1) of the Directive provides that the Directive shall apply to all Union citizens who move to or reside in a Member State other than that of which they are a national and to their family members who accompany or join them. In the case of *Metock* (case C-127/08) the Court of Justice of the European Union held that the rights of accompanying or joining family members apply irrespective of whether the family member is already residing lawfully in another Member State with the Union citizen (or was so residing prior to moving to the host Member State). *Regulation 2(3) and (4)* makes changes to the 2006 Regulations to reflect that judgment.

As with *Singh*, this interaction is beyond being characterised as the UK simply implementing the CJEU's judgment, as it is required to do. The executive used the space left by the Court, around the minimum standard, to resolve the rights issue at the national level to achieve its own objectives, here being to restrict immigration and tighten border control.

Despite passing the 2011 Amendment Regulations, the UK did not amend Regulation 9 of the 2006 Regulations which, when read with Regulation 13,

[30] 2011 Regulations, regs 2(3), (4).

provided that a non-EEA national family member's right to residency depended upon: (i) the family member having lived with the UK national in another EEA country before residing in the UK; and (ii) the UK national having resided in the other EEA state as a 'worker or self-employed person'. Regulation 11 of the 2006 Regulations which provided that a non-EEA national's residency in the UK is dependent upon acquiring: (i) an EEA family permit; (ii) a residence card; or (iii) a permanent residence card, was also not amended. Accordingly, the UK used the space left by the CJEU strategically and still retained those regulations which imposed conditions of entry into, and residence in, the UK on non-EEA nationals. This response to the CJEU's 'exercise of comity' was typical across Member States. As Lansbergen says:

> The political reaction to *Metock* has shown strong indications that while Member States are bound under Community law to comply with the ruling, they will seek to moderate its effects by adopting an expansive interpretation of the circumstances in which the Directive allows for the refusal or withdrawal of the rights contained therein.[31]

There is also evidence of understanding on the part of each party to the interaction as to the institutional competence and strength of the other. In coming to its finding, the CJEU acknowledged the state's motivation of restricting population growth or, at least, its motivation of resisting a 'great increase in the number of persons able to benefit from a right of residence in the community'.[32] The CJEU stated:

> The refusal of the host Member State to grant rights of entry and residence to the family members of a Union citizen *is such as to discourage that citizen from moving to or residing in that Member State, even if his family members are not already lawfully resident in the territory of another Member State.*[33]

The CJEU also acknowledged the political nature of this rights issue and the traditional competence of states in the areas of immigration and border control. The Court characterised the states' arguments as follows:

> The Minister for Justice and several of the governments that have submitted observations contend, however, that, in a context typified by strong pressure of migration, it is necessary to control immigration at the external borders of the Community, which presupposes an individual examination of all the circumstances surrounding a first entry into Community territory. An interpretation of Directive 2004/38 prohibiting a host Member State from requiring prior lawful residence in another Member State would undermine the ability of the Member States to control immigration at their external frontiers.[34]

[31] Anja Lansbergen, 'Metock, Implementation of the Citizens' Rights Directive and Lessons for EU Citizenship' (2009) 31 *Journal of Social Welfare and Family Law* 285, 294.

[32] Case C-127/08 *Metock and Others* (n 16) para 72.

[33] ibid 64 (emphasis added).

[34] ibid 71.

On the other side of the interaction, there is also evidence of the UK acknowledging the institutional competence and strength of the CJEU to set down a minimum standard of reasonableness with respect to a non-national in Mr Metock's position. The fact that the UK executive did not amend Regulations 9 or 11 of the 2006 Regulations appears to reflect the CJEU's guidance set out above as to how the state could use the space left to it, around the minimum standard, to achieve its own goals. As was the case with the interactions surrounding *Singh*, this seems to indicate a recognition and acknowledgment on the part of the UK executive of the CJEU's competence to set the minimum standard of rights protection.

The CJEU had made a specific point of saying that it was not all nationals who could derive these rights of entry and residence in a Member State, but only family members. The UK executive's retention of Regulation 9 of the 2006 Regulations ensured that only 'true' family members could benefit from residency. Similarly, the CJEU had also suggested in its judgment that a state could still adopt necessary measures to refuse rights conferred by the 2004 Directive to prevent fraud. Retaining Regulation 11 of the 2006 Regulations and its requirement that a third-country national must in these circumstances obtain and show certain permits and residence cards did just that, as did later amendments made by the Parliament to the 2014 Immigration Act which implemented measures to prevent 'sham marriages'. Although she pointed to the CJEU's judgment in *Metock* as the reason legislative changes were needed to deal with 'sham marriages', Home Secretary Theresa May MP stated, in the second reading speech for the 2014 Act:

> New clause 11 is intended to ensure that the marriage and civil partnership provisions work as effectively as possible. Importantly, part 4 of the Bill will establish a new referral and investigation scheme to prevent sham marriages and civil partnerships from gaining an immigration advantage. Increasingly, sham marriages are being used as a back-door route around immigration rules. The ability to do that has been extended by the Metock case in the European Court, which has enabled people from outside the EU married to someone within the EU to gain free movement rights.[35]

B. Was this Dialogue Normatively Advantageous?

There is evidence that the democratic dialogue under scrutiny here produced a 'better' protection of rights, at least to some extent, in the sense of drawing on both legal constitutionalism and political constitutionalism.

The CJEU appeared in the two cases to reason in such a way as we would expect a Court to reason. It focused on the individual's situation and on the interests of a minority, namely, non-nationals who seek to enter and remain in the country. The focus of the CJEU in *Singh* and *Metock* was on the non-EEA national's enjoyment of the right of movement and establishment (ie, to re-enter and remain) for

[35] HC deb 30 January 2014, vol 574, col 1029.

the purpose of reunification of the non-national with their spouse or other family member.[36] The Court was not focused on the impact on the majority or on the wider population of allowing such immigration by non-nationals in circumstances such as those of Mr Singh and Mr Metock. Evidence of this 'individually focused' reasoning by the ECJ in *Singh* can be seen by the following passages from the judgment:

> A national of a Member State might be deterred from leaving his country of origin in order to pursue an activity as an employed or self-employed person as envisaged by the Treaty in the territory of another Member State if, on returning to the Member State of which he is a national in order to pursue an activity there as an employed or self-employed person, the conditions of his entry and residence were not at least equivalent to those which he would enjoy under the Treaty or secondary law in the territory of another Member State.
>
> He would in particular be deterred from so doing if his spouse and children were not also permitted to enter and reside in the territory of his Member State of origin under conditions at least equivalent to those granted them by Community law in the territory of another Member State.[37]

The CJEU in *Metock* focused on the individual non-national and on the implications of the measure for the individual and the individual's family. The Court raised Article 8 of the ECHR,[38] and also stated:

> That interpretation is consistent with the purpose of Directive 2004/38, which aims to facilitate the exercise of the fundamental right of residence of Union citizens in a Member State other than that of which they are a national. *Where a Union citizen founds a family after becoming established in the host Member State, the refusal of that Member State to authorise his family members who are nationals of non-member countries to join him there would be such as to discourage him from continuing to reside there and encourage him to leave in order to be able to lead a family life in another Member State or in a non-member country.*[39]

The Advocate General's Opinion in *Singh*, on which the judgment drew heavily, further demonstrated this focus on the individual's rights as opposed to the greater population's interests. We can see this particularly in the following statements in the Advocate General's Opinion, where he focuses on the individual and on the obstacles faced by the individual, as well as by their family unit:

> I think it is necessary, therefore, to ascertain in specific terms what rights are granted by Community legislation to nationals of Member States who seek to exercise their right of establishment and what the purpose and scope of those rights are.
>
> Nevertheless, the question of principle remains, and in my view it would be illogical to uphold an interpretation of the rule which, *by denying the right of residence to members*

[36] Case C-370/90 *Surinder Singh* (n 3) paras 3–6; Case C-127/08 *Metock and Others* (n 16) para 75.
[37] Case C-370/90 *Surinder Singh* (n 3) paras 19–20.
[38] Case C-127/08 *Metock and Others* (n 16) para 79.
[39] ibid 89 (emphasis added).

> *of the family of a citizen who returns to his own country after working in another Member State, would result in an unjustified obstacle to freedom of movement for workers within Community territory and a difference in the treatment of two workers in the same circumstances solely by reason of their different nationalities.*[40]

The UK Parliament, on the other hand, again reasoned in a way that one might expect a legislature to reason: namely, in such a way as to balance competing groups and interests to reflect that it is a democratically representative and accountable body. The UK executive's focus in its response to *Singh* and its motivation behind the response was, as discussed above, primarily to prevent the evasion of its national immigration legislation. Accordingly, its focus can be characterised as being on upholding the law made in the interests of the majority by a democratic body, elected by that majority. The UK executive also seemed to reason in such a way as to demonstrate a focus on the greater population and its interests, in its response to *Metock*. The executive, in that response, emphasised the need to restrict immigration and instil border control which, intuitively, imports a motivation to *protect* the majority from immigration. As the CJEU stated in the *Metock* judgment, describing the state's reasoning and motivations:

> The Minister for Justice submits in particular that that interpretation would have *serious consequences for the Member States* by bringing about a great increase in the number of persons able to benefit from a right of residence in the Community.[41]

In characterising the UK response to *Metock*, Theresa May even explicitly stated that the executive's response was, in effect, one solely motivated by the 'national interest':

> I thank my hon. Friend, who is absolutely right, and I recognise the concerns that he and other Members have raised about the European Court of Justice. Of course, it is not just another member state that has to abide by the implications of the Metock judgment; we all have to abide by them. There has been an increase in sham marriages following that judgment – it related to the rights of those married to EU nationals – and we now have to deal with that issue. One of the reasons we have considered these measures very carefully is the question of the operation of the European Court of Justice. As I have said, however, the measures that we wish to rejoin are those that will be of benefit and *I believe that they are in our national interest.*[42]

There was some evidence, however, with respect to this case study on non-nationals who seek to enter and remain for the purpose of family reunification, that the protection of rights produced, although it drew on both legal and political constitutionalism, did not necessarily produce an appropriate balance between the two.

As we saw with the ECtHR and its relationship with the UK Parliament on aspects of whether non-nationals can enter and remain in a country, the CJEU's

[40] Case C-370/90 *Surinder Singh* (n 7) paras 12–13 (emphasis added).
[41] Case C-127/08 *Metock and Others* (n 16) paras 71–72 (emphasis added).
[42] HC deb 9 July 2013, vol 566, col 191 (emphasis added).

very entry into the realm of immigration law seemed to be viewed by the UK Parliament at times as the CJEU overstepping its institutional authority. As evidenced by the following statement by Theresa May in the House of Commons, this sometimes reached a point where the UK Parliament called into question its participation in the European project more generally:

> In the Metock case, for example, the European Court of Justice made a ruling that extended free movement rights to illegal migrants if they are married to a European economic area national who is exercising those rights. Since the Metock judgment, we have seen a steady increase in sham marriages involving EEA nationals. However, the UK cannot fix that issue alone, despite there being agreement on both sides of the House.
>
> Let me be clear: I am not saying that there is never a role for the European Court of Justice. If that was the case, we would never opt into any new measures. *However, as a question of policy, we need carefully to consider the Court's ability to interfere in our criminal justice system and weigh that against any benefits that the measure may bring.*[43]

A year later, May further argued that the CJEU's judgment in *Metock* went beyond the Court's jurisdiction. She said:

> The point I have made to my right hon. Friend, and others in the past, is that of course *there is a question about the jurisdiction of the European Court of Justice*, and we have already opted into measures post the Lisbon treaty where the Court operates. We have seen decisions by the ECJ that have been unhelpful – perhaps I can put it like that – such as the Metock case, or the case I referred to earlier when making a statement to the House. *We believe that the Court should not have the final say over matters such as substantive criminal law or international relations, and that is why we are not rejoining more than 20 minimum standards measures on matters such as racism and xenophobia.* That is why we will not be rejoining the EU–US extradition agreement, and we should be able to renegotiate as we see fit. I am clear that we should have the final say over our laws.[44]

A similar sentiment was also present in Christopher Chope MP's statements in the House of Commons. Having discussed and cited as an example *Metock* specifically, Chope went on to indicate that the enjoyment of non-nationals of a right to enter and remain in a country is, in effect, a matter for Parliament and, accordingly, for the British people. Significantly, it is *not* a matter for the CJEU:

> In essence, what happened was that we joined the European Economic Community, the fundamentals of which include freedom of movement, but over a period of time freedom of movement has been extended by treaty, directive, regulation and case law into areas that nobody could ever have contemplated. *None of those extensions was discussed with the British people and hardly any of them were discussed with our Parliament.*[45]

[43] HC deb 12 June 2013, vol 564, col 426 (emphasis added).
[44] HC deb 10 July 2014, vol 584, col 489 (emphasis added).
[45] HC deb 17 January 2014, vol 573, col 1146 (emphasis added).

Chris Heaton-Harris MP also demonstrated a belief that the CJEU in *Metock* had overstepped its role and participated in 'activism' and, in effect, domestic legislative behaviour in 're-writing' law. Heaton-Harris labelled this functioning of the CJEU as a 'great concern':

> One particular case illustrates the great concern about the Court's judicial activism: the Metock case in 2008 … In other words, this highly controversial ruling *rewrote EU law and Irish immigration law, so there is a reason to be concerned about the possibility of the Court's being involved in such decisions.*[46]

He subsequently added:

> I have been lobbying very hard for the block opt-out to be enacted, but does she understand the concerns of some of us on the Back Benches about the activist nature of the European Court of Justice? *We have only to consider the Metock case in Ireland, which led to that member state having to change its immigration rules domestically, to understand why there is such concern.* I look forward to taking part in the debate.[47]

Additionally, there is evidence of increased deliberation in the interactions. In the *Singh* judgment, the ECJ raised the views of the Commission of the European Communities, and expressly drew on the Report for the Hearing, written by Judge-Rapporteur Fernand Grévisse. The Report for the Hearing itself in turn mentioned the applicant's reliance on 'several academic commentators in support of his submissions' and, specifically, 'the opinion expressed by a number of writers that "it is now clear that nationals of one Member State may on their return to their own Member State rely on Article 52 of the EEC Treaty)"'.[48]

In *Metock*, 10 Member States intervened and, as Advocate General Poiares Maduro noted in his Opinion for the case, this was a significant number:

> The constitutional significance of the subject explains the liveliness of the debate, with no less than 10 Member States intervening in support of the respondent in the main proceedings to challenge the interpretation put forward by the applicants in the main proceedings and the Commission of the European Communities.[49]

By setting out these different voices and drawing on the submissions from a diverse range of actors in its judgments, and by then interacting with the UK Parliament, the CJEU in effect brought these views to the attention of the domestic legislature, which might not have otherwise engaged with them.

There is also some evidence that a system of checks and balances between the institutions was produced. The CJEU provided a 'check' on the UK executive and Parliament. It ensured that the rights protection owed to non-nationals (specifically non-EEA nationals and third-country nationals who could not show prior lawful residence in an EU Member State) seeking to enter and remain in a country

[46] HC deb 12 June 2013, vol 564, col 431 (emphasis added).
[47] HC deb 9 July 2013, vol 566, col 191 (emphasis added).
[48] Case C-370/90 *Surinder Singh* Report for the Hearing I-4275.
[49] Case C-127/08 *Metock and Others* Advocate General Poiares Maduro (11 June 2008) I-6247.

for the purpose of family reunification did not go below a minimum standard. That standard was that states cannot regulate entry and residence of family members of Union citizens. In turn, the UK executive and Parliament, 'checked' that the CJEU had stayed within its mandate, as was demonstrated by the fact that Parliament, at times, openly stated that it considered the CJEU to have 'overstepped' its institutional authority and competence.

II. Conclusion

The UK did retain control over its 'laws, money and borders' when it was subject to EU law and to the CJEU's jurisdiction. The UK Parliament and the CJEU engaged in democratic dialogue and, significantly, the normative claims of democratic dialogue model were, for the most part, achieved when the institutions engaged in dialogue with one another. This was despite the fact that EU law applied in the UK automatically. The dialogue did not, however, take place to the same extent as we have seen occurred between Parliament and the ECtHR in chapter three.

Conclusion

On 20 March 2025, the House of Lords took note of the seventy-fifth anniversary of the ECtHR. While some members of the House of Lords lauded the ECtHR's many achievements, many took the opportunity to criticise the relationship between the UK Parliament and the ECtHR, pointing out the Court's alleged institutional overreach. Lord Lilley ended his contribution with the following statement:

> The claim that if Britain left it would be joining Belarus and Russia is puerile. We would be joining other common-law countries, including democracies such as Australia, New Zealand and Canada, which uphold human rights without relying on a supranational court. Like them, we would make our laws democratically, not hand over the right to make laws to an international court, giving it the power to legislate rather than enforce the law.[1]

Lord Wolfson of Tredegar later added:

> The fact is that over the past years our ability to manage immigration has been hindered by interpretations of international laws, including the ECHR, which are a long way from the intentions of the states when they signed up to those treaties and conventions.[2]

The two Lords are Conservatives, but their views are not partisan. On 18 June 2025, the Labour Party's Shabana Mahmood MP, in giving a speech to the Council of Europe in her capacity as the UK's Minister for Justice, stated:

> [W]hen the application of rights begins to feel out of step with common sense – when it conflicts with fairness or disrupts legitimate government action – trust begins to erode … [i]f a foreign national commits a serious crime, they should expect to be removed from the country … when legal outcomes feel disconnected from public reasonableness, it is our job to respond … [w]hich is why we are clarifying how Convention rights – particularly Article 8 – operate in relation to our immigration rules. The right to family life is fundamental. But it has too often been used in ways that frustrate deportation, even where there are serious concerns about credibility, fairness, and risk to the public.
>
> …
>
> When people come to believe that rights only exist to protect the rule-breaker – not the rule-follower – those who would undermine the entire idea of universal human rights – the populists – will seize the space we leave behind. So, what should we do? *We cannot leave these questions to the courts alone.*[3]

[1] HL deb 20 March 2025, vol 844, col 1364.

[2] HL deb 20 March 2025, vol 844, col 1393.

[3] Rt Hon Shabana Mahmood MP, 'Lord Chancellor speech at the Council of Europe' (Strasbourg, 18 June 2025) (emphasis added).

This book has demonstrated that the courts have not dealt with these questions alone. Rather, the UK Parliament and the ECtHR are, and have been, in a relationship of democratic dialogue. This relationship has been interactive and dynamic, and the institutions have consciously worked together to produce moderated protections of rights which reflect a minimum standard of legal rights protection, and achieve the government's agenda. This has been the case even in the highly contentious and highly politicised area of immigration and where the enjoyment of a non-national's right to enter and remain in a country is under scrutiny. The same was also shown to be true for the relationship the UK Parliament previously had with the CJEU.

Significantly, the book demonstrated that the relationship between the ECtHR and the UK Parliament has normative benefits, as did the relationship that the Parliament had with the CJEU. The UK Parliament and these 'foreign' courts were shown to work together to produce protections of rights that reflected the strengths of how each institution reasons about rights, and their interactions led to greater and more diverse deliberation. The stability of the relationships was maintained by the capacity of each institution to effectively disengage from the interaction, in circumstances where one institution overstepped its institutional competence and authority. This capacity functioned to set up a system of checks and balances between the institutions.

It is, however, important to recognise the limitations of the argument presented in this book. First, the findings set out in chapters three and four may be surprising and perhaps disappointing to those who most strongly support a legal protection of rights and who especially support the role of international courts in the protection of rights. An analysis of outcomes demonstrates that intervention by the international court in each instance seemed to be what triggered an ultimate weakening of rights for non-nationals – a minority group – which international courts are charged to protect. In each of the many examples studied in the previous chapters, the UK Parliament responded to the ECtHR and the CJEU by expanding a right to enter and remain in the UK to include certain types of non-nationals who had hitherto been excluded (such as those with particular family ties in the UK), but then by also significantly restricting the enjoyment of the right for many more categories of non-nationals.

Second, the findings in chapters three and four may not be satisfying to political constitutionalists, who strongly believe in a political protection of rights. The chapters demonstrated that democratic dialogue gave the ECtHR and the CJEU an ability to uniquely influence UK policy and legislation in the area of immigration. This is despite the fact that this is an area which is conventionally understood to fall almost exclusively within the state's sovereign prerogative, and which the relevant international conventions do not contemplate. We saw that interactions between these international courts and the UK Parliament have, for example, meant that non-nationals will enjoy protection to enter and remain in particularly vulnerable circumstances such as when parents without this protection would be separated from their dependent children and when the proposed deportation would result in a violation of the non-nationals' other ECHR rights, such as the right to liberty and security.

Third, and relatedly, although the book has proposed the model of transnational democratic dialogue, I have not argued that this model is better or worse than legal or political constitutionalism. I have only offered a new approach to the traditional debate between legal and political constitutionalism, and suggested that this new approach is a viable alternative and one that may not suffer from the inaccuracies of those approaches.

Transnational democratic dialogue is grounded in practice and has unique normative benefits. Just after the ECtHR's interim measures decision on Rwanda, Baroness Warwick of Undercliffe stated:

> Myths about the HRA may start in the *Daily Mail* but they become part of the popular discourse about human rights. To counter that, we need a better understanding of our fundamental rights, how the UK's human rights framework works and how our rights are enforced.[4]

The relationship between the ECtHR and the UK Parliament is clearly not perfect, nor was the relationship that existed between the UK Parliament and the CJEU. However, the democratic dialogue model gives us a clear and persuasive framework by which to understand how these institutions have interacted with one another. With this framework, we have a tool to evaluate governmental and legislative plans in relation to human rights and to scrutinise the government's public justifications for those plans because we now know that the UK Parliament having a dynamic relationship with a 'foreign' court does not undermine or infringe its own sovereignty, as we are so often told it does.

[4] HL deb 14 July 2022, vol 823, col 1643.

BIBLIOGRAPHY

Literature

Abdelgawad, EL, 'Dialogue and the Implementation of the European Court of Human Rights' Judgments' (2016) 34 *Netherlands Quarterly of Human Rights* 340.

Ackerman, B, 'Why Dialogue?' (1989) 86 *Journal of Philosophy* 5.

Addis, M, Morrow P, and Liberty, *Your Rights: The Liberty Guide to Human Rights* (Pluto Press 2005).

Ahmed, T and de Jesús Butler, I, 'The European Union and Human Rights: An International Law Perspective' (2006) 17 *European Journal of International Law* 771.

Aleinikoff, TA, 'International Legal Norms and Migration: A Report' in TA Aleinikoff and V Chetail (eds), *Migration and International Legal Norms* (TMC Asser Press 2003).

Aleinikoff, TA and Chetail, V, *Migration and International Legal Norms* (TMC Asser 2003).

Allan, TRS, *Law, Liberty, and Justice: The Legal Foundations of British Constitutionalism* (Oxford University Press 1994).

—— 'Constitutional Dialogue and the Justification of Judicial Review' (2003) 23 *Oxford Journal of Legal Studies* 563.

—— *The Sovereignty of Law: Freedom, Constitution and Common Law* (Oxford University Press 2013).

—— 'The Moral Unity of Public Law' (2017) 67 *University of Toronto Law Journal* 1.

Ambrus, M, 'The European Court of Human Rights and Standards of Proof: An Evidentiary Approach towards the Margin of Appreciation' in L Gruszcynski and W Wouter (eds), *Deference in International Courts and Tribunals: Standard of Review and Margin of Appreciation* (Oxford University Press 2014).

Amos, M, 'The Dialogue between the United Kingdom and the European Court of Human Rights' (2012) 61 *ICLQ* 557.

Anagnostou, D and Mungiu-Pippidi, A, 'Domestic Implementation of Human Rights Judgments in Europe: Legal Infrastructure and Government Effectiveness Matter' (2014) 25 *European Journal of International Law* 205.

Anderson, K, 'The Ottawa Convention Banning Landmines, the Role of International Non-Governmental Organizations and the Idea of International Civil Society' (2000) 11 *European Journal of International Law* 91.

Arden, M, *Human Rights and European Law: Building New Legal Orders* (Oxford University Press 2015).

Arnardóttir, OM, 'The "Procedural Turn" under the European Convention on Human Rights and Presumptions of Convention Compliance' (2017) 15 *International Journal of Constitutional Law* 9.

Arnull, A, 'Judicial Dialogue in the European Union' in J Dickson and P Eleftheriadis (eds), *Philosophical Foundations of European Union Law* (Oxford University Press 2012).

Avbelj, M, 'The Emergence and Growth of Transnational Law' in M Avbelj, *The European Union under Transnational Law: A Pluralist Appraisal* (Hart Publishing 2018).

Ayala, C, 'The Judicial Dialogue between International and National Courts in the Inter-American Human Rights System' in M Scheinin, H Krunke and M Askenova (eds), *Judges as Guardians of Constitutionalism and Human Rights* (Edward Elgar 2016).

Barnard, C and Peers, S (eds), *European Union Law*, 2nd edn (Oxford University Press 2017).

Barton, JH, Stacy, HM and Greely, HT, *International Law and the Future of Freedom* (Stanford University Press 2014).

Bateup, C, 'The Dialogic Promise – Assessing the Normative Potential of Theories of Constitutional Dialogue' (2005) 71 *Brooklyn Law Review* 1109.

Baumgärtel, M, *Demanding Rights: Europe's Supranational Courts and the Dilemma of Migrant Vulnerability* (Cambridge University Press 2019).
Baumgärtel, M and Oomen, B, 'Pulling Human Rights Back in? Local Authorities, International Law and the Reception of Undocumented Migrants' (2019) 51 *Journal of Legal Pluralism and Unofficial Law* 172.
Bellamy, R, 'The Democratic Legitimacy of International Human Rights Conventions: Political Constitutionalism and the European Convention on Human Rights' (2014) 25 *European Journal of International Law* 1019.
Benhabib, S, 'Dialogic Constitutionalism and Judicial Review' (2020) 9 *Global Constitutionalism* 506.
Benvenisti, E, 'Margin of Appreciation, Consensus, and Universal Standards Symposium Issue: The Proliferation of International Tribunals: Piecing Together the Puzzle' (1998) 31 *New York University Journal of International Law and Politics* 843.
—— 'The Margin of Appreciation, Subsidiarity and Global Challenges to Democracy' (2018) 9 *Journal of International Dispute Settlement* 240.
Benvenisti, E and Downs, GW, 'National Courts, Domestic Democracy, and the Evolution of International Law' (2009) 20 *European Journal of International Law* 59.
—— 'Toward Global Checks and Balances' (2009) 20 *Constitutional Political Economy* 366.
—— *Between Fragmentation and Democracy: The Role of National and International Courts* (Cambridge University Press 2017).
Besson, S, 'The Reception Process in Ireland and the United Kingdom' in H Keller and A Stone Sweet (eds), *A Europe of Rights: The Impact of the ECHR on National Legal Systems* (Oxford University Press 2008).
—— 'Human Rights and Democracy in a Global Context: Decoupling and Recoupling' (2011) 4 *Ethics & Global Politics* 19.
Bickel, A, *The Least Dangerous Branch*, 2nd edn (Yale University Press 1962).
Blauberger, M, 'National Responses to European Court Jurisprudence' (2014) 37 *West European Politics* 457.
Bohman, J, 'Survey Article: The Coming of Age of Deliberative Democracy' (1998) 6 *Journal of Political Philosophy* 400.
Boll, AM, 'Nationality and Obligations of Loyalty in International and Municipal Law' (2005) 24 *Australian Year Book of International Law* 37.
Bolton, JR, 'Is There Really Law in International Affairs?' (2000) 10 *Transnational Law & Contemporary Problems* 1.
Bossuyt, MJ, *Guide to the 'Travaux Préparatoires' of the International Covenant on Civil and Political Rights* (M Nijhoff 1987).
Bryde, B-O, 'The Constitutional Judge and the International Constitutionalist Dialogue' (2005) 80 *Tulane Law Review* 203.
Buchanan, A and Keohane, RO, 'The Legitimacy of Global Governance Institutions' (2006) 20 *Ethics & International Affairs* 405.
Buchanan, A and Powell, R, 'Constitutional Democracy and the Rule of International Law: Are They Compatible?' (2008) 16 *Journal of Political Philosophy* 326.
Carozza, PG and González, P, 'The Final Word? Constitutional Dialogue and the Inter-American Court of Human Rights: A Reply to Jorge Contesse' (2017) 15 *International Journal of Constitutional Law* 436.
Chetail, V, 'Freedom of Movement and Transnational Migrations: A Human Rights Perspective' in T Alexander Aleinikoff and V Chetail (eds), *Migration and International Legal Norms* (TMC Asser Press 2003).
—— 'The Human Rights of Migrants in General International Law: From Minimum Standards to Fundamental Rights International Migrants Bill of Rights: Essay' (2013) 28 *Georgetown Immigration Law Journal* 225.
—— *International Migration Law* (Oxford University Press 2019).
Clayton, G and Firth, G, *Immigration and Asylum Law* (Oxford University Press 2021).

Clément-Wilz, L, 'The Advocate General: A Key Actor of the Court of Justice of the European Union' (2012) 14 *Cambridge Yearbook of European Legal Studies* 587.

Conant, LJ, *Justice Contained: Law and Politics in the European Union* (Cornell University Press 2002).

Contesse, J, 'The Final Word? Constitutional Dialogue and the Inter-American Court of Human Rights' (2017) 15 *International Journal of Constitutional Law* 414.

Contreras, P, 'National Discretion and International Deference in the Restriction of Human Rights: A Comparison between the Jurisprudence of the European and the Inter-American Court of Human Rights' (2012) 11 *Northwestern University Journal of International Human Rights* 28.

Dauvergne, C, 'Sovereignty, Migration and the Rule of Law in Global Times' (2004) 67 *MLR* 588.

De Búrca, G, 'Developing Democracy beyond the State' (2008) 46 *Columbia Journal of Transnational Law* 221.

—— 'After the EU Charter of Fundamental Rights: The Court of Justice as a Human Rights Adjudicator?' (2013) 20 *Maastricht Journal of European and Comparative Law* 168.

De Vittor, F, 'Nationality and Freedom of Movement' in S Forlati and A Annoni (eds), *The Changing Role of Nationality in International Law* (Taylor & Francis Group 2013).

Delahunty, RJ and Yoo, J, 'Against Foreign Law' (2005) 29 *Harvard Journal of Law & Public Policy* 291.

Desmond, A, 'The Private Life of Family Matters: Curtailing Human Rights Protection for Migrants under Article 8 of the ECHR?' (2018) 29 *European Journal of International Law* 261.

Di Pascale, A, 'Exceptional Duties to Admit Aliens' in R Plender (ed), *Issues in International Migration Law* (Brill 2015).

Dixon, R, 'Creating Dialogue about Socioeconomic Rights: Strong-Form versus Weak-Form Judicial Review Revisited' (2007) 5 *International Journal of Constitutional Law* 391.

—— 'The Supreme Court of Canada, Charter Dialogue, and Deference' (2009) 47 *Osgoode Hall Law Journal* 235.

Donald, A and Leach, P, 'The Role of Parliament Following Judgments of the European Court of Human Rights' in M Hunt, H Hooper and P Yowell (eds), *Parliaments and Human Rights: Redressing the Democratic Deficit* (Hart Publishing 2015).

Douglas-Scott, S, 'A Tale of Two Courts: Luxembourg, Strasbourg and the Growing European Human Rights Acquis' (2006) 43 *CML Review* 629.

—— 'The European Union and Human Rights after the Treaty of Lisbon' (2011) 11 *Human Rights Law Review* 645.

Dulitzky, AE, 'An Inter-American Constitutional Court – The Invention of the Conventionality Control by the Inter-American Court of Human Rights' (2015) 50 *Texas International Law Journal* 45.

Dunbar, R, 'The Application of International Law in the Court of Justice of the European Union: Proportionality Rising' (2021) 22 *German Law Journal* 557.

Dworkin, R, *Taking Rights Seriously* (Harvard University Press 1977).

—— 'The Forum of Principle' (1981) 56 *New York University Law Review* (1950) 469.

—— 'A New Philosophy for International Law' (2013) 41 *Philosophy & Public Affairs* 2.

Dzehtsiarou, K, 'Does Consensus Matter? Legitimacy of European Consensus in the Case Law of the European Court of Human Rights' [2011] *Public Law* 534.

Edwards, A, 'The Meaning of Nationality in International Law in an Era of Human Rights' in A Edwards and L Van Waas (eds), *Nationality and Statelessness under International Law* (Cambridge University Press 2014).

Eisgruber, CL, *Constitutional Self-Government* (Harvard University Press 2001).

Ekins, R, 'Constitutional Conversations in Britain (in Europe)' in G Sigalet, G Webber and R Dixon (eds), *Constitutional Dialogue*, 1st edn (Cambridge University Press 2019).

Ely, JH, *Democracy and Distrust: A Theory of Judicial Review* (Harvard University Press 1980).

Evans, AC, 'The Political Status of Aliens in International Law, Municipal Law and European Community Law' (1981) 30 *ICLQ* 20.

Evans, C and Evans, S, 'Evaluating the Human Rights Performance of Legislatures' (2006) 6 *Human Rights Law Review* 545.

Fabbrini, F and Maduro, MP, 'Supranational Constitutional Courts' (Social Science Research Network 2017) SSRN Scholarly Paper 2990277.

Fasone, C and Lupo, N, 'Constitutional Review and the Powers of National Parliaments in EU Affairs: Erosion or Protection?' in D Jancic (ed), *National Parliaments after the Lisbon Treaty and the Euro Crisis* (Oxford University Press 2017).

Feikert-Ahalt, C, 'United Kingdom' (2016) 1 *National Parliaments – The Law Library of Congress* 114.

Feldman, D, 'Democracy, Law and Human Rights: Politics as Challenge and Opportunity' in M Hunt, H Hooper and P Yowell (eds), *Parliaments and Human Rights: Redressing the Democratic Deficit* (Bloomsbury Publishing 2015).

Flynn, T, 'Review of Constitutional Pluralism in the European Union and Beyond, Jan Komárek' (2013) 76 *MLR* 782.

—— *The Triangular Constitution: Constitutional Pluralism in Ireland, the EU and the ECHR* (Hart Publishing 2019).

Follesdal, A, 'The Legitimacy of International Human Rights Review: The Case of the European Court of Human Rights' (2009) 40 *Journal of Social Philosophy* 595.

Forowicz, M, *The Reception of International Law in the European Court of Human Rights* (Oxford University Press 2010).

Frese, A and Olsen, HP, 'Spelling It Out – Convergence and Divergence in the Judicial Dialogue between CJEU and ECtHR' (2019) 88 *Nordic Journal of International Law* 429.

Friedman, B, 'Dialogue and Judicial Review' (1992) 91 *Michigan Law Review* 577.

Fripp, E, Moffatt, R and Wilford, E, *The Law and Practice of Expulsion and Exclusion from the United Kingdom: Deportation, Removal, Exclusion and Deprivation of Citizenship* (Bloomsbury Publishing 2014).

Gammeltoft-Hansen, T, *Access to Asylum: International Refugee Law and the Globalisation of Migration Control* (Cambridge University Press 2011).

Gardbaum, S, 'The New Commonwealth Model of Constitutionalism' (2001) 49 *American Journal of Comparative Law* 707.

—— *The New Commonwealth Model of Constitutionalism: Theory and Practice* (Cambridge University Press 2013).

Gearey, A, Morrison, W and Jago, R, *The Politics of the Common Law: Perspectives, Rights, Processes, Institutions*, 2nd edn (Routledge-Cavendish 2013).

Gearty, C, 'Democracy and Human Rights in the European Court of Human Rights: A Critical Appraisal' (2000) 51 *Northern Ireland Legal Quarterly* 381.

Geddis, A, 'Inter-Institutional "Rights Dialogue" under the New Zealand Bill of Rights Act' in T Campbell, K Ewing and A Tomkins (eds), *The Legal Protection of Human Rights: Sceptical Essays* (Oxford University Press 2011).

Goldsworthy, J, 'Homogenizing Constitutions' (2003) 23 *OJLS* 483.

Goodfellow, M, *Hostile Environment: How Immigrants Became Scapegoats* (Verso Books 2020).

Goodwin-Gill, GS, 'The Limits of the Power of Expulsion in Public International Law' (1976) 47 *British Yearbook of International Law* 55.

—— *International Law and the Movement of Persons between States* (Clarendon Press 1978).

Goodwin-Gill, GS and McAdam, J, *The Refugee in International Law*, 3rd edn (Oxford University Press 2007).

Grant, JP and Barker, JC, *Parry and Grant Encyclopaedic Dictionary of International Law*, 3rd edn (Oxford University Press 2009).

Grieve, D, 'Speech on Understanding the Human Rights Act and European Convention on Human Rights', *London Common Law and Commercial Bar Lecture* (2012).

Griffith, JAG, 'The Political Constitution' (1979) 42 *MLR* 1.

Griffiths, M and Yeo, C, 'The UK's Hostile Environment: Deputising Immigration Control' (2021) 41 *Critical Social Policy* 521.

Grossman, N, 'Legitimacy and International Adjudicative Bodies' (2009) 41 *George Washington International Law Review* 107.

Guerra, LL, 'Dialogues between the Strasbourg Court and National Courts' in A Müller and HE Kjos (eds), *Judicial Dialogue and Human Rights*, 1st edn (Cambridge University Press 2017).
Guiraudon, V, 'Citizenship Rights for Non-Citizens: France, Germany and the Netherlands' in C Joppke (ed), *Challenge to the Nation-State: Immigration in Western Europe and the United States* (Oxford University Press 1998).
—— 'European Courts and Foreigners' Rights: A Comparative Study of Norms Diffusion' (2000) 34 *International Migration Review* 1088.
Habermas, J, *Between Facts and Norms: Contributions to a Discourse Theory of Law and Democracy* (William Rehg tr, MIT Press 1996).
Haddad, H, 'Judicial Institution Builders: NGOs and International Human Rights Courts' in C Smith (ed), *Globalizing Human Rights: Emerging Issues and Approaches* (Routledge 2013).
Hailbronner, K and Goglin, J, 'Aliens' in R Wolfrum (ed), *The Max Planck Encyclopedia of Public International Law* (Oxford University Press 2013).
Harpaz, G, 'The European Court of Justice and Its Relations with the European Court of Human Rights: The Quest for Enhanced Reliance, Coherence and Legitimacy' (2009) 46 *CML Rev* 105.
Hart, N, 'Complementary Protection and Domestic Courts: The Extent, Method, Purpose and Effects of Judicial Dialogue' in A Müller and HE Kjos (eds), *Judicial Dialogue and Human Rights* (Cambridge University Press 2017).
Held, D, *Models of Democracy* (Stanford University Press 2006).
Helfer, LR and Slaughter, A-M, 'Toward a Theory of Effective Supranational Adjudication' (1997) 107 *Yale Law Journal* 273.
Henrard, K, 'The Shifting Parameters of Nationality' (2018) 65 *Netherlands International Law Review* 269.
Hickman, T, 'Constitutional Dialogue, Constitutional Theories and the Human Rights Act 1998' [2005] *Public Law* 306.
—— *Public Law after the Human Rights Act* (Hart Publishing 2010).
Hiebert, JL, 'New Constitutional Ideas: Can New Parliamentary Models Resist Judicial Dominance When Interpreting Rights Symposium: Comparative Avenues in Constitutional Law – Innovative Models of Constitutionalism' (2003) 82 *Texas Law Review* 1963.
Higgins, R, 'The Right in International Law of an Individual to Enter, Stay in and Leave a Country' (1973) 49 *International Affairs* 341.
Hirschl, R, *Towards Juristocracy: The Origins and Consequences of the New Constitutionalism* (Harvard University Press 2004).
Hoffmann, L, 'The Universality of Human Rights' (2009) 125 *LQR* 416.
Hogg, PW and Bushell, AA, 'The Charter Dialogue between Courts and Legislatures (Or Perhaps the Charter of Rights Isn't Such a Bad Thing after All)' (1997) 35 *Osgoode Hall Law Journal* 75.
Hogg, PM, Thornton, AAB and Wright, WK, 'Charter Dialogue Revisited – or Much Ado about Metaphors Charter Dialogue: Ten Years Later' (2007) 45 *Osgoode Hall Law Journal* 1.
Hoof, GJH, *Rethinking the Sources of International Law* (Brill 1983).
Horne, A and Tyrrell, H, 'Sovereignty, Privilege and the European Convention on Human Rights' in A Horne and A Le Sueur (eds), *Parliament: Legislation and Accountability* (Hart Publishing 2016).
Horspool, M, *European Union Law*, 9th edn (Oxford University Press 2016).
Hovell, D, 'A Dialogue Model: The Role of the Domestic Judge in Security Council Decision-Making International Law and Practice: Symposium on Domestic Courts as Agents of Development of International Law' (2013) 26 *Leiden Journal of International Law* 579.
Jackson, S, 'Designing Human Rights Legislation: Dialogue, the Commonwealth Model and the Roles of Parliaments and Courts' (2007) 13 *Auckland University Law Review* 89.
Jägerskiöld, S, 'The Freedom of Movement' in L Henkin (ed), *The International Bill of Rights: The Covenant on Civil and Political Rights* (Columbia University Press 1981).
Jaklic, K, *Constitutional Pluralism in the EU* (Oxford University Press 2014).
Jenkins, D, 'There and Back Again: The Strange Journey of Special Advocates and Comparative Law Methodology' (2010) 42 *Columbia Human Rights Law Review* 279.
Jessup, PC, *Transnational Law* (Yale University Press 1956).

Joppke, C and Marzal, E, 'Courts, the New Constitutionalism and Immigrant Rights: The Case of the French Conseil Constitutionnel' (2004) 43 *European Journal of Political Research* 823.
Kälin, W, 'Aliens, Expulsion and Deportation' in *Max Planck Encyclopedia of International Law* (Oxford University Press 2010).
Kanstroom, D, 'Deportation as a Global Phenomenon: Reflections on the ILC Draft Articles on the Expulsion of Aliens' (2017) 30 *Harvard Human Rights Journal* 49.
Kavanagh, A, 'Participation and Judicial Review: A Reply to Jeremy Waldron' (2003) 22 *Law and Philosophy* 451.
—— 'The Lure and the Limits of Dialogue Public Law for the Twenty-First Century' (2016) 66 *University of Toronto Law Journal* 83.
Kerr, J, 'The Conversation between Strasbourg and National Courts: Dialogue or Dictation' (2009) 44 *Irish Jurist* 1.
Kesby, A, *The Right to Have Rights: Citizenship, Humanity, and International Law* (Oxford University Press 2012).
King, J, 'Dialogue, Finality and Legality' in G Sigalet, G Webber and R Dixon (eds), *Constitutional Dialogue: Rights, Democracy, Institutions* (Cambridge University Press 2019).
Kingsley, JJ, 'Legal Transplantation: Is This What the Doctor Ordered and Are the Blood Types Compatible – The Application of Interdisciplinary Research to Law Reform in the Developing World: A Case Study of Corporate Governance in Indonesia' (2004) 21 *Arizona Journal of International and Comparative Law* 493.
Klaassen, M, 'Between Facts and Norms: Testing Compliance with Article 8 ECHR in Immigration Cases' (2019) 37 *Netherlands Quarterly of Human Rights* 157.
Koh, H, 'The 1994 Roscoe Pound Lecture: Transnational Legal Process' (1996) 75 *Nebraska Law Review* 181.
—— 'Why Transnational Law Matters' (2006) 24 *Penn State International Law Review* 745.
Krotoszynski, RJ, Jr, 'I'd Like to Teach the World to Sing (In Perfect Harmony): International Judicial Dialogue and the Muses – Reflections of the Perils and the Promise of International Judicial Dialogue 2006 Survey of Books Relating to the Law – Part V: International and Comparative Law' (2005) 104 *Michigan Law Review* 1321.
Kumm, M, 'Who Is the Final Arbiter of Constitutionality in Europe? Three Conceptions of the Relationship Between the German Federal Constitutional Court and the European Court of Justice' (1999) 36 *CML Rev* 351.
—— 'The Jurisprudence of Constitutional Conflict: Constitutional Supremacy in Europe before and after the Constitutional Treaty' (2005) 11 *European Law Journal* 262.
—— 'The Cosmopolitan Turn in Constitutionalism: On the Relationship between Constitutionalism in and beyond the State' in JL Dunoff and JP Trachtman (eds), *Ruling the World? Constitutionalism, International Law, and Global Governance* (Cambridge University Press 2009).
Kumm, M and Comella, VF, 'The Future of Constitutional Conflict in the European Union: Constitutional Supremacy after the Constitutional Treaty' in J Weiler and C Eisgruber (eds), Jean Monnet Working Paper No 5/04 (2004).
Lansbergen, A, 'Metock, Implementation of the Citizens' Rights Directive and Lessons for EU Citizenship' (2009) 31 *Journal of Social Welfare and Family Law* 285.
Leclair, J, 'Judicial Review in Canadian Constitutional Law: A Brief Overview' (2004) 36 *George Washington International Law Review* 543.
Legg, A, *The Margin of Appreciation in International Human Rights Law Deference and Proportionality* (Oxford University Press 2012).
Letsas, G, 'The ECHR as a Living Instrument: Its Meaning and Legitimacy' in A Føllesdal, B Peters and G Ulfstein (eds), *Constituting Europe: The European Court of Human Rights in a National, European and Global Context* (Cambridge University Press 2013).
Lyer, KR and Webb, P, 'Effective Parliamentary Oversight of Human Rights' in A Follesdal, G Ulfstein and M Saul (eds), *The International Human Rights Judiciary and National Parliaments: Europe and Beyond* (Cambridge University Press 2017).
MacCormick N, 'Beyond the Sovereign State' (1993) 56 *MLR* 1.

—— 'The Maastricht-Urteil: Sovereignty Now' (1995) 1 *European Law Journal* 259.

—— *Questioning Sovereignty: Law, State, and Nation in the European Commonwealth* (Oxford University Press 1999).

Macfarlane, E, 'Dialogue or Compliance? Measuring Legislatures' Policy Responses to Court Rulings on Rights' (2013) 34 *International Political Science Review* 39.

Maduro, MP, 'Interpreting European Law – Judicial Adjudication in a Context of Constitutional Pluralism' (2007) 2 *European Journal of Legal Studies* 18.

—— 'Three Claims of Constitutional Pluralism' in M Avbelj and J Komárek, *Constitutional Pluralism in the European Union and Beyond* (Hart Publishing 2012).

Manfredi, CP and Kelly, JB, 'Six Degrees of Dialogue: A Response to Hogg and Bushell Forum' (1999) 37 *Osgoode Hall Law Journal* 513.

Martin, D, 'The Authority and Responsibility of States' in TA Aleinikoff and V Chetail (eds), *Migration and International Legal Norms* (TMC Asser Press 2003).

Martinsen, DS, 'Judicial Policy-Making and Europeanization: The Proportionality of National Control and Administrative Discretion' (2011) 18 *Journal of European Public Policy* 944.

Mayerfeld, J, *The Promise of Human Rights: Constitutional Government, Democratic Legitimacy, and International Law* (University of Pennsylvania Press 2016).

McCrudden, C, 'A Common Law of Human Rights? Transnational Judicial Conversations on Constitutional Rights' (2000) 20 *Oxford Journal of Legal Studies* 499.

McDonald, L, 'Rights, "Dialogue" and Democratic Objections to Judicial Review' (2004) 32 *Federal Law Review* 1.

McDougal, MS, Lasswell, HD and Chen, L, 'The Protection of Aliens From Discrimination and World Public Order: Responsibility of States Conjoined with Human Rights' (1976) 70 *American Journal of International Law* 432.

McGoldrick, D, 'Affording States a Margin of Appreciation: Comparing the European Court of Human Rights and the Inter-American Court of Human Rights' in CM Buckley, A Donald and P Leach (eds), *Towards Convergence in International Human Rights Law: Approaches of Regional and International Systems* (Brill 2016).

McLachlan, C, *Foreign Relations Law* (Cambridge University Press 2014).

Mégret, F, 'Transnational Mobility, the International Law of Aliens, and the Origins of Global Migration Law' (2017) 111 *American Journal of International Law Unbound* 13.

Menkel-Meadow, C, 'Why and How to Study "Transnational" Law' (2011) 1 *UC Irvine Law Review* 97.

Meuwese, A and Snel, M, '"Constitutional Dialogue": An Overview' (2013) 9 *Utrecht Law Review* 123.

Monti, G, *European Union Law: Cases and Materials*, 2nd edn (Cambridge University Press 2010).

Motomura, H, 'Immigration Law After a Century of Plenary Power: Phantom Constitutional Norms and Statutory Interpretation' (1990) 100 *Yale Law Journal* 545.

Mowbray, AR, 'The Role of the European Court of Human Rights in the Promotion of Democracy' [1999] *Public Law* 703.

Müller, A and Kjos, HE, 'Introduction' in A Müller and HE Kjos (eds), *Judicial Dialogue and Human Rights* (Cambridge University Press 2017).

Nafziger, JAR, 'The General Admission of Aliens under International Law' (1983) 77 *American Journal of International Law* 804.

Nagel, T, 'The Problem of Global Justice' (2005) 33 *Philosophy & Public Affairs* 113.

Nickel, JW, *Making Sense of Human Rights*, 2nd edn (Blackwell 2007).

Nowak, M, *U.N. Covenant on Civil and Political Rights: CCPR Commentary*, 2nd rev edn (NP Engel 2005).

Nußberger, A, 'The ECtHR's Use of Decisions of International Courts and Quasi-Judicial Bodies' in A Müller and HE Kjos (eds), *Judicial Dialogue and Human Rights*, 1st edn (Cambridge University Press 2017).

O'Cinneide, C, 'Saying "No" to Strasbourg: When Are National Parliaments Justified in Refusing to Give Effect to Judgments of International Human Rights Courts?' in M Saul, A Follesdal and G Ulfstein (eds), *The International Human Rights Judiciary and National Parliaments: Europe and Beyond* (Cambridge University Press 2017).

Okowa, PN, 'Case Concerning Ahmadou Sadio Diallo (Republic of Guinea v Democratic Republic of the Congo) Preliminary Objections' (2008) 57 *ICLQ* 219.

O'Leary, S, 'A Tale of Two Cities: Fundamental Rights Protection in Strasbourg and Luxembourg' (2018) 20 *Cambridge Yearbook of European Legal Studies* 3.

Oxford English Dictionary, 'Alien' (Oxford University Press 2012).

Pasquet, L, 'Dialogue or Interaction? A Non-Cosmopolitan Reading of Transjudicial Communication' in A Müller and HE Kjos (eds), *Judicial Dialogue and Human Rights*, 1st edn (Cambridge University Press 2017).

Paunio, E, 'Conflict, Power, and Understanding – Judicial Dialogue between the ECJ and National Courts' (2010) 4 *No Foundations: An Interdisciplinary Journal of Law and Justice* 5.

Payandeh, M, 'The Concept of International Law in the Jurisprudence of HLA Hart' (2010) 21 *European Journal of International Law* 967.

Pérez, AT, 'Judicial Dialogue and Fundamental Rights in the European Union: A Quest for Legitimacy' in G Jacobsohn and M Schor (eds), *Comparative Constitutional Theory* (Edward Elgar 2018).

Perruchoud, R, 'State Sovereignty and Freedom of Movement' in B Opeskin, J Redpath-Cross and R Perruchoud (eds), *Foundations of International Migration Law* (Cambridge University Press 2012).

Peters, A, 'Dual Democracy' in J Klabbers, A Peters and G Ulfstein (eds), *The Constitutionalization of International Law* (Oxford University Press 2009).

—— 'Extraterritorial Naturalizations: Between the Human Right to Nationality, State Sovereignty and Fair Principles of Jurisdiction' (2010) 53 *German Yearbook of International Law* 624.

Phuong, C, 'Minimum Standards for Return Procedures and International Human Rights Law' (2007) 9 *European Journal of Migration and Law* 105.

Pinto-Duschinsky, M, *Bringing Rights Back Home: Making Human Rights Compatible with Parliamentary Democracy in the UK* (Policy Exchange 2011).

Plender, R, 'Nationality Law and Immigration Law' in R Plender (ed), *Issues in International Migration Law* (Brill 2015).

Rawls, J, *Political Liberalism*, expanded edn (Columbia University Press 2005).

Roach, KW, 'Sharpening the Dialogue Debate: The Next Decade of Scholarship' (2007) 45 *Osgoode Hall Law Journal* (1960) 169.

—— 'Constitutional, Remedial, and International Dialogues about Rights: The Canadian Experience Symposium: Globalization and the Judiciary' (2004) 40 *Texas International Law Journal* 537.

—— 'Dialogic Judicial Review and Its Critics' (2004) 23 *Supreme Court Law Review* 49.

—— *The Supreme Court on Trial: Judicial Activism or Democratic Dialogue* (Irwin 2016).

Rosas, A, 'Fundamental Rights in the Luxembourg and Strasbourg Courts' in C Baudenbacher, P Tresselt and T Orlygsson (eds), *The EFTA Court: Ten Years On* (Hart Publishing 2005).

—— 'The European Court of Justice in Context: Forms and Patterns of Judicial Dialogue' (2007) 1 *European Journal of Legal Studies* 1.

Rubenfeld, J, 'Unilateralism and Constitutionalism' (2004) 79 *New York University Law Review* 1971.

Rubenstein, K and Lenagh-Maguire, N, 'More or Less Secure? Nationality Questions, Deportation and Dual Nationality' in A Edwards and L Van Waas (eds), *Nationality and Statelessness under International Law* (Cambridge University Press 2014).

Rubio-Marín, R, 'Introduction' in R Rubio-Marín (ed), *Human Rights and Immigration* (Oxford University Press 2014).

Schauer, F, 'Dialogue and Its Discontents' in G Sigalet, G Webber and R Dixon (eds), *Constitutional Dialogue*, 1st edn (Cambridge University Press 2019).

Schmidt, SK, 'Beyond Compliance: The Europeanization of Member States through Negative Integration and Legal Uncertainty' (2008) 10 *Journal of Comparative Policy Analysis: Research and Practice* 299.

Schor, M, 'Mapping Comparative Judicial Review' (2008) 7 *Washington University Global Studies Law Review* 257.

——'Constitutional Dialogue and Judicial Supremacy' in G Jacobsohn and M Schor (eds), *Comparative Constitutional Theory* (Edward Elgar 2018).
Sigalet, G, Webber, G and Dixon, R, 'Introduction: The "What" and "Why" of Constitutional Dialogue' in G Sigalet, G Webber and R Dixon (eds), *Constitutional Dialogue*, 1st edn (Cambridge University Press 2019).
Sirota, L, 'Constitutional Dialogue: The New Zealand Bill of Rights Act and the Noble Dream' (2017) 27 *New Zealand Universities Law Review* 897.
Slaughter, A-M, 'A Typology of Transjudicial Communication Symposium: Human Rights International Law' (1994) 29 *University of Richmond Law Review* 99.
——'Judicial Globalization' (2000) 40 *Virginia Journal of International Law* 1103.
——'A Global Community of Courts Focus: Emerging Fora for International Litigation (Part 2)' (2003) 44 *Harvard International Law Journal* 191.
——*A New World Order* (Princeton University Press 2004).
Song, S, *Immigration and Democracy* (Oxford University Press 2018).
Spano, R, 'Universality or Diversity of Human Rights?: Strasbourg in the Age of Subsidiarity' (2014) 14 *Human Rights Law Review* 487.
Spielmann, D, 'Allowing the Right Margin: The European Court of Human Rights and The National Margin of Appreciation Doctrine – Waiver or Subsidiarity of European Review?' (2012) 14 *Cambridge Yearbook of European Legal Studies* 381.
Spiro, PJ, 'A New International Law of Citizenship' (2011) 105 *American Journal of International Law* 694.
Stephenson, S, 'Constitutional Reengineering: Dialogue's Migration from Canada to Australia' (2013) 11 *International Journal of Constitutional Law* 870.
Stone Sweet, A, *The Birth of Judicial Politics in France: The Constitutional Council in Comparative Perspective* (Oxford University Press 1992).
—— 'Constitutionalism, Legal Pluralism, and International Regimes' (2009) 16 *Indiana Journal of Global Legal Studies* 621.
Strumia, F, 'European Citizenship and EU Immigration: A Demoi-Cratic Bridge between the Third Country Nationals' Right to Belong and the Member States' Power to Exclude: European Citizenship and EU Immigration' (2016) 22 *European Law Journal: Review of European Law in Context* 417.
Thwaites, R, 'The Life and Times of the Genuine Link' (2018) 49 *Victoria University of Wellington Law Review* 645.
Thym, D, 'Respect for Private and Family Life under Article 8 ECHR in Immigration Cases: A Human Right to Regularize Illegal Stay' (2008) 57 *ICLQ* 87.
——'Residence as De Facto Citizenship? Protection of Long-Term Residence under Article 8 ECHR' in R Rubio Marín (ed), *Human Rights and Immigration* (Oxford University Press 2014).
Tolley, MC, 'Parliamentary Scrutiny of Rights in the United Kingdom: Assessing the Work of the Joint Committee on Human Rights' (2009) 44 *Australian Journal of Political Science* 41.
Torbisco-Casals, N, 'The Legitimacy of International Courts: The Challenge of Diversity' (2021) 52 *Journal of Social Philosophy* 491.
Tremblay, LB, 'The Legitimacy of Judicial Review: The Limits of Dialogue between Courts and Legislatures' (2005) 3 *International Journal of Constitutional Law* 617.
Tushnet, MV, 'New Forms of Judicial Review and the Persistence of Rights- and Democracy-Based Worries' (2003) 38 *Wake Forest Law Review* 813.
Tzanakopoulos, A, 'Judicial Dialogue as a Means of Interpretation' in HP Aust and G Nolte (eds), *The Interpretation of International Law by Domestic Courts: Uniformity, Diversity, Convergence* (Oxford University Press).
Voeten, E, 'The Politics of International Judicial Appointments: Evidence from the European Court of Human Rights' (2007) 61 *International Organization* 669.

Von Bogdandy, A and Venzke, I, 'In Whose Name? An Investigation of International Courts' Public Authority and Its Democratic Justification' (2012) 23 *European Journal of International Law* 7.
Von Staden, A, 'The Democratic Legitimacy of Judicial Review beyond the State: Normative Subsidiarity and Judicial Standards of Review' (2012) 10 *International Journal of Constitutional Law* 1023.
Waldron, J, 'The Core of the Case against Judicial Review' (2006) 115 *Yale Law Journal* 1346.
—— 'Refining the Question about Judges' Moral Capacity' (2008) 7 *International Journal of Constitutional Law* 69.
—— 'Judges as Moral Reasoners' (2009) 7 *International Journal of Constitutional Law* 2.
Walters, W, 'Deportation, Expulsion, and the International Police of Aliens' (2002) 6 *Citizenship Studies* 265.
Waters, MA, 'Mediating Norms and Identity: The Role of Transnational Judicial Dialogue in Creating and Enforcing International Law' (2004) 93 *Georgetown Law Journal* 487.
Webber, GCN, 'The Unfulfilled Potential of the Court and Legislature Dialogue' (2009) 42 *Canadian Journal of Political Science/Revue canadienne de science politique* 443.
Weis, P, *Nationality and Statelessness in International Law*, 2nd edn (Sijthoff & Noordhoff 1979).
Weissbrodt, D, *The Human Rights of Non-Citizens* (Oxford University Press 2008).
Wheatley, S, 'A Democratic Rule of International Law' (2011) 22 *European Journal of International Law* 525.
Wojnowska-Radzinska, J, *The Right of an Alien to Be Protected against Arbitrary Expulsion in International Law* (Brill Nijhoff 2015).
Yeo, C, *Welcome to Britain: Fixing Our Broken Immigration System* (Biteback Publishing 2020).
Young, AL, *Parliamentary Sovereignty and the Human Rights Act* (Hart Publishing 2009).
—— 'Deference, Dialogue and the Search for Legitimacy' (2010) 30 *Oxford Journal of Legal Studies* 815.
—— 'Is Dialogue Working under the Human Rights Act 1998?' [2011] *Public Law* 773.
—— *Democratic Dialogue and the Constitution* (Oxford University Press 2017).

Reports

Aguiar, M, 'Report of the Committee on Migration, Refugees and Demography of the Council of Europe on the Non-Expulsion of Long-Term Immigrants' (2001).
'Dialogue across the Atlantic: Selected Case-Law of the European and Inter-American Human Rights Courts' (Wolf Legal Publishers 2016).
European Migration Network, 'Misuse of the Right to Family Reunification: Marriages of Convenience and False Declarations of Parenthood' (International Organization for Migration 2012).
Greer, S, 'The Margin of Appreciation: Interpretation and Discretion under the European Convention on Human Rights' (Council of Europe 2000).
High Commissioner on National Minorities, 'The Bolzano/Bozen Recommendations on National Minorities in Inter-State Relations' (Organization for Security and Co-operation in Europe 2008).
Pascouau, Y, 'Conditions for Family Reunification under Strain: A Comparative Study in Nine EU Member States' (European Policy Centre 2011).
'Research Report: References to the Inter-American Court of Human Rights and Inter-American Instruments in the Case-Law of the European Court of Human Rights' (Council of Europe/European Court of Human Rights 2016).
Reynolds, S, 'Obstacles to the Right of Free Movement and Residence for EU Citizens and Their Families: Country Report for the United Kingdom' (Directorate-General for Internal Policies, European Parliament 2016).
Shaw, J et al, 'Getting to Grips with EU Citizenship: Understanding the Friction between UK Immigration Law and EU Free Movement Law' (Edinburgh Law School Citizenship Studies 2013).
White, H, 'Parliamentary Scrutiny of Government' (Institute for Government 2015).

UK Government Documents

Cabinet Office, 'Retained EU Law Dashboard' (UK Government 2022): www.gov.uk/government/publications/retained-eu-law-dashboard.
'Explanatory Memorandum to the Statement of Changes in Immigration Rules Presented to Parliament on 13 June 2012 (HC 194)' (2012).
'Explanatory Notes: Immigration and Social Security Co-Ordination (EU Withdrawal) Bill' (House of Commons 2018).
Home Office, 'Statement of Intent: Family Migration' (2012).
—— 'Immigration Bill European Convention on Human Rights Memorandum by the Home Office' (2014).
—— 'Immigration Bill Factsheet: Overview of the Bill' (2013).
—— 'Immigration Rules on Family and Private Life (HC 194) Grounds of Compatibility with Article 8 of the European Convention on Human Rights' (2012).
—— 'Memorandum of Understanding between the Government of the United Kingdom of Great Britain and Northern Ireland and the Government of the Republic of Rwanda for the Provision of an Asylum Partnership Arrangement' (2022).
Johnson, B, 'PM Speech on Action to Tackle Illegal Migration: 14 April 2022' (*UK Government*).
Johnston, N, 'Prisoners' Voting Rights: Developments since May 2015' (House of Commons Library 2020) Briefing Paper Number 07461.
Joint Committee on Human Rights, 'Enhancing Parliament's Role in Relation to Human Rights Judgments' (House of Commons 2010) Fifteenth Report of Session 2009–2010.
Mahmood, S MP, 'Lord Chancellor speech at the Council of Europe' (Strasbourg, 18 June 2025).
'Statement of Changes in Immigration Rules – Merits of Statutory Instruments Committee' (House of Lords 2010).
UK Ministry of Justice, Human Rights Act Reform: A Modern Bill of Rights. A Consultation to Reform the Human Rights Act 1998 (2021).
'What Is the Role of Parliament?' (UK Parliament).

EU Documents

'About Parliament' (European Parliament): www.europarl.europa.eu/about-parliament/en/home.
Bratza, N, Speech given at the High Level Conference, Brighton (18–20 April 2012).
Explanations Relating to the Charter of Fundamental Rights [2007] OJ C 303/02.
Information Note on References from National Courts for a Preliminary Ruling [2005] OJ C 143/1.
Recommendations to National Courts and Tribunals in Relation to the Initiation of Preliminary Ruling Proceedings [2012] OJ C 338/1.

UN Documents

Canepa v Canada [1997] UN Doc CCPR/C/59/D/558/1993.
Francesco Madafferi v Australia [2004] UN Doc CCPR/C/81/D/1011/2001.
International Law Commission, 'Draft Articles on Diplomatic Protection with Commentaries', *Report of the International Law Commission on the Work of its 58th Session* (UN Doc A/61/10 2006).
—— 'Draft Articles on the Expulsion of Aliens, with Commentaries', *Report of the International Law Commission on the Work of its 64th Session* (UN Doc A/67/10 2012).

—— 'Draft Articles on the Expulsion of Aliens, with Commentaries', *Report of the International Law Commission on the Work of its 66th Session* (UN Doc A/69/10 2014).
—— 'Expulsion of Non-Nationals: Memorandum by the Secretariat', *58th Session* (UN Doc A/CN4/565 2006).
Office of the United Nations High Commissioner for Human Rights, 'Discussion Paper: Expulsions of Aliens in International Human Rights Law' (2006).
Stewart v Canada [1996] UN Doc CCPR/C/58/D/538/1993.
United Nations High Commissioner for Refugees, 'Advisory Opinion on the Extraterritorial Application of Non-Refoulement Obligations under the 1951 Convention Relating to the Status of Refugees and Its 1967 Protocol' (2007).
United Nations Human Rights Committee, 'General Comment No 15: The Position of Aliens under the Covenant' (UN Doc HRI/GEN/1/Rev.9 1986).
—— 'General Comment No 27, Freedom of Movement' (UN Doc CCPR/C/21/Rev.1/Add.9 1999).

Newspaper Articles and Blogs/Electronic Links

Bet, M and Elsom, J, 'Rwanda WILL Keep Taking Illegal Migrants Even If Britain Quits ECHR' *Sun* (4 April 2024): www.thesun.co.uk/news/27126580/rishi-sunak-echr-rwanda-boats-flights/.
Çalı, B, 'ESIL Reflection: The Disciplinary Account of the Authority of International Law: Does It Stand Firm against Its External Critics?' (European Society of International Law, 9 May 2016).
Cambien, N, 'The Impact of Union Citizenship on Member State Immigration Laws: Some Potentially Perverse Side-Effects Resulting from Recent ECJ Case Law' (Social Science Research Network 2012) SSRN Scholarly Paper ID 2189492: papers.ssrn.com/abstract=2189492.
Elgot, J, 'Liz Truss Halts Dominic Raab's Bill of Rights Plan' *Guardian* (7 September 2022): www.theguardian.com/law/2022/sep/07/liz-truss-halts-dominic-raab-bill-of-rights-plan.
—— 'Tory MPs to Push for UK Exit from European Convention on Human Rights' *Guardian* (5 February 2023): www.theguardian.com/politics/2023/feb/05/tory-mps-to-push-for-uk-exit-from-european-convention-of-human-rights.
Goldsmith, J, 'The Trump Onslaught on International Law and Institutions' (*Lawfare*, 17 March 2017): www.lawfareblog.com/trump-onslaught-international-law-and-institutions.
Malnick, E, 'Dominic Raab: I'll Overhaul the Human Rights Act to Stop Strasbourg Dictating to Us' *Telegraph* (16 October 2021): www.telegraph.co.uk/politics/2021/10/16/dominic-raab-sets-plans-overhaul-human-rights-act-reform-judicial/.
Mason, R, 'UK Would Be Outlier with Russia If It Left ECHR, Law Society Says' *Guardian* (9 August 2023): www.theguardian.com/world/2023/aug/09/uk-could-leave-european-convention-on-human-rights-to-stop-channel-migrant-boats.
Morton, B, 'Keir Starmer Pledges to Close Loophole That Let Gazan Family Settle in UK' *BBC News* (12 February 2025): www.bbc.com/news/articles/cpdx0yn6v7lo.
Piri, F, 'Dominic Raab's Attack on the ECHR Should Frighten Us All' *euronews* (28 October 2021): www.euronews.com/2021/10/28/dominic-raab-s-attack-on-the-echr-should-frighten-us-all-view.
Walker, P, 'Skilled Visa Rules, Deportations and Higher Fees: What's in the Immigration White Paper' *Guardian* (12 May 2025): www.theguardian.com/uk-news/2025/may/12/whats-in-uk-immigration-white-paper-visa-rules-deportations-fees.
Weaver, M, 'Suella Braverman Says "We Will Do Whatever It Takes" If Strasbourg Thwarts Rwanda Plan' *Guardian* (28 August 2023): www.theguardian.com/politics/2023/aug/28/suella-braverman-strasbourg-rwanda-european-convention-human-rights.

INDEX

www.ingramcontent.com/pod-product-compliance
Ingram Content Group UK Ltd.
Pitfield, Milton Keynes, MK11 3LW, UK
UKHW021031041026
15470UKWH00013B/1280

9 781509 984497